Building Distributed Applications in Gin

A hands-on guide for Go developers to build and deploy distributed web apps with the Gin framework

Mohamed Labouardy

BIRMINGHAM—MUMBAI

Building Distributed Applications in Gin

Copyright © 2021 Packt Publishing

Group Product Manager: Kunal Chaudhari

Acquisition Editor: Denim Pinto

Publishing Product Manager: Ashish Tiwari

Senior Editor: Rohit Singh

Content Development Editor: Ananya Endow

Technical Editor: Gaurav Gala

Copy Editor: Safis Editing

Project Coordinator: Deeksha Thakkar

Proofreader: Safis Editing

Indexer: Vinayak Purushotham

Production Designer: Joshua Misquitta

Published: June 2021

Production reference: 2200821

Published by Packt Publishing Ltd.

Livery Place

35 Livery Street

Birmingham `

B3 2PB, UK.

ISBN 978-1-80107-485-8

www.packt.com

I want to thank my wife, Mounia. You've always supported me, always patiently listened while I struggled to get this done, and always made me believe I could finish this. I love you.

Thanks as well to all the folks at Packt who worked with me on the production and promotion of the book. It was truly a team effort.

Contributors

About the author

Mohamed Labouardy is the CTO and cofounder of Crew.work, and a DevSecOps evangelist. He is the founder of Komiser.io, a regular conference speaker, and the author of several books about serverless and distributed applications.

You can find him on Twitter (`@mlabouardy`).

This book is dedicated to my parents, even though they will never know unless someone tells them about this.

About the reviewer

Dmitry Goryunov was born in 1987 in Tomsk, a really nice city in Siberia that many talented engineers call their home. His first coding experience was writing macros for Ultima Online at the age of 12.

Ever since 2007, throughout his entire career, he has enjoyed building distributed software systems. Currently, he lives in Berlin and works for Zalando SE, where he is solving MLOps challenges for natural language processing systems.

Table of Contents

3
Managing Data Persistence with MongoDB

4
Building API Authentication

5
Serving Static HTML in Gin

6

Scaling a Gin Application

Section 3: Beyond the Basics

7

Testing Gin HTTP Routes

Assessments

Other Books You May Enjoy

Index

Preface

Gin is a high-performance HTTP web framework used to build web applications and microservices in Go. This book is designed to teach you the ins and outs of the Gin framework with the help of practical examples.

You'll start by exploring the basics of the Gin framework, before progressing to build a real-world RESTful API. Along the way, you'll learn how to write custom middleware and understand the routing mechanism, as well as how to bind user data and validate incoming HTTP requests. The book also demonstrates how to store and retrieve data at scale with a NoSQL database such as MongoDB, and how to implement a caching layer with Redis. Next, you'll understand how to secure and test your API endpoints with authentication protocols such as OAuth 2 and JWT. Later chapters will guide you through rendering HTML templates on the server side and building a frontend application with the React web framework to consume API responses. Moreover, you'll deploy your application on **Amazon Web Services (AWS)** and scale it on Kubernetes. Finally, you'll learn how to automate the deployment process with a CI/CD pipeline and how to troubleshoot and debug a Gin application in production with Prometheus and the ELK stack.

By the end of this Gin book, you will be able to design, build, and deploy a production-ready distributed application from scratch using the Gin framework.

Who this book is for

This book is for Go developers who are comfortable with the Go language and are seeking to learn about REST API design and development with the Gin framework.

What this book covers

Chapter 1, Getting Started with Gin, gives a foundational understanding of what the Gin framework is, how it works, and what its features are. It also supplies guidelines for setting up the Go runtime and a Gin "Hello World" example.

Chapter 2, Setting up API Endpoints, covers how to build a complete RESTful API from scratch and how to generate its documentation with OpenAPI.

Chapter 3, Managing Data Persistence with MongoDB, illustrates how to store and retrieve data at scale with a NoSQL database such as MongoDB. It also covers how to optimize the API response time with Redis.

Chapter 4, Building API Authentication, is dedicated to the best practices and recommendations to follow to secure API endpoints. It demonstrates the usage of authentication protocols, including JWT, Auth0, and session cookies.

Chapter 5, Serving Static HTML in Gin, demonstrates how to build a **single-page application** (**SPA**) with a REST backend backed by a Gin RESTful API. It also shows how to render HTML templates with Gin and how to build a self-contained web application.

Chapter 6, Scaling a Gin Application, shows how to improve the performance and scalability of a Gin distributed web application with Docker and RabbitMQ.

Chapter 7, Testing Gin HTTP Routes, explores how to run automated tests with Docker. This involves running Go unit tests and integration tests, and inspecting security vulnerabilities with Snyk.

Chapter 8, Deploying the Application on AWS, demonstrates how to deploy the Gin distributed application on a server backed by AWS EC2 and how to scale it for a heavy workload on Kubernetes.

Chapter 9, Implementing a CI/CD Pipeline, introduces the CI/CD practices we should follow to automate the build, test, and deployment of a Gin application. It also covers how to implement the practices with CircleCI using a Pipeline as Code approach.

Chapter 10, Capturing Gin Application Metrics, goes a step further in order to show you how to troubleshoot and monitor with ease a running Gin application in production.

To get the most out of this book

This book is written for anyone who works on Linux, macOS, or Windows. You will need Go installed and an AWS account. You will also need Git in order to clone the repository with the source code provided with this book. Similarly, you are expected to have a basic knowledge of Go. Beginner-level knowledge of the Go programming language is required to make the most of this book.

Even though these are the basic requirements, we will guide you through the installations whenever required.

Software/hardware covered in the book	OS requirements
Visual Studio Code 1.56.2	Windows, macOS, and Linux (any)
Go Swagger 0.27.0	Windows, macOS, and Linux (any)
Postman 8.5.1	Windows, macOS, and Linux (any)
cURL	Windows, macOS, and Linux (any)
Docker CE 20.10.6	Windows, macOS, and Linux (any)
Docker Compose 1.29.1	Windows, macOS, and Linux (any)
AWS CLI 2.2.6	Windows, macOS, and Linux (any)
Node.JS LTS	Windows, macOS, and Linux (any)
React 17.0.1	Windows, macOS, and Linux (any)
Auth0, CircleCI, Snyk, and AWS accounts	

If you are using the digital version of this book, we advise you to type the code yourself or access the code via the GitHub repository (link available in the next section). Doing so will help you avoid any potential errors related to the copying and pasting of code.

Last, keep in mind that this book is not intended to replace online resources, but rather aims to complement them. So, you will obviously need internet access to complete your reading experience at some points through the provided links.

Download the example code files

You can download the example code files for this book from GitHub at `https://github.com/PacktPublishing/Building-Distributed-Applications-in-Gin`. In case there's an update to the code, it will be updated on the existing GitHub repository.

We also have other code bundles from our rich catalog of books and videos available at `https://github.com/PacktPublishing/`. Check them out!

Download the color images

We also provide a PDF file that has color images of the screenshots/diagrams used in this book. You can download it here: `https://static.packt-cdn.com/downloads/9781801074858_ColorImages.pdf`.

Conventions used

There are a number of text conventions used throughout this book.

`TestIndexHandler`: Indicates code words in text, database table names, folder names, filenames, file extensions, pathnames, dummy URLs, user input, and Twitter handles. Here is an example: "To write a unit test, start with a `main_test.go` and define a method to return an instance of the Gin router."

A block of code is set as follows:

```
pm.test("More than 10 recipes", function () {
    var jsonData = pm.response.json();
    pm.expect(jsonData.length).to.equal(10)
});
```

Any command-line input or output is written as follows:

```
$ go tool cover -html=coverage.out
```

Bold: Indicates a new term, an important word, or words that you see onscreen. For example, words in menus or dialog boxes appear in the text like this. Here is an example: "Click on **Launch** and assign a key-pair or create a new SSH key pair. Then click on **Create instance**."

> **Tips or important notes**
> Appear like this.

Get in touch

Feedback from our readers is always welcome.

General feedback: If you have questions about any aspect of this book, mention the book title in the subject of your message and email us at `customercare@packtpub.com`.

Errata: Although we have taken every care to ensure the accuracy of our content, mistakes do happen. If you have found a mistake in this book, we would be grateful if you would report this to us. Please visit www.packtpub.com/support/errata, selecting your book, clicking on the Errata Submission Form link, and entering the details.

Piracy: If you come across any illegal copies of our works in any form on the Internet, we would be grateful if you would provide us with the location address or website name. Please contact us at copyright@packt.com with a link to the material.

If you are interested in becoming an author: If there is a topic that you have expertise in and you are interested in either writing or contributing to a book, please visit authors. packtpub.com.

Share your thoughts

Once you've read *Building Distributed Applications in Gin*, we'd love to hear your thoughts! Scan the QR code below to go straight to the Amazon review page for this book and share your feedback.

https://packt.link/r/1801074852

Your review is important to us and the tech community and will help us make sure we're delivering excellent quality content.

Section 1: Inside the Gin Framework

In this part, we will cover the hype and performance benefits of the Gin Framework. This part will also cover how to write a simple Gin-based application. As such, it includes the following chapter:

- *Chapter 1, Getting Started with Gin*

1
Getting Started with Gin

This chapter will give you a foundational understanding of what the Gin framework is, how it works, and its features. We'll also supply guidelines for setting up the Go runtime and development environment. Moreover, we'll discuss the advantages of using Gin as a web framework for building distributed applications. We will finish this chapter by learning to write our first Gin-based web application.

In this chapter, we will cover the following topics:

- What is Gin?
- Go runtime and **integrated development environment** (IDE)
- Go modules and dependency management
- Writing a Gin web application

By the end of this chapter, you will be able to build a basic HTTP server with the Gin web framework.

Technical requirements

To follow along with this chapter, you will need the following:

- Some programming experience. The code in this chapter is pretty simple, but it helps to know something about Go.

- A tool to edit your code with. Any text editor you have will work fine. Most text editors have good support for Go. The most popular are **Visual Studio Code (VSCode)** (free), GoLand (paid), and Vim (free).

- A command terminal. Go works well using any Terminal on Linux and Mac, and on PowerShell or CMD in Windows.

The code bundle for this chapter is hosted on GitHub at `https://github.com/PacktPublishing/Building-Distributed-Applications-in-Gin/tree/main/chapter01`.

What is Gin?

Before deep diving into the Gin web framework, we need to understand why Go is a top choice when it comes to building scalable and distributed applications.

Go (also referred to as Golang) is an open source programming language, developed by Robert Griesemer, Rob Pike, and Ken Thompson within Google in 2007. It is a compiled, statically typed language designed to enable users to easily write reliable, scalable, and highly efficient applications. The key features of Go are as follows:

- **Simple and consistent**: Go has a rich set of library packages with powerful standard libraries for testing, error management, and concurrency.

- **Fast and scalable**: Go is a general-purpose programming language developed for the multi-core reality of today's computers. It has built-in concurrency with Goroutines and channels. Goroutines provide lightweight, threaded execution. Declaring a Goroutine is as simple as adding the go keyword before a function.

- **Efficient**: Go provides efficient execution and compilation. Go is also statically linked, which means that the compiler invokes a linker in the last step that resolves all library references. This means we would get one binary executable after compiling a Go program with no external dependencies. Moreover, it offers efficient memory utilization with a built-in garbage collector (Go exhibits many similarities with low-level programming languages such as C or C++).

- **Community and support**: Go is backed by Google and has an ever growing ecosystem and numerous contributors to the language on GitHub. Moreover, many online resources (tutorials, videos, and books) are available for getting started with Go.

Go has become hugely popular among enterprises and the open source community. Based on the StackOverflow Developer Survey 2020 (`https://insights.stackoverflow.com/survey/2020`), Go is in the top 5 of the most loved programming languages:

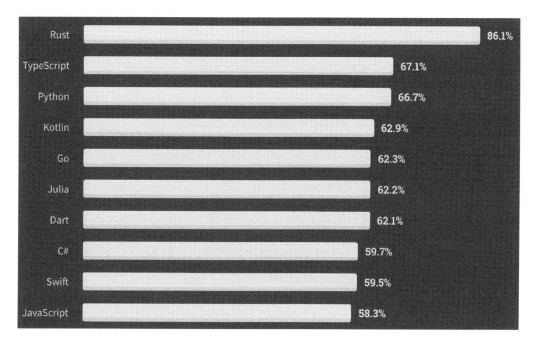

Figure 1.1 – Most loved programming languages according to the StackOverflow Survey 2020

Golang is known to be the number one choice when it comes to building large-scale, complex tools and cloud-based applications. The following image highlights the main open source projects that have been developed using Go:

- **Docker**: A solution that's used to create, deploy, and run applications using containers.

- **Kubernetes**: A container orchestration platform for managing containers across a fleet of nodes/machines.

- **Etcd**: A reliable distributed key-value store used to store data for a distributed system or application.

- **InfluxDB**: A scalable time-series database designed to handle high write and query loads.

- **CoreOS**: A lightweight operating system designed to deploy container-based applications.

- **Terraform**: An infrastructure-as-code tool for building, changing, and versioning cloud infrastructure.

- **CockroachDB**: A cloud-native SQL database for data-intensive applications.

- **Consul**: A distributed store with service discovery, service mesh, and health check monitoring capabilities:

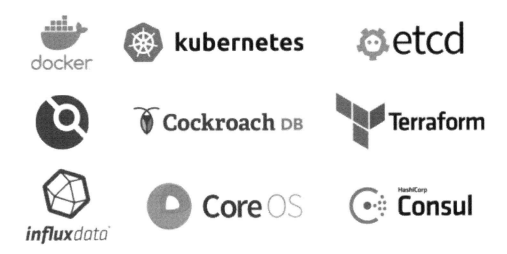

Figure 1.2 – Open source tools powered by Go

As we can see, Go is a solid language for distributed systems and infrastructure tools. Docker, Kubernetes, Prometheus, and others are built using Go.

Go is also known for building web applications of all shapes and sizes. This is partly due to the fantastic work that has been put into making the standard library clean, consistent, and easy to use. Perhaps one of the most important packages for any budding Go web developer is the net/http package. This package allows you to build HTTP servers in Go with its powerful compositional constructs.

To build a web application, you'll need to build an HTTP server. The client (for example, a browser) makes an HTTP request with some information; the server then processes that request and returns a response. The response can be in JSON, XML, or HTML format:

Figure 1.3 – HTTP client-server communication

This pattern of request-response is one of the key focal points in building web applications in Go.

While the net/http package allows you to craft a web application easily, the routing mechanism is not so powerful, especially for complex applications. That's where a web framework comes into play. The top Golang web frameworks are listed in the following table:

Framework	GitHub Repository	Stars	First Release
Gin	https://github.com/gin-gonic/gin	48.2k+	2014
Macaron	https://github.com/go-macaron/macaron	3.1k+	2016
Martini	https://github.com/go-martini/martini	11.2k+	2013
Echo	https://github.com/labstack/echo	18.9k+	2016
Mux	https://github.com/gorilla/mux	13.4k+	2016

Gin is possibly the most used and largest running Go web framework. The framework has already harvested 48,210 stars and 5,100 forks in GitHub, which shows that the framework is very popular. This modular framework can be extended easily with minimal fuss. It is great to use because many components can be reused with a direct `net/http` package.

> **Important note**
> Another strong but conservative framework is Gorilla/Mux. It has one of the biggest online communities with many resources on the internet to teach you how to build end-to-end web applications.

According to the official documentation `https://gin-gonic.com/docs/`, Gin is described as follows:

> *"Gin is an HTTP web framework written in Go (Golang). It features a Martini-like API with much better performance -- up to 40 times faster. If you need smashing performance, get yourself some Gin".*

Gin is a minimalistic web framework suitable for building web applications, microservices, and RESTful APIs. It reduces boilerplate code by creating reusable and extensible pieces of code: you can write a piece of middleware that can be plugged into one or more request handlers. Moreover, it comes with the following key features:

- **Well documented**: The documentation for Gin is broad and comprehensive. Most tasks that you will need to do relating to the router can be found easily in the docs.

- **Simplicity**: Gin is a pretty minimalistic framework. Only the most essential features and libraries are included, with little to no boilerplate to bootstrap applications, making Gin a great framework for developing highly available REST APIs.

- **Extensible**: The Gin community has created numerous pieces of well-tested middleware that make developing for Gin a charm. Features include compression with GZip, authentication with an authorization middleware, and logging with external solutions such as Sentry.

- **Performance**: Gin runs 40x faster than Martini and runs comparatively well compared to other Golang frameworks. The following is the results of a benchmark I ran against multiple Go libraries:

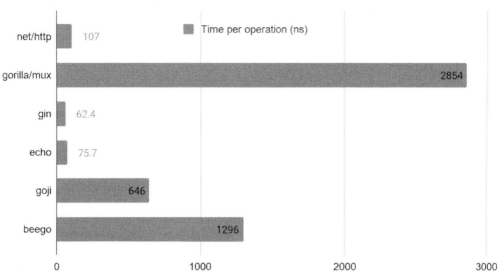

Figure 1.4 – Golang web framework benchmarks

> **Important note**
>
> This benchmark was performed on a macOS High Sierra, 2.7 GHz Intel Core i7, 16 GB DDR3 computer, with Go 1.15.6 as the runtime environment.

That being said, before you can write your first line of Go code, you'll need to set up the environment. Let's start by installing Go.

Setting up the Go environment

At the time of writing this book, the latest version of Go is Go 1.15.6. To install Go, you can either download or use the official binary distributions, or you can install Go from the source code (`https://github.com/golang/go`).

> **Important note**
>
> The official binary distributions are available for FreeBSD (release 8 and above), Linux (2.6.23 and above), macOS (Snow Leopard and above), and Windows (XP and above). Both the 32-bit (386) and 64-bit (amd64) x86 processor architectures are supported. For FreeBSD and Linux, the ARM processor architecture is also supported.

To install Go, download the distribution package from the `https://golang.org/dl/` web page, as shown here, and choose the file that's appropriate for your platform:

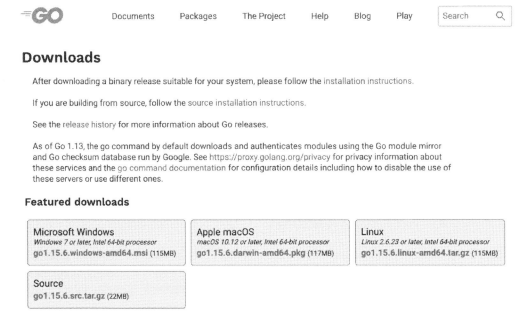

Figure 1.5 – Golang available packages

Once you have the distribution package, install Go according to your platform of choice. We will cover this in the following sections.

Linux/FreeBSD

To install Go on Linux or FreeBSD, you must download `go.-.tar.gz`. The latest Go for Linux on a 64-bit architecture is `go1.15.6.linux-amd64.tar.gz`:

```
wget -c https://golang.org/dl/go1.15.6.linux-amd64.tar.gz
//64bit
```

```
wget -c https://golang.org/dl/go1.15.6.linux-386.tar.gz
//32bit
```

Download the archive and extract it into the `/usr/local` folder. Then, run the following command as root or through sudo:

```
tar -C /usr/local -xzf go1.15.6.linux-amd64.tar.gz
```

Add `/usr/local/go/bin` to the `PATH` environment variable. You can do this by adding the following line to `$HOME/.profile or /etc/profile` (for a system-wide installation):

```
export PATH=$PATH:/usr/local/go/bin
```

Verify that you've installed Go by opening a command prompt and typing the following command:

```
go version
```

This command should display the installed version of Go:

```
mlabouardy@Mohameds-MBP-001 ~ % go version
go version go1.15.6 darwin/amd64
mlabouardy@Mohameds-MBP-001 ~ %
```

Figure 1.6 – Installed version of Go

Let's move on to see how to set up a Go environment on Windows.

Windows

To install Go on Windows, you can either use the MSI installer or the ZIP archive. Installing from MSI is easier. The latest Go for Windows on a 64-bit architecture is `go1.15.6.windows-amd64.msi`. You will then need to execute one of the following commands based on your system:

```
wget -c https://golang.org/dl/go1.15.6.windows-amd64.msi
//64bit
```

```
wget -c https://golang.org/dl/go1.15.6.windows-386.msi
//32bit
```

Open the MSI file you downloaded and follow the prompts to install Go. By default, the installer will place Go at `C:\Go` and set up `C:\Go\bin` in your `PATH` environment variable. You can change the location as needed:

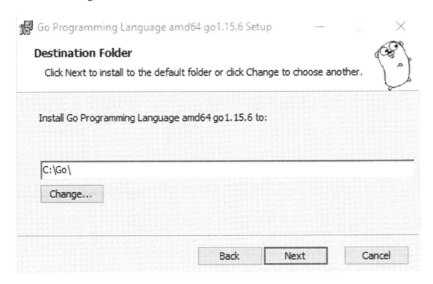

Figure 1.7 – Golang installation wizard

After installing Go, you will need to close and reopen any open command prompts so that changes to the environment that have been made by the installer are reflected in the command prompt.

> **Important note**
>
> Using the ZIP archive is easy as well. Extract the files into a directory (for example, `C:\Go`) and add the `bin` subdirectory to your `PATH` variable.

Once installed, click on the **Start** menu. Then, in the menu's search box, type cmd. After, press the *Enter* key. In the command prompt window that appears, type the `go version` command, as shown here:

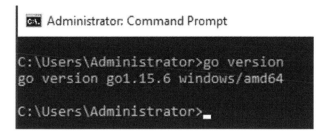

Figure 1.8 – Installed version of Go

You'll see **go version go1.15.6 windows/amd64**, as shown in the preceding screenshot. With that, you're all set up!

MacOS

For MacOS, you can download the appropriate PKG file; that is, go1.15.6.darwin-amd64.pkg (at the time of writing this book). Once downloaded, run through the installation wizard. The package will install the distribution to /usr/local/go and place the /usr/local/go/bin directory in your PATH environment variable:

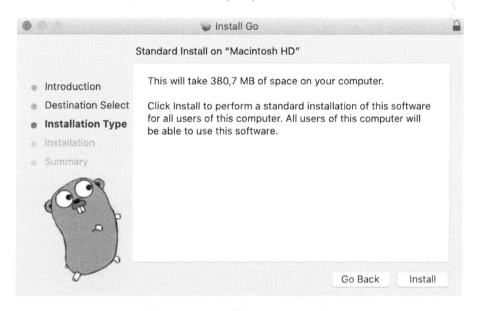

Figure 1.9 – Installing Go on MacOS

You'll need to restart your terminal, or run this command in your Terminal:

```
source ~/.profile
```

Alternatively, you can use Homebrew to install Go. This can be as simple as doing the following:

```
brew install golang@1.15.6
```

The Terminal window will give you feedback regarding the installation process of Go. It may take a few minutes before the installation is complete. Verify that you've installed Go by opening a command prompt and typing the `go version` command.

> **Important note**
> In the future, to update Go, you can run the following commands to update Homebrew and then update Go. You don't have to do this now as you've just installed the latest version:

```
brew update
```
```
brew upgrade golang
```

Now that you've installed Go, you need to set it up properly. Go development tools are designed to work with code maintained in public repositories, and the model is the same, regardless of whether you're developing an open source program or something else. Go code is developed in a workspace. A workspace is made up of three directories, namely the following:

- `bin`: This will contain all you Go executable binaries.
- `src`: This will store your source files, which are organized in packages, with one subdirectory in the `src` directory representing one package.
- `pkg`: This will store your package objects.

The default directory for the Go workspace is the home directory with a `go` subdirectory or `$HOME/go`. Issue the following command to create the directory structure for your Go workspace:

```
mkdir -p $HOME/go/{bin,src,pkg}
```

The -p option tells mkdir to create all the parents in the directory, even if they don't currently exist. Using {bin, src, pkg} creates a set of arguments for mkdir and tells it to create the bin, src, and pkg directories. This will ensure the following directory structure is now in place:

```
The go, bin and  src folders should be at the same level
(remove extra spaces from go and src folders, so the folders
are aligned with bin folder)
$HOME
    └── go
    ├── bin
    └── src
```

Next, you need to set the GOPATH environment variable, as follows:

```
export GOPATH=$HOME/go
export PATH=$PATH:$GOPATH/bin
```

You can verify your $PATH has been updated by using the echo command and inspecting the output:

```
echo $PATH
```

You should see your $GOPATH/bin in your home directory. If you were logged in as USER, you will see /Users/USER/go/bin in the path:

```
/Users/USER/go/bin:/usr/local/sbin:/usr/local/bin:/usr/bin:/
bin:/usr/sbin:/sbin
```

With the Go workspace and GOPATH created, we can go ahead and set up the development environment.

Integrated development environment

Throughout this book, I will be using an **IDE** to write RESTful API and services. Using an IDE can boost your productivity since it provides rich features such as autocompletion, highlighting code, a powerful built-in debugger, and custom extensions. There are many IDEs available. In this book, I will be using **VSCode**.

To install VSCode, download the appropriate package based on your system from
`https://code.visualstudio.com/download`:

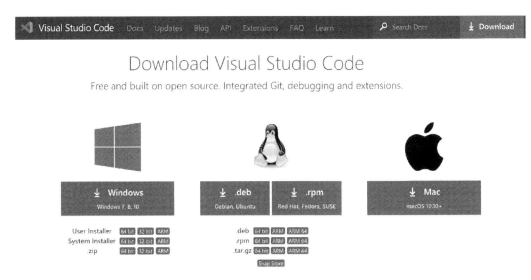

Figure 1.10 – VS Code – available packages

> **Note**
> Mac users can also use `Brew` to install VSCode with the following command:
>
> `brew install --cask visual-studio-code`

Once downloaded, run the setup wizard and follow the instructions. Once the installation
is complete, launch VSCode. You will be presented with the following start screen:

Figure 1.11 – VSCode user interface

VSCode supports all the popular programming languages and Git integration by default. You can also install extensions to extend the functionality of VSCode. The VS Code marketplace contains a huge list of free community plugins and extensions. To enable support for Golang, you need to install an extension called **Go** by navigating to the **Extensions** tab from the left sidebar:

Figure 1.12 – Golang extension for VSCode

Click on the **Install** button and then restart VSCode for the changes to take effect.

Installing Go tools

Next, we will install the following Go tools, which are a set of packages that help improve your development workflow and overall experience while writing code:

Tool	Description
gocode	Similar to JavaDoc, it generates HTML pages of API documentation from Go source files.
gopkgs	Auto-completes unimported packages on file save.
golint	This tool detects when an error is silently ignored.
godef	Print where symbols are defined in the Go source code.

> **Important Note**
>
> A complete list of the available Go tools can be found at `https://pkg.go.dev/golang.org/x/tools`.

To install the tools, click on **View | Command Pallete**, or use the *Ctrl + Shift + P* shortcut and type `goinstall update/tools`:

Figure 1.13 – Available Go tools on VSCode

Check all the dependencies and click on **OK**. It will take some time to download all the dependencies:

```
Tools environment: GOPATH=/Users/mlabouardy/go
Installing 9 tools at /Users/mlabouardy/go/bin in module mode.
  gopkgs
  go-outline
  gotests
  gomodifytags|
  impl
  goplay
  dlv
  golint
  gopls

Installing github.com/uudashr/gopkgs/v2/cmd/gopkgs (/Users/mlabouardy/go/bin/gopkgs) SUCCEEDED
Installing github.com/ramya-rao-a/go-outline (/Users/mlabouardy/go/bin/go-outline) SUCCEEDED
Installing github.com/cweill/gotests/... (/Users/mlabouardy/go/bin/gotests) SUCCEEDED
Installing github.com/fatih/gomodifytags (/Users/mlabouardy/go/bin/gomodifytags) SUCCEEDED
Installing github.com/josharian/impl (/Users/mlabouardy/go/bin/impl) SUCCEEDED
Installing github.com/haya14busa/goplay/cmd/goplay (/Users/mlabouardy/go/bin/goplay) SUCCEEDED
```

Figure 1.14 – Go tools installation

With Go installed and configured on your computer, you are now ready to install the Gin framework.

Installing and configuring Gin

Gin is a third-party package. To install Gin in Go projects, we need to use the `go get` command. The command takes the URL of the package to be installed as an argument. Issue the following command to install the `gin` package from GitHub:

```
go get github.com/gin-gonic/gin
```

> **Note**
>
> If you're running Go 1.16 and above, you need to disable Go modules via the `GO111MODULE=off` option.

When checking out the `gin` package, the `go get` command creates a Gin directory in the `$GOPATH/src` path. The directory will contain the source code of the Gin framework:

```
mlabouardy@Mohameds-MBP-001 gin % ls
AUTHORS.md                README.md                context_appengine.go    errors.go
gin_integration_test.go   logger_test.go           recovery_test.go         test_helpers.go
BENCHMARKS.md             auth.go                  context_test.go          errors_1.13_test.go
gin_test.go               middleware_test.go       render                   testdata
CHANGELOG.md              auth_test.go             debug.go                 errors_test.go
githubapi_test.go         mode.go                  response_writer.go       tree.go
CODE_OF_CONDUCT.md        benchmarks_test.go       debug_test.go            examples
go.mod                    mode_test.go             response_writer_test.go  tree_test.go
CONTRIBUTING.md           binding                  deprecated.go            fs.go
go.sum                    path.go                  routergroup.go           utils.go
LICENSE                   codecov.yml              deprecated_test.go       gin.go
internal                  path_test.go             routergroup_test.go      utils_test.go
Makefile                  context.go               doc.go                   ginS
logger.go                 recovery.go              routes_test.go           version.go
mlabouardy@Mohameds-MBP-001 gin % pwd
/Users/mlabouardy/go/src/github.com/gin-gonic/gin
```

Figure 1.15 – Gin package source code

Begin by creating the `hello-world` project directory under `$GOHOME/src/hello-world` or any directory that seems appropriate:

```
mkdir -p $GOHOME/src/hello-world
cd $GOHOME/src/hello-world
```

Open the folder with VSCode and create a `main.go` file inside the project folder that contains the following content:

```
package main

import "github.com/gin-gonic/gin"

func main() {
    router := gin.Default()
    router.GET("/", func(c *gin.Context) {
        c.JSON(200, gin.H{
            "message": "hello world",
        })
    })
    router.Run()
}
```

The first line, `package main`, indicates that this is the main module in this project. The `import` section is for importing the `gin` package. This package provides us with the `router` variable, which is declared right below `import` and the API context to be used while we send the response in our `main` function.

Next, we create an HTTP `GET` method on the root (`/`) resource and define a function to be called when HTTP requests hit the root endpoint. The function sends a JSON response with a status code of 200 (OK) with a body of `"message": "test successful"`.

Finally, we must deploy the router on port `8080` using the `router.Run()` method. The following diagram summarizes how an HTTP request is processed in Gin:

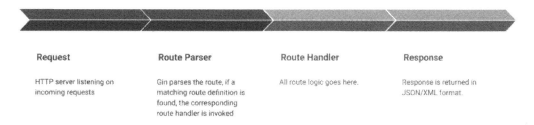

Request	Route Parser	Route Handler	Response
HTTP server listening on incoming requests	Gin parses the route, if a matching route definition is found, the corresponding route handler is invoked	All route logic goes here.	Response is returned in JSON/XML format.

Figure 1.16 – Parsing incoming HTTP requests with Gin

To run the app, execute the following command from the terminal session:

```
go run main.go
```

All the files and commands executed henceforth will be within this directory. If you followed the setup process, you should see the following output in your Terminal:

```
mlabouardy@Mohameds-MBP-001 hello-world % go run main.go
[GIN-debug] [WARNING] Creating an Engine instance with the Logger and Recovery middleware
 already attached.

[GIN-debug] [WARNING] Running in "debug" mode. Switch to "release" mode in production.
 - using env:   export GIN_MODE=release
 - using code:  gin.SetMode(gin.ReleaseMode)

[GIN-debug] GET    /                         --> main.main.func1 (3 handlers)
[GIN-debug] Environment variable PORT is undefined. Using port :8080 by default
[GIN-debug] Listening and serving HTTP on :8080
```

Figure 1.17 – Gin server logs

Point your favorite browser to `http://localhost:8080`. You should see a "`hello world`" message:

Figure 1.18 – Hello world example

Awesome – you have successfully started an HTTP server in Go with the Gin framework.

Back to the terminal, Gin will trace the HTTP requests:

```
[GIN-debug] GET    /                        --> main.main.func1 (3 handlers)
[GIN-debug] Environment variable PORT is undefined. Using port :8080 by default
[GIN-debug] Listening and serving HTTP on :8080
[GIN] 2021/01/06 - 14:44:03 | 200 |    63.056µs |           ::1 | GET      "/"
```

Figure 1.19 – Tracing incoming HTTP requests

You can use a cURL command to issue an HTTP request:

```
curl -X GET http://localhost:8080
```

Alternatively, you can use an advanced REST client such as Postman. You can download the right version based on your platform from the following URL: `https://www.getpostman.com/apps`.

Once it has downloaded, run the wizard and open Postman. Set the fields as follows:

- HTTP method: `GET`
- URL: `http://localhost:8080`
- Headers: Set `Content-Type` to `application/json`

The request should be configured like so:

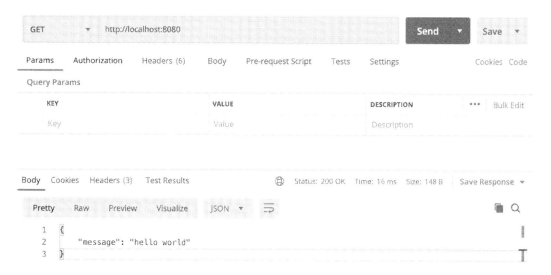

Figure 1.20 – GET request with the Postman client

It's worth mentioning that by default, the HTTP server is listening on port 8080. However, if the port is being used by another application, you can define a different port by adding an argument to the Run method:

```
r.Run(":5000")
```

This command will run the server on port 5000, as shown in the following screenshot:

```
mlabouardy@Mohameds-MBP-001 hello-world % go run main.go
[GIN-debug] [WARNING] Creating an Engine instance with the Logger and Recovery middleware
 already attached.

[GIN-debug] [WARNING] Running in "debug" mode. Switch to "release" mode in production.
 - using env:   export GIN_MODE=release
 - using code:  gin.SetMode(gin.ReleaseMode)

[GIN-debug] GET    /                        --> main.main.func1 (3 handlers)
[GIN-debug] Listening and serving HTTP on :5000
[GIN] 2021/01/06 - 15:02:57 | 200 |      156.441µs |            ::1 | GET      "/"
```

Figure 1.21 – Running the Gin server on port 5000

Note that the `port` parameter needs to be passed as a string, prepended by colon punctuation.

You should now be familiar with the basics of building and running a simple web application. In the next few sections, we will cover how to enhance those functionalities with third-party packages. But before we do that, let's cover how to manage Go dependencies.

Dependency management in Golang

For now, the code is stored locally. However, it's recommended to store the source code in a remote repository for versioning. That's where a solution such as GitHub comes into play. Sign up for a free account at `https://github.com`. Then, create a new GitHub repository called `hello-world`:

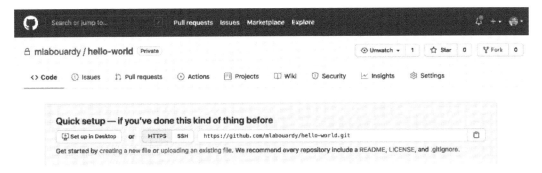

Figure 1.22 – New GitHub repository

Next, initialize the repository with the following commands:

```
git init
git remote add origin https://github.com/mlabouardy/hello-
world.git
```

Commit the `main.go` file to the remote repository by executing the following commands:

```
git add .
git commit -m "initial commit"
git push origin master
```

Your repository should now look like this:

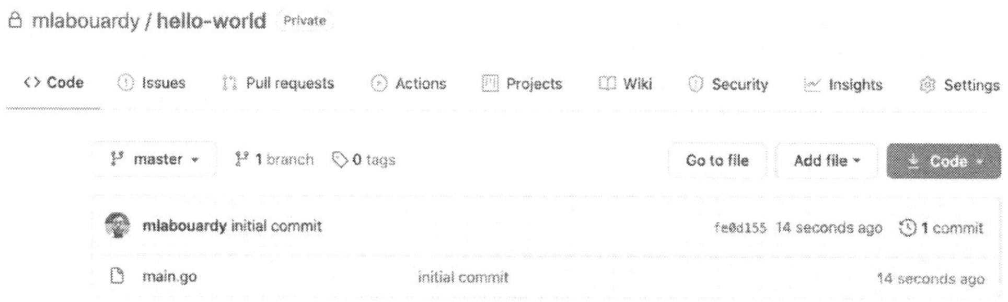

Figure 1.23 – Versioning main.go in Git

We can stop here. However, if you're working within a team, you will need some way to ensure all team members are using the same Go version and packages. That's where Go modules come into the picture. Go modules were introduced in 2018 to make dependency management a lot easier.

> **Note**
>
> Starting with Go 1.16, Go modules are the default way to manage external dependencies.

In the project folder, run the following command to create a new module:

```
go mod init hello-world
```

This command will create a go.mod file that contains the following content. The file defines projects requirements and locks dependencies to their correct versions (similar to package.json and package-lock.json in Node.js):

```
module github.com/mlabouardy/hello-world
```

```
go 1.15
```

To add the Gin package, we can issue the `go get` command. Now, our `go.mod` file will look like this:

```
module github.com/mlabouardy/hello-world
```

```
go 1.15
```

```
require github.com/gin-gonic/gin v1.6.3
```

A new file called `go.sum` will be generated upon adding the Gin framework (the output was cropped for brevity). You may assume it's a lock file. But in fact, `go.mod` already provides enough information for 100% reproducible builds. The other file is just for validation purposes: it contains the expected cryptographic checksums of the content of specific module versions. You can think of it as an additional security layer to ensure that the modules your project depends on do not change unexpectedly, whether for malicious or accidental reasons:

```
github.com/davecgh/go-spew v1.1.0/go.mod h1:J7Y8YcW2NihsgmVo/
mv3lAwl/skON4iLHjSsI+c5H38=
github.com/davecgh/go-spew v1.1.1/go.mod h1:J7Y8YcW2NihsgmVo/
mv3lAwl/skON4iLHjSsI+c5H38=
github.com/gin-contrib/sse v0.1.0 h1:Y/
yl/+YNO8GZSjAhjMsSuLt29uWRFHdHYUb5lYOV9qE=
github.com/gin-contrib/sse v0.1.0/go.mod
h1:RHrZQHXnP2xjPF+u1gW/2HnVO7nvIa9PG3Gm+fLHvGI=
github.com/gin-gonic/gin v1.6.3
h1:ahKqKTFpO5KTPHxWZjEdPScmYaGtLo8Y4DMHoEsnp14=
github.com/gin-gonic/gin v1.6.3/go.mod
h1:75u5sXoLsGZoRN5Sgbi1eraJ4GU3++wFwWzhwvtwp4M=
github.com/go-playground/assert/v2 v2.0.1/go.mod h1:VDjEfimB/
XKnb+ZQfWdccd7VUvScMdVu0Titje2rxJ4=
github.com/go-playground/locales v0.13.0
h1:HyWk6mgj5qFqCT5fjGBuRArbVDfE4hi8+e8ceBS/t7Q=
github.com/go-playground/locales v0.13.0/go.mod
```

You can list your dependencies with the following command:

```
go list -m all
```

The output is as follows:

```
github.com/mlabouardy/hello-world
github.com/davecgh/go-spew v1.1.1
github.com/gin-contrib/sse v0.1.0
github.com/gin-gonic/gin v1.6.3
github.com/go-playground/assert/v2 v2.0.1
github.com/go-playground/locales v0.13.0
github.com/go-playground/universal-translator v0.17.0
github.com/go-playground/validator/v10 v10.2.0
github.com/golang/protobuf v1.3.3
github.com/google/gofuzz v1.0.0
github.com/json-iterator/go v1.1.9
github.com/leodido/go-urn v1.2.0
github.com/mattn/go-isatty v0.0.12
github.com/modern-go/concurrent v0.0.0-20180228061459
e0a39a4cb421
github.com/modern-go/reflect2 v0.0.0-20180701023420
4b7aa43c6742
github.com/pmezard/go-difflib v1.0.0
github.com/stretchr/objx v0.1.0
github.com/stretchr/testify v1.4.0
github.com/ugorji/go v1.1.7
github.com/ugorji/go/codec v1.1.7
golang.org/x/sys v0.0.0-20200116001909-b77594299b42
golang.org/x/text v0.3.2
golang.org/x/tools v0.0.0-20180917221912-90fa682c2a6e
gopkg.in/check.v1 v0.0.0-20161208181325-20d25e280405
gopkg.in/yaml.v2 v2.2.8
```

> **Important Note**
> To remove unused dependencies, you can use the go mod tidy command.

Finally, add the `go.mod` and `go.sum` files to the remote repository using the following commands:

```
git add .
git commit -m "dependency management"
git push origin master
```

The updated repository will look as follows:

Figure 1.24 – Managing dependencies with Go modules

It's worth mentioning that the downloaded modules are stored locally in your $GOPATH/ pkg/mod directory. However, sometimes, it's useful to store the modules or third-party packages that your project depends on and place them in a folder, so that they can be checked into version control. Fortunately, Go modules support vendoring:

```
go mod vendor
```

This command will create a `vendor` directory in your project folder that contains all your third-party dependencies. You can now commit this folder to your remote Git repository to ensure the stability of your future builds, without having to rely on external services:

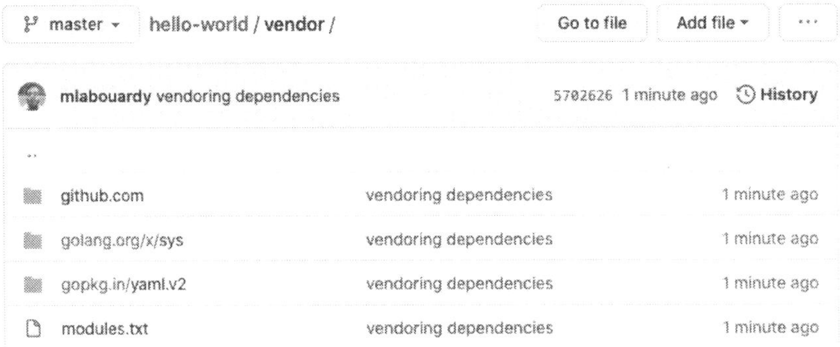

Figure 1.25 – Vendoring dependencies

Sometimes, you may wonder why a specific package is a dependency. You can answer this by analyzing or visualizing the project dependencies. To do so, we can use the `go mod graph` command to display the list of modules in the `go.mod` file:

```
go mod graph | sed -Ee 's/@[^[:blank:]]+//g' | sort | uniq
>unver.txt
```

This command will generate a new file called `unver.txt` containing the following content (the output has been cropped for brevity):

```
github.com/gin-contrib/sse github.com/stretchr/testify
github.com/gin-gonic/gin github.com/gin-contrib/sse
github.com/gin-gonic/gin github.com/go-playground/validator/v10
github.com/gin-gonic/gin github.com/golang/protobuf
github.com/gin-gonic/gin github.com/json-iterator/go
github.com/gin-gonic/gin github.com/mattn/go-isatty
github.com/gin-gonic/gin github.com/stretchr/testify
github.com/gin-gonic/gin github.com/ugorji/go/codec
github.com/gin-gonic/gin gopkg.in/yaml.v2
```

Then, create a `graph.dot` file containing the following content:

```
digraph {
    graph [overlap=false, size=14];
    root="$(go list -m)";
    node [ shape = plaintext, fontname = "Helvetica",
           fontsize=24];
    "$(go list -m)" [style = filled,
                     fillcolor = "#E94762"];
```

This content will generate a graph structure using the DOT language. We can use DOT to describe graphs (directed or not). That being said, we will inject the output of `unvert.txt` into the `graph.dot` file with the following commands:

```
cat unver.txt | awk '{print "\""$1"\" -> \""$2"\""};' >>graph.
dot
echo "}" >>graph.dot
sed -i '' 's+\("github.com/[^/]*/\)\([^"]*"\)+\1\\n\2+g' graph.
dot
```

This results in a module dependency graph:

```
mlabouardy@Mohameds-MBP-001 hello-world % cat graph.dot
digraph {
        graph [overlap=false, size=14];
        root="github.com/mlabouardy/hello-world";
        node [  shape = plaintext, fontname = "Helvetica", fontsize=24];
        "github.com/mlabouardy/hello-world" [style = filled, fillcolor = "#E94762"];
"github.com/gin-contrib/sse" -> "github.com/stretchr/testify"
"github.com/gin-gonic/gin" -> "github.com/gin-contrib/sse"
"github.com/gin-gonic/gin" -> "github.com/go-playground/validator/v10"
"github.com/gin-gonic/gin" -> "github.com/golang/protobuf"
"github.com/gin-gonic/gin" -> "github.com/json-iterator/go"
"github.com/gin-gonic/gin" -> "github.com/mattn/go-isatty"
"github.com/gin-gonic/gin" -> "github.com/stretchr/testify"
"github.com/gin-gonic/gin" -> "github.com/ugorji/go/codec"
"github.com/gin-gonic/gin" -> "gopkg.in/yaml.v2"
"github.com/go-playground/locales" -> "golang.org/x/text"
"github.com/go-playground/universal-translator" -> "github.com/go-playground/locales"
"github.com/go-playground/validator/v10" -> "github.com/go-playground/assert/v2"
"github.com/go-playground/validator/v10" -> "github.com/go-playground/locales"
"github.com/go-playground/validator/v10" -> "github.com/go-playground/universal-translator"
"github.com/go-playground/validator/v10" -> "github.com/leodido/go-urn"
"github.com/json-iterator/go" -> "github.com/davecgh/go-spew"
"github.com/json-iterator/go" -> "github.com/google/gofuzz"
"github.com/json-iterator/go" -> "github.com/modern-go/concurrent"
"github.com/json-iterator/go" -> "github.com/modern-go/reflect2"
"github.com/json-iterator/go" -> "github.com/stretchr/testify"
"github.com/leodido/go-urn" -> "github.com/stretchr/testify"
"github.com/mattn/go-isatty" -> "golang.org/x/sys"
"github.com/mlabouardy/hello-world" -> "github.com/gin-gonic/gin"
"github.com/stretchr/testify" -> "github.com/davecgh/go-spew"
"github.com/stretchr/testify" -> "github.com/pmezard/go-difflib"
"github.com/stretchr/testify" -> "github.com/stretchr/objx"
"github.com/stretchr/testify" -> "gopkg.in/yaml.v2"
"github.com/ugorji/go" -> "github.com/ugorji/go/codec"
"github.com/ugorji/go/codec" -> "github.com/ugorji/go"
"golang.org/x/text" -> "golang.org/x/tools"
"gopkg.in/yaml.v2" -> "gopkg.in/check.v1"
```

Figure 1.26 – Module dependency graph

We can now render the results with Graphviz. This tool can be installed with the following commands, based on your operation system:

- **Linux**: You can download the official package based on your package manager. For Ubuntu/Debian, use the following command:

```
apt-get install graphviz
```

- **MacOS**: You can use the Homebrew utility for MacOS:

```
brew install graphviz
```

- **Windows**: You can use the Chocolatey (`https://chocolatey.org/install`) package manager for Windows:

```
choco install graphviz.portable
```

Once Graphviz has been installed, execute the following command to convert the `graph.dot` file into `.svg` format:

```
sfdp -Tsvg -o graph.svg graph.dot
```

A `graph.svg` file will be generated. Open the file with the following command:

```
open graph.svg
```

This results in the following directed graph:

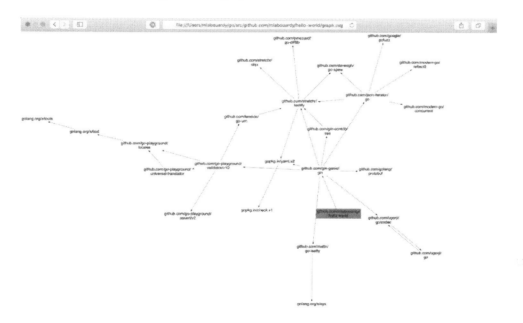

Figure 1.27 – Visually analyzing module dependencies

This graph perfectly shows the dependencies among the modules/packages of the *hello-world* project.

> **Note**
>
> Another way of generating a dependencies graph is by using the `modgv` utility (`https://github.com/lucasepe/modgv`). This tool converts `go mod graph` output into GraphViz's DOT language with a single command.

Now that the source code has been versioned in GitHub, we can go further and explore how to write a custom function handler for Gin routes.

Writing a custom HTTP handler

You can create a handler function that takes `*gin.Context` as an argument and serves a JSON response with a status code of 200. Then, you can register the handler using the `router.Get()` function:

```
package main

import "github.com/gin-gonic/gin"

func IndexHandler(c *gin.Context){
    c.JSON(200, gin.H{
        "message": "hello world",
    })
}

func main() {
    router := gin.Default()
    router.GET("/", IndexHandler)
    router.Run()
}
```

> **Important note**
>
> Separating the handler function from the router will be useful in the advanced chapters of this book, when unit testing is tackled.

The biggest strength of the Gin framework is its ability to extract segments from the request URL. Consider the following example:

```
/users/john
/hello/mark
```

This URL has a dynamic segment:

- Username: Mark, John, Jessica, and so on

You can implement dynamic segments with the following `:variable` pattern:

```
func main() {
    router := gin.Default()
    router.GET("/:name", IndexHandler)
    router.Run()
}
```

The last thing we must do is get the data from the variable. The `gin` package comes with the `c.Params.ByName()` function, which takes the name of the parameter and returns the value:

```
func IndexHandler(c *gin.Context) {
    name := c.Params.ByName("name")
    c.JSON(200, gin.H{
        "message": "hello " + name,
    })
}
```

Rerun the app with the `go run` command. Hit the `http://localhost:8080/` `mohamed` link on your browser; the user will be returned:

```
{"message":"hello mohamed"}
```

Figure 1.28 – Example of the path parameter

Now, we know that every time we hit the GET /user route, we get a response of "hello user." If we hit any other route, it should respond with a 404 error message:

Figure 1.29 – Error handling in Gin

Gin can also handle HTTP requests and responses in XML format. To do so, define a user struct with firstName and lastName as attributes. Then, use the c.XML() method to render XML:

```go
func main() {
    router := gin.Default()
    router.GET("/", IndexHandler)
    router.Run()
}

type Person struct {
    XMLName  xml.Name `xml:"person"`
    FirstName  string    `xml:"firstName,attr"`
    LastName   string    `xml:"lastName,attr"`
}

func IndexHandler(c *gin.Context) {
    c.XML(200, Person{FirstName: "Mohamed",
                      LastName: "Labouardy"})
}
```

Now, rerun the application. If you navigate to http://localhost:8080, the server will return an XML response, as follows:

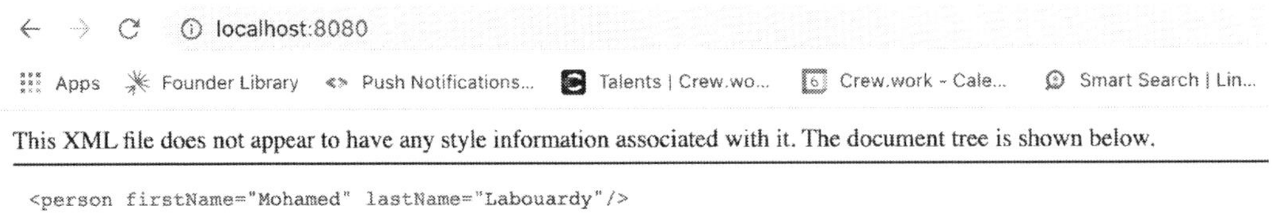

```
<person firstName="Mohamed" lastName="Labouardy"/>
```

Figure 1.30 – XML response

Congratulations! At this point, you have a Go programming workspace set up on your local machine, as well as Gin configured. Now, you can begin a coding project!

Summary

In this chapter, we gave you an introduction to the Go programming language. We learned how to set up the runtime and development environments. We also understood the GOPATH environment variable, which is a workspace definition in Go, and we now know that all packages and projects reside on that path.

Later, we explored the different Go web frameworks and learned why Gin is the most popular for building distributed web applications. Finally, we learned how to write our first hello world project with Gin from scratch.

In the next chapter, we will get our hands dirty and start building a distributed RESTful API with the Gin framework.

Questions

1. Why is Golang popular?
2. Which are the best Golang frameworks for web development?
3. What's a Go module?
4. What's the default port of an HTTP server written in the Gin framework?
5. What methods are used to render JSON and XML responses?

Further reading

- *Hands-On Serverless Applications with Go*, Mohamed Labouardy, by Packt Publishing
- *Hands-On RESTful Web Services with Go - Second Edition*, Naren Yellavula, by Packt Publishing

Section 2: Distributed Microservices

The second part of this book is a deep dive into the Gin framework. It includes a practical example of building a real-world production-ready RESTful API in Go and explains how to communicate with different microservices based on REST to build distributed web applications. This section includes the following chapters:

- *Chapter 2, Setting up API Endpoints*
- *Chapter 3, Managing Data Persistence with MongoDB*
- *Chapter 4, Building API Authentication*
- *Chapter 5, Serving Static HTML in Gin*
- *Chapter 6, Scaling a Gin Application*

2
Setting Up API Endpoints

In the previous chapter, we learned how to build our first Gin web application. In this one, we're going to build a complete RESTful API from scratch. Along the way, we will explore HTTP methods and advanced routing features. We'll also cover how to write the OpenAPI Specification and how to generate API documentation.

In this chapter, we will cover the following topics:

- Exploring API functionality
- Implementing HTTP routes
- Writing the OpenAPI Specification

By the end of this chapter, you'll be familiar with the routing mechanisms of Gin, HTTP methods, and data validation.

Technical requirements

To follow along with this chapter, you'll need the following:

- A laptop (Windows, Linux, or macOS) with Golang version 1.15.6 set up so that you can easily execute the commands provided

- A general understanding of the RESTful API and the Go programming language

The code bundle for this chapter is hosted on GitHub at `https://github.com/PacktPublishing/Building-Distributed-Applications-in-Gin/tree/main/chapter02`.

Exploring API functionality

To illustrate how to build a RESTful API, we will build a cooking application. We will cover how to integrate, deploy, and test the app using the Gin framework. The application will do the following:

- Display the recipes that are submitted by the users, along with their ingredients and instructions.

- Allow anyone to post a new recipe.

The application architecture and flow are shown in the following diagram:

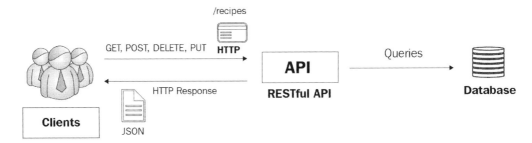

Figure 2.1 – Recipes application architecture

The architecture is composed of a microservice written with the Gin framework and a database for data persistency. The microservice exposes a RESTful API to manage the recipes through the HTTP protocol.

> **Note**
> Later in this book, we will cover how to build a frontend application with the React web framework so that we can consume the RESTful API.

Before we get started, we need to create a GitHub repository where the code source will be stored. To structure the code within Git branches, we will use the GitFlow model. This approach consists of the following branches:

- **master**: This branch corresponds to the current production code. You can't commit directly, except for hotfixes. Git tags can be used to tag all the commits in the master branch with a version number (for instance, for using the semantic versioning convention, `https://semver.org/`, which has three parts: major, minor, and patch, so a tag with version 1.2.3 has 1 as its major version, 2 as its minor version, and 3 as its patch version).

- **preprod**: This is a release branch and is a mirror of production. It can be used to test all the new features that are developed on the develop branch before they are merged to the master branch.

- **develop**: This is the development integration branch, which contains the latest integrated development code.

- **feature/X**: This is an individual feature branch that's being developed. Each new feature resides in its own branch, and they're generally created for the latest develop branch.

- **hotfix/X**: When you need to solve something in production code, you can use the hotfix branch and open a pull request for the master branch. This branch is based on the master branch.

The following schema illustrates the GitFlow approach:

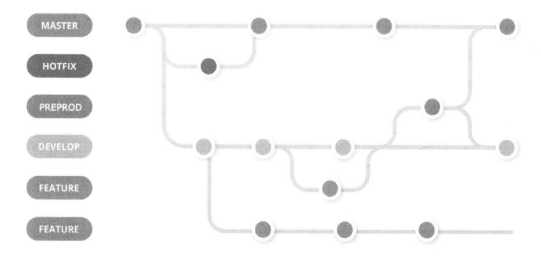

Figure 2.2 – GitFlow model – main branches

Once the GitHub repository has been created, clone it to your Go workspace and create three main branches called `develop`, `preprod`, and `master`. This will help you organize the project and isolate the code under development from the code running in production. This branching strategy is a slimmer version of the GitFlow workflow branching model (don't forget to replace the GitHub URL with a link to your repository):

```
git clone https://github.com/mlabouardy/recipes-api.git
cd recipes-api
touch README.md
git checkout -b preprod
git push origin preprod
git checkout -b develop
git push origin develop
```

This will create a new directory called `recipes-api`. Let's make this directory the root of a module by executing the following command. This will enable us to manage project dependencies with the `go.mod` and `go.sum` files:

```
go mod init
```

Open the project folder on VSCode and create a `main.go` file with the following code. The `main` function will initialize a new Gin router and run an HTTP server on port `8080` by invoking the `Run()` method of our Gin instance:

```go
package main

import "github.com/gin-gonic/gin"

func main() {
    router := gin.Default()
    router.Run()
}
```

> **Note**
>
> Make sure that you install the `gin` package with the `go get` command. Refer to the previous chapter for a step-by-step guide.

Push the changes to the Git remote repository. For now, we will push the changes directly to the `develop` branch. We will learn how to open pull requests in the next section:

```
git add .
git commit -m "boilerplate"
git push origin develop
```

The updated repository should look as follows:

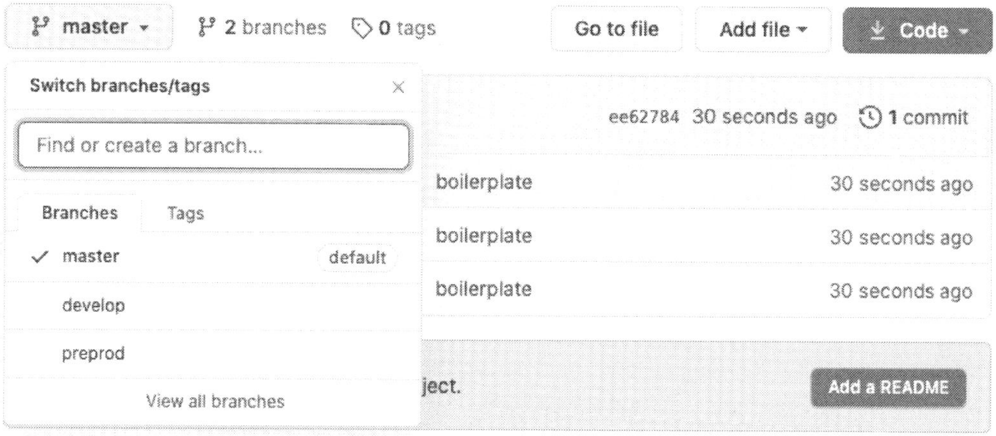

Figure 2.3 – GitHub branches

> **Note**
>
> If you're working with a team of developers, you will need to issue the `go mod download` command to install the required dependencies after cloning the project from GitHub.

In the next sub-section, we'll see how you can define the data model.

Defining the data model

Before digging into the routes definition, we need to define a model that will hold information about a recipe. We can create our model by defining a Go struct. This model will contain the properties/fields of a recipe. Declare the following struct in the `main.go` file:

```
type Recipe struct {
    Name            string    `json:"name"`
```

```
    Tags            []string    `json:"tags"`
    Ingredients     []string    `json:"ingredients"`
    Instructions    []string    `json:"instructions"`
    PublishedAt     time.Time   `json:"publishedAt"`
}
```

Our `Recipe` model is self-explanatory. Each recipe should have a name, a list of ingredients, a list of instructions or steps, and a publication date. Moreover, each recipe belongs to a set of categories or tags (for example, vegan, Italian, pastry, salads, and so on), as well as an ID, which is a unique identifier to differentiate each recipe in the database. We will also specify the tags on each field using backtick annotation; for example, `json:"NAME"`. This allows us to map each field to a different name when we send them as responses, since JSON and Go have different naming conventions.

Once the struct has been defined, push the changes to a new branch based on the `develop` branch:

```
git checkout -b feature/datamodel
git add main.go
git commit -m "recipe data model"
git push origin feature/datamodel
```

Once you've pushed these changes to your repository, the **Compare & pull request** button will appear in GitHub. Click on it and open a pull request by clicking on the **Create pull request** button to merge `feature/datamodel` with the `develop` branch:

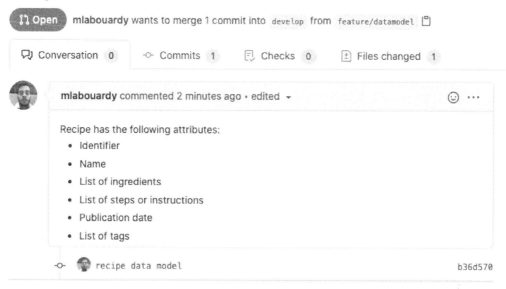

Figure 2.4 – GitHub pull request

Merge the changes to the `develop` branch and delete the `feature/datamodel` branch:

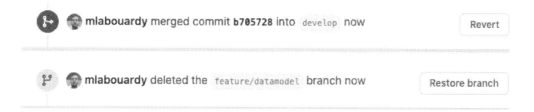

Figure 2.5 – Merging the pull request into the develop branch

With the data model defined, we can look at the route handler definitions. The API will expose various endpoints. Let's take a look at them now.

HTTP endpoints

The following table shows the list of HTTP endpoints that we can use:

HTTP Method	Resource	Description
GET	`/recipes`	Returns a list of recipes
POST	`/recipes`	Creates a new recipe
PUT	`/recipes/{id}`	Updates an existing recipe
DELETE	`/recipes/{id}`	Deletes an existing recipe
GET	`/recipes/search?tag=X`	Searches for recipes by tags

Now, we are going to establish the endpoints of our API. We will set this up by creating all our endpoints in the `main` function. Every endpoint needs a separate function to handle the request. We will define them in the `main.go` file.

> **Note**
>
> In the next chapter, we will cover how to structure the Go project according to the standard Go layout.

Implementing HTTP routes

In this section, we will create function handlers to handle POST, GET, PUT, and DELETE HTTP requests. So, let's jump right into it.

POST /recipes

First, let's implement the endpoint responsible for creating a new recipe. Create a POST method on the `/recipes` resource. Then, define a `NewRecipeHandler` method for that path. The `main.go` file should look something like this:

```
package main

import (
    "time"
    "github.com/gin-gonic/gin"
)

type Recipe struct {
```

```
    ID          string      `json:"id"`
    Name        string      `json:"name"`
    Tags        []string    `json:"tags"`
    Ingredients []string    `json:"ingredients"`
    Instructions []string   `json:"instructions"`
    PublishedAt time.Time   `json:"publishedAt"`
}


func NewRecipeHandler(c *gin.Context) {

}


func main() {
    router := gin.Default()
    router.POST("/recipes", NewRecipeHandler)
    router.Run()
}
```

Before writing the code of the NewRecipeHandler method, we need to define a global variable called recipes to store the list of recipes. This variable will be used temporarily and will be replaced in the next chapter with a database for data persistency. To initialize the recipes variable, we can use the init() method, which will be executed during the startup of the application:

```
var recipes []Recipe
func init() {
    recipes = make([]Recipe, 0)
}
```

Here, we will define the logic behind NewRecipeHandler. The c.ShouldBindJSON function marshals the incoming request body into a Recipe struct and then assigns a unique identifier with an external package called xid. Next, it assigns a publication date with the time.Now() function and appends the recipe to the list of recipes, which will keep it in memory. If the request body is invalid, then the handler will return an error (400 status code). Otherwise, the handler will return a 200 status code:

```
func NewRecipeHandler(c *gin.Context) {
    var recipe Recipe
    if err := c.ShouldBindJSON(&recipe); err != nil {
```

```
        c.JSON(http.StatusBadRequest, gin.H{
            "error": err.Error()})
        return
    }
    recipe.ID = xid.New().String()
    recipe.PublishedAt = time.Now()
    recipes = append(recipes, recipe)
    c.JSON(http.StatusOK, recipe)
}
```

In the previous code, we used a built-in status code constants such as `http.StatusOK` and `http.StatusBadRequest` instead of a hardcoded HTTP status code. We're also setting the response type to JSON.

Before running the application, we need to download the `xid` package, which is used to generate a unique ID:

```
go get github.com/rs/xid
```

The new dependency will be added automatically to the `go.sum` and `go.mod` files. Run the server, as follows:

```
go run main.go
```

An HTTP server will be deployed on port `8080`:

```
[GIN-debug] [WARNING] Creating an Engine instance with the Logger and Recovery middleware already attached.

[GIN-debug] [WARNING] Running in "debug" mode. Switch to "release" mode in production.
 - using env:   export GIN_MODE=release
 - using code:  gin.SetMode(gin.ReleaseMode)

[GIN-debug] POST   /recipes                  --> main.NewRecipeHandler (3 handlers)
[GIN-debug] Environment variable PORT is undefined. Using port :8080 by default
[GIN-debug] Listening and serving HTTP on :8080
```

Figure 2.6 – Gin server logs

To test it out, issue a POST request with the Postman client at `http://localhost:8080/recipes` with the following JSON in the request body:

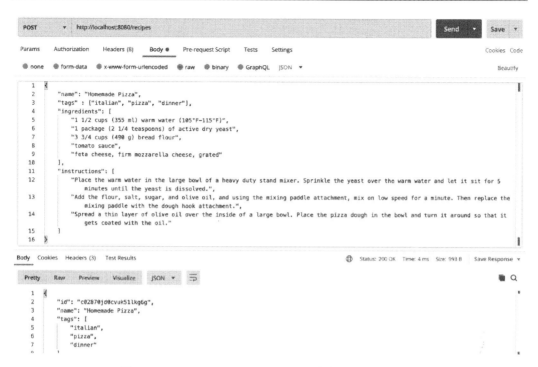

Figure 2.7 – Issuing a POST request with the Postman client

The preceding command will add the recipe to the array of recipes and return it with an assigned ID and publication date.

Another alternative to Postman is to use the cURL command. Use the following cURL command with the POST verb, followed by a JSON document:

```
curl --location --request POST 'http://localhost:8080/recipes' \
--header 'Content-Type: application/json' \
--data-raw '{
    "name": "Homemade Pizza",
    "tags" : ["italian", "pizza", "dinner"],
    "ingredients": [
        "1 1/2 cups (355 ml) warm water (105°F-115°F)",
        "1 package (2 1/4 teaspoons) of active dry yeast",
        "3 3/4 cups (490 g) bread flour",
        "feta cheese, firm mozzarella cheese, grated"
    ],
    "instructions": [
```

```
        "Step 1.",
        "Step 2.",
        "Step 3."
    ]
}' | jq -r
```

> **Note**
>
> The jq utility https://stedolan.github.io/jq/ is used to
> format the response body in JSON format. It's a powerful command-line JSON
> processor.

With the POST endpoint working as expected, we can push the code changes to a new feature branch:

```
git checkout -b feature/new_recipe
git add .
git commit -m "new recipe endpoint"
git push origin feature/new_recipe
```

Once committed, raise a pull request to merge the feature/new_recipe branch with the develop branch:

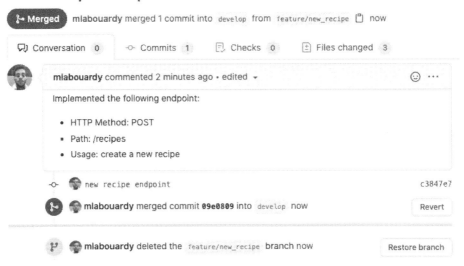

Figure 2.8 – Merging a new recipe endpoint feature branch into the develop branch

Make sure to delete the feature branch once the changes have been merged.

Now that the POST /recipes endpoint has been created, we can implement a GET /recipes endpoint to list all the recipes we have added using the POST/recipes endpoint.

GET /recipes

Similar to the previous endpoint, register a GET method on the /recipes resource and attach ListRecipesHandler. The function will be invoked when an incoming GET request is received on the /recipes resource. The code is straightforward; it marshals the recipes array to JSON with the c.JSON() method:

```
func ListRecipesHandler(c *gin.Context) {
    c.JSON(http.StatusOK, recipes)
}


func main() {
    router := gin.Default()
    router.POST("/recipes", NewRecipeHandler)
    router.GET("/recipes", ListRecipesHandler)
    router.Run()
}
```

Redeploy the app with the go run main.go command:

```
[GIN-debug] [WARNING] Creating an Engine instance with the Logger and Recovery middleware already attached.

[GIN-debug] [WARNING] Running in "debug" mode. Switch to "release" mode in production.
 - using env:   export GIN_MODE=release
 - using code:  gin.SetMode(gin.ReleaseMode)

[GIN-debug] POST   /recipes                  --> main.NewRecipeHandler (3 handlers)
[GIN-debug] GET    /recipes                  --> main.ListRecipesHandler (3 handlers)
[GIN-debug] Environment variable PORT is undefined. Using port :8080 by default
[GIN-debug] Listening and serving HTTP on :8080
```

Figure 2.9 – Exposing a GET endpoint

To test the endpoint, issue a GET request on `http://localhost:8080/recipes`. Here, an empty array will be returned:

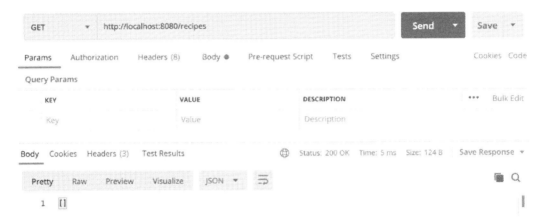

Figure 2.10 – Fetching a list of recipes

The corresponding `cURL` command is as follows:

```
curl -s --location --request GET 'http://localhost:8080/
recipes' \
--header 'Content-Type: application/json'
```

The empty array is due to the fact the `recipes` variable is only available during the runtime of the application. In the next chapter, we will cover how to connect the RESTful API to a database such as MongoDB for data persistency. But for now, we can initialize the `recipes` array upon starting the application by placing the initialization code in the `init()` method.

The loading mechanism will be based on a JSON file that contains a list of recipes that I have created in advance. The complete list is available in this book's GitHub repository:

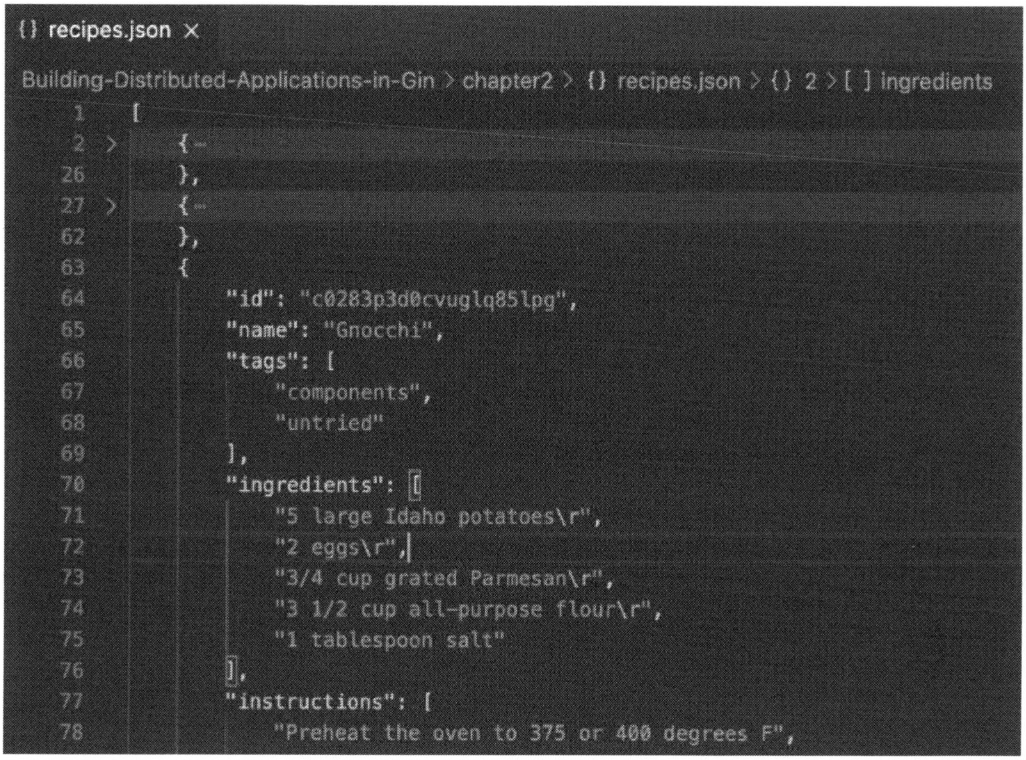

Figure 2.11 – List of recipes in JSON format

We will read the JSON file with the `ioutil.ReadFile()` method and then convert the content into an array of recipes with the following code snippet:

```go
func init() {
    recipes = make([]Recipe, 0)
    file, _ := ioutil.ReadFile("recipes.json")
    _ = json.Unmarshal([]byte(file), &recipes)
}
```

Don't forget to import `encoding/json` and `io/ioutil` before you rerun the application and issue a GET request on the `/recipes` endpoint. This time, a list of recipes will be returned in JSON format:

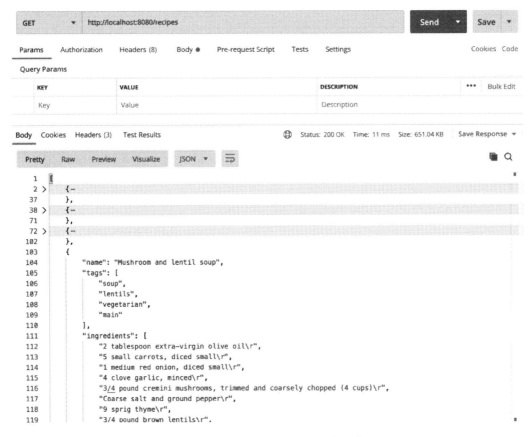

Figure 2.12 – GET /recipes returning a list of recipes

You can use the `curl` and `jq` commands to count the number of recipes that are returned by the request:

```
curl -s -X GET 'http://localhost:8080/recipes' | jq length
```

The `recipes.json` file contains 492 recipes; therefore, the HTTP request should return 492 recipes:

```
mlabouardy@Mohameds-MBP-001 chapter2 % curl -s -X GET 'http://localhost:8080/recipes' | jq length
492
```

Figure 2.13 – Using jq to count JSON items

Commit the new endpoint code to Git by creating a new feature branch with the following commands:

```
git checkout -b feature/fetch_all_recipes
git add .
git commit -m "list recipes endpoint"
git push origin feature/fetch_all_recipes
```

Once the changes have been pushed, create a pull request and merge the branch into `develop`:

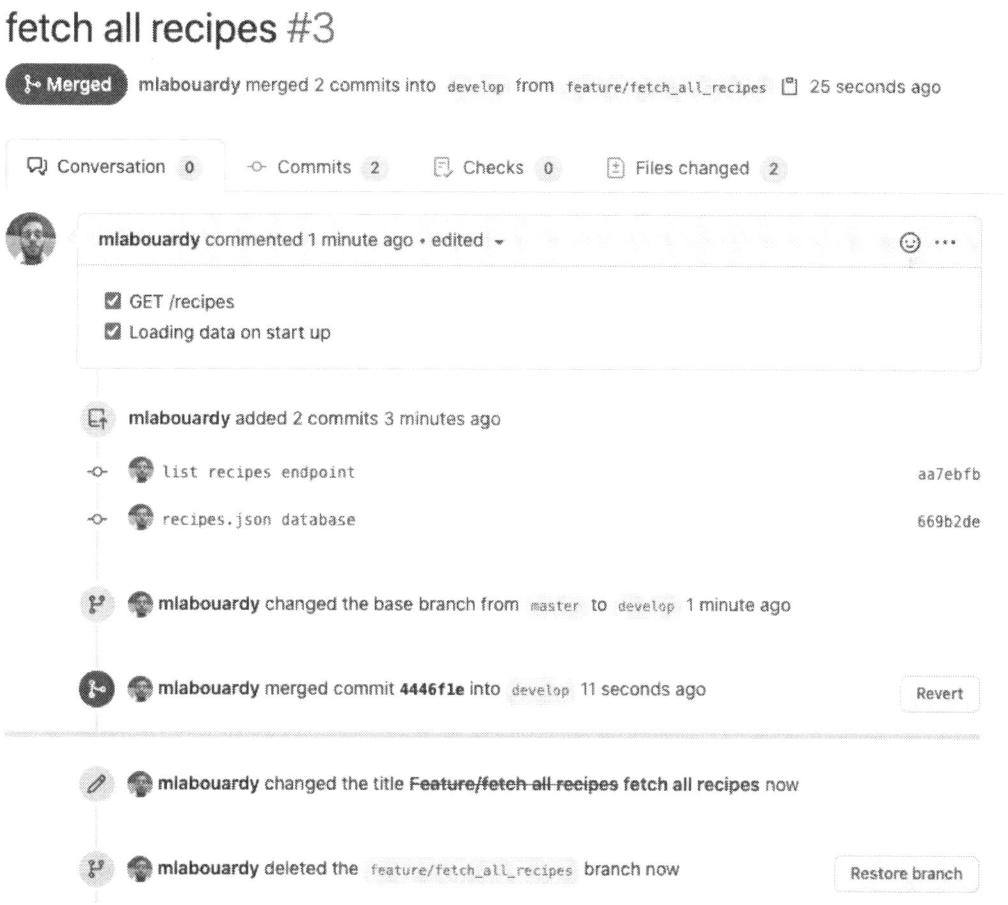

fetch all recipes #3

⑂ Merged   mlabouardy merged 2 commits into `develop` from `feature/fetch_all_recipes`   📋 25 seconds ago

💬 Conversation 0	⦿ Commits 2	☑ Checks 0	± Files changed 2

mlabouardy commented 1 minute ago · edited ▾   ☺ ···

☑ GET /recipes
☑ Loading data on start up

mlabouardy added 2 commits 3 minutes ago

⦿   list recipes endpoint   aa7ebfb

⦿   recipes.json database   669b2de

mlabouardy changed the base branch from `master` to `develop` 1 minute ago

mlabouardy merged commit **4446f1e** into `develop` 11 seconds ago   Revert

mlabouardy changed the title ~~Feature/fetch all recipes~~ fetch all recipes now

mlabouardy deleted the `feature/fetch_all_recipes` branch now   Restore branch

Figure 2.14 – Merging the list of recipes endpoint feature branch into the develop branch

PUT /recipes/{id}

To update an existing recipe, we will use the PUT verb with a path query parameter called ID, representing the identifier of the recipe to be updated. Register an endpoint on the / recipes/:id resource inside your main function:

```
router.PUT("/recipes/:id", UpdateRecipeHandler)
```

The UpdateRecipeHandler endpoint's handler code is provided in the following snippet. It fetches the recipe ID from the request URL with the c.Param() method, converts the request body into a Recipe struct, and loops through the list of recipes, looking for the recipe to update. If it's not found, an error message is sent with a 404 code error; otherwise, the recipe is updated with the new values from the request body:

```go
func UpdateRecipeHandler(c *gin.Context) {
    id := c.Param("id")
    var recipe Recipe
    if err := c.ShouldBindJSON(&recipe); err != nil {
        c.JSON(http.StatusBadRequest, gin.H{
            "error": err.Error()})
        return
    }

    index := -1
    for i := 0; i < len(recipes); i++ {
        if recipes[i].ID == id {
            index = i
        }
    }

    if index == -1 {
        c.JSON(http.StatusNotFound, gin.H{
            "error": "Recipe not found"})
        return
    }

    recipes[index] = recipe
```

```
    c.JSON(http.StatusOK, recipe)
}
```

Relaunch the server, then issue a POST request to create a new recipe. To illustrate how the update endpoint is working, we will create a recipe for a margherita pizza with the following sample JSON:

```
{
    "name": "Homemade Pizza",
    "tags" : ["italian", "pizza", "dinner"],
    "ingredients": [
        "pizza dough",
        "tomato sauce",
        "olive oil",
        "7 ounces fresh mozzarella cheese, cut into
         1/2-inch cubes",
        "5 - 6 large fresh basil leaves"
    ],
    "instructions": []
}
```

To test it out, once again with the Postman client, issue a new POST request on `http://localhost:8080/recipes` with this JSON document:

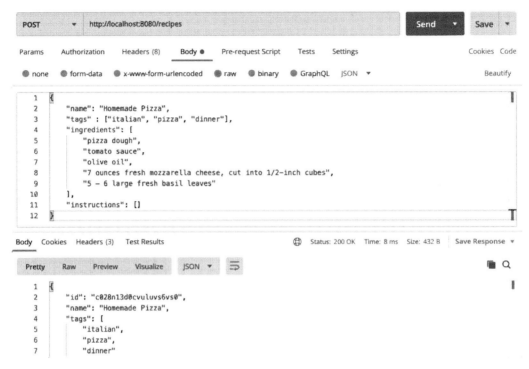

Figure 2.15 – Adding a new recipe

The Homemade Pizza recipe will be created, and you will have received the ID of the new recipe (in our example, it is c2inb6q3k1kc2p0uqetg). Let's say we want to update the recipe and change it to Shrimp scampi pizza. This time, we can use the PUT method and provide the ID of the recipe as a path parameter:

Figure 2.16 – Updating an existing recipe

The request will return a 200 status code. To verify that the changes have taken effect, we can use the GET /recipes endpoint:

Figure 2.17 – Verifying the changes are being applied to the recipe

Push the new endpoint to a new feature branch and merge the branch into develop:

```
git checkout -b feature/update_recipe
git add .
git commit -m "update recipe endpoint"
git push origin feature/update_recipe
```

DELETE /recipes/{id}

To delete a recipe, we need to register the DELETE HTTP route inside our main function, as follows:

```
router.DELETE("/recipes/:id", DeleteRecipeHandler)
```

The DeleteRecipeHandler function's code will get the target recipe ID from the request parameter and loop through the list of recipes. If no matching recipe is found, an error message of "Recipe not found" will be sent with a 404 status code. Otherwise, the recipe index on the array will be used and the recipe will be deleted based on the index:

```go
func DeleteRecipeHandler(c *gin.Context) {
    id := c.Param("id")
    index := -1
    for i := 0; i < len(recipes); i++ {
        if recipes[i].ID == id {
            index = i
        }
    }

    if index == -1 {
        c.JSON(http.StatusNotFound, gin.H{
            "error": "Recipe not found"})
        return
    }

    recipes = append(recipes[:index], recipes[index+1:]...)
    c.JSON(http.StatusOK, gin.H{
        "message": "Recipe has been deleted"})
}
```

To test the delete endpoint, use the Postman client or issue a cURL command in the terminal session:

```
curl -v -sX DELETE http://localhost:8080/recipes/
c0283p3d0cvuglq85log | jq -r
```

If the target recipe exists, then it will be deleted, and you will see that a success message is returned:

```
[mlabouardy@Mohameds-MBP-001 chapter2 % curl -v -sX DELETE http://localhost:8080/recipes/c0283p3d0cvuglq85log | jq -r
*   Trying ::1...
* TCP_NODELAY set
* Connected to localhost (::1) port 8080 (#0)
> DELETE /recipes/c0283p3d0cvuglq85log HTTP/1.1
> Host: localhost:8080
> User-Agent: curl/7.64.1
> Accept: */*
>
< HTTP/1.1 200 OK
< Content-Type: application/json; charset=utf-8
< Date: Sun, 17 Jan 2021 19:29:06 GMT
< Content-Length: 37
<
{ [37 bytes data]
* Connection #0 to host localhost left intact
* Closing connection 0
{
  "message": "Recipe has been deleted"
}
```

Figure 2.18 – Deleting a recipe

Otherwise, an error message will be returned:

```
[mlabouardy@Mohameds-MBP-001 chapter2 % curl -v -sX DELETE http://localhost:8080/recipes/c0283p3d0cvuglq85log | jq -r
*   Trying ::1...
* TCP_NODELAY set
* Connected to localhost (::1) port 8080 (#0)
> DELETE /recipes/c0283p3d0cvuglq85log HTTP/1.1
> Host: localhost:8080
> User-Agent: curl/7.64.1
> Accept: */*
>
< HTTP/1.1 404 Not Found
< Content-Type: application/json; charset=utf-8
< Date: Sun, 17 Jan 2021 19:30:39 GMT
< Content-Length: 28
<
{ [28 bytes data]
* Connection #0 to host localhost left intact
* Closing connection 0
{
  "error": "Recipe not found"
}
```

Figure 2.19 – An error 404 message is returned if the recipe is not found

Once again, store the changes in a feature branch and merge the changes into `develop`:

```
git checkout -b feature/delete_recipe
git add .
git commit -m "delete recipe endpoint"
git push origin feature/delete_recipe
```

GET /recipes/search

The final endpoint allows users to search for recipes based on tags or keywords:

```
router.GET("/recipes/search", SearchRecipesHandler)
```

The `SearchRecipesHandler` handler code snippet is as follows (don't forget to import `strings`):

```
func SearchRecipesHandler(c *gin.Context) {
    tag := c.Query("tag")
    listOfRecipes := make([]Recipe, 0)

    for i := 0; i < len(recipes); i++ {
        found := false
        for _, t := range recipes[i].Tags {
            if strings.EqualFold(t, tag) {
                found = true
            }
        }
        if found {
            listOfRecipes = append(listOfRecipes,
                recipes[i])
        }
    }

    c.JSON(http.StatusOK, listOfRecipes)
}
```

The HTTP handler fetches the tag value given in the query parameter with the `c.Query` method.

You can test the endpoint by looking for Italian recipes with a GET request at `http://localhost:8080/recipes/search?tag=italian`:

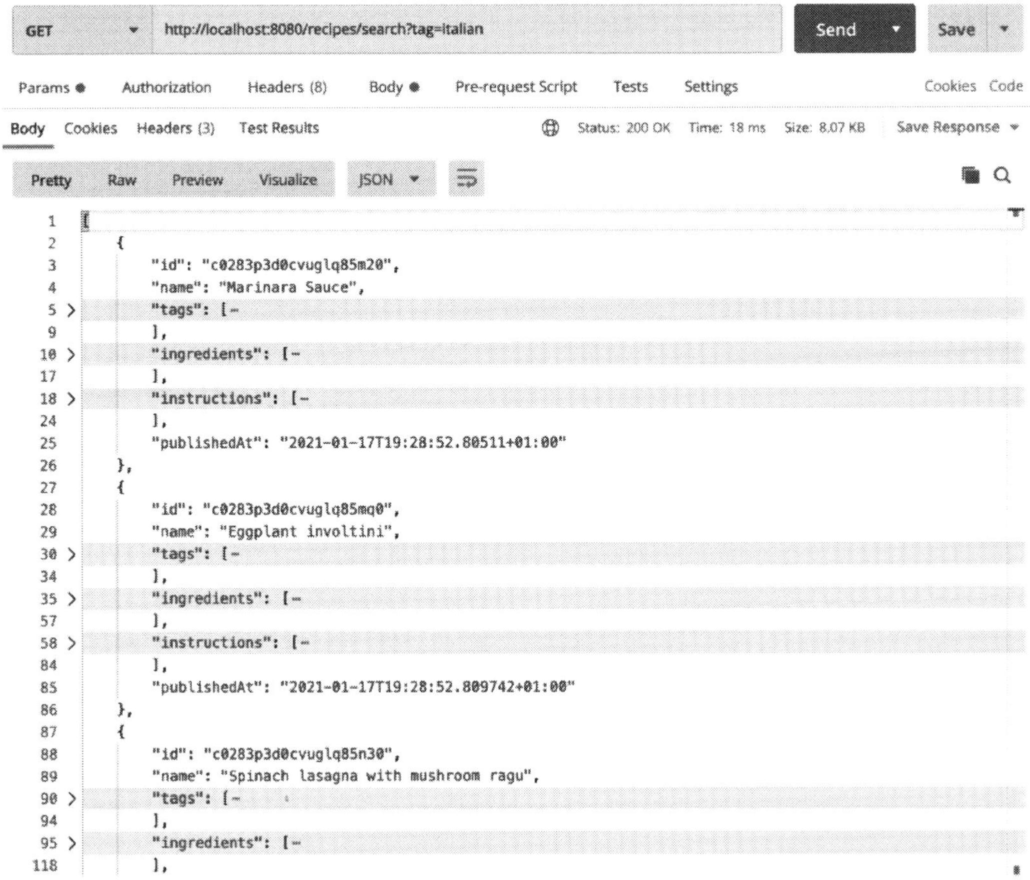

Figure 2.20 – Searching for recipes with a query parameter

Finally, push the search endpoint code to the remote repository by creating a new feature branch:

```
git checkout -b feature/search_recipe
git add .
git commit -m "search recipe by tag"
git push origin feature/search_recipe
```

> **Note**
>
> Before each commit, make sure to run the `go mod tidy` command to ensure your `go.mod` and `go.sum` files are clean and accurate.

So far, we have covered how to build a RESTful API in Golang with the Gin framework. However, without meaningful documentation of the API, users won't be able to use it.

Documentation should be part of your development cycle, to help you maintain a scalable API. That's why, in the next section, we will explore how to use the **OpenAPI Specification (OAS)**.

Writing the OpenAPI Specification

The OpenAPI Specification (formerly known as the Swagger Specification) is an API description format or API definition language. It allows you to describe an API, including the following information:

- General information about the API

- The available paths and operations (HTTP methods)

- The expected inputs (query or path parameters, request body, and so on) and responses (HTTP status code, response body, and so on) for each operation

Finding an easy way to generate the OpenAPI definition from an existing API can be challenging. The good news is that Swagger tools can help you do this with ease.

Installing Go Swagger

To get started, install the `go-swagger` tool from the official guide at `https://goswagger.io/install.html` or download the binary from GitHub at `https://github.com/go-swagger/go-swagger/releases`. At the time of writing this book, the latest stable version is v0.25.0:

🔲 sha1sum.txt	441 Bytes
🔲 sha256sum.txt	687 Bytes
🔲 swagger_darwin_amd64	16.6 MB
🔲 swagger_linux_386	12.7 MB
🔲 swagger_linux_amd64	15.3 MB
🔲 swagger_linux_arm	12.7 MB
🔲 swagger_linux_arm64	14 MB
🔲 swagger_windows_386.exe	13.1 MB
🔲 swagger_windows_amd64.exe	15.6 MB
📄 Source code (zip)	
📄 Source code (tar.gz)	

Figure 2.21 – Go Swagger binary – latest release

Make sure to add it to the `PATH` environment variable. Then, issue the following command to verify the installation:

```
go-swagger version
```

The preceding command should display the following output:

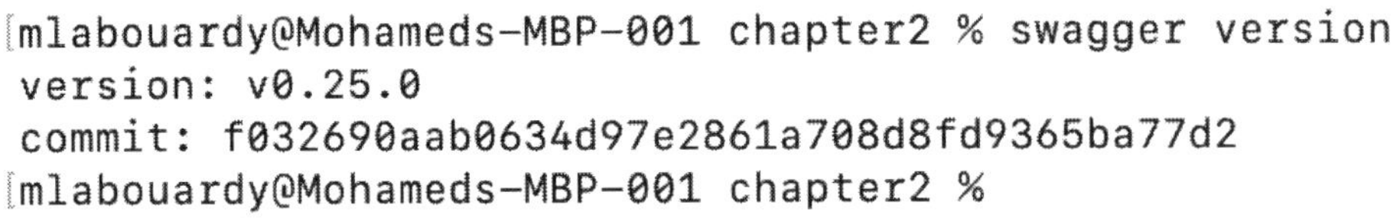

```
[mlabouardy@Mohameds-MBP-001 chapter2 % swagger version
version: v0.25.0
commit: f032690aab0634d97e2861a708d8fd9365ba77d2
[mlabouardy@Mohameds-MBP-001 chapter2 %
```

Figure 2.22 – Go Swagger version

Now, it's time to write our OpenAPI Specification for the recipes API.

> **Note**
>
> An alternative to `go-swagger` is `swag` (`https://github.com/swaggo/swag`). This tool can be used to convert Go annotations into Swagger documentation.

Swagger metadata

We'll start by providing some basic information about the API with the `swagger:meta` annotation. This annotation has the following properties:

Property	Description
Schemes	The transfer protocols supported by your API are HTTP and HTTPS.
Host	The host where the API is served (for instance, `localhost:8080`).
BasePath	The default base path for the API (for example, `/v1`).
Version	The current version of the API. Multiple versioning strategies can be used. In this book, we will be using semantic versioning (`https://semver.org/`).
Contact	The API owner or author.
Consumes	A list of default MIME type values, one per line for the content the API receives (for example, `application/json`).
Produces	A list of default MIME type values, one per line for the content the API sends. A full list can be found here: `https://developer.mozilla.org/en-US/docs/Web/HTTP/Basics_of_HTTP/MIME_types`.

Add the following comments at the top of the `main` package:

```
// Recipes API
//
// This is a sample recipes API. You can find out more about
the API at https://github.com/PacktPublishing/Building-
Distributed-Applications-in-Gin.
//
//   Schemes: http
```

```
//   Host: localhost:8080
//   BasePath: /
//   Version: 1.0.0
//   Contact: Mohamed Labouardy
// <mohamed@labouardy.com> https://labouardy.com
//
//   Consumes:
//   - application/json
//
//   Produces:
//   - application/json
// swagger:meta
package main
```

These comments include things such as the API's description, version, base URL, and so on. There are more fields that you can include (a full list is available at `https://goswagger.io/use/spec/meta.html`).

To generate the OpenAPI Specification, we will use the `swagger` command-line tool. The CLI will parse the `main.go` file. If the parser encounters a comment that matches the Swagger annotation or any supported tags, it will generate the corresponding block of the specification.

On your Terminal, issue the following command to generate a `spec` file:

```
swagger generate spec -o ./swagger.json
```

This command will generate the specification in JSON format. You can generate the spec in YAML format as well by just appending the output with the `.yml` or `.yaml` extension.

The content of the generated `swagger.json` file will look as follows:

```
{
 "consumes": [
    "application/json"
 ],
 "produces": [
    "application/json"
 ],
 "schemes": [
```

```
    "http"
],
"swagger": "2.0",
"info": {
    "description": "This is a sample recipes API. You can
    find out more about the API at https://github.com/
PacktPublishing/Building-Distributed-Applications-in-Gin.",
    "title": "Recipes API",
    "contact": {
        "name": "Mohamed Labouardy",
        "url": "https://labouardy.com",
        "email": "mohamed@labouardy.com"
    },
    "version": "1.0.0"
},
"host": "localhost:8080",
"basePath": "/",
"paths": {}
}
```

Another cool thing with the Swagger command line is its embedded UI. You can load the generated spec in the Swagger UI locally with the following command:

```
swagger serve ./swagger.json
```

The UI will be exposed on port `http://localhost:49566`:

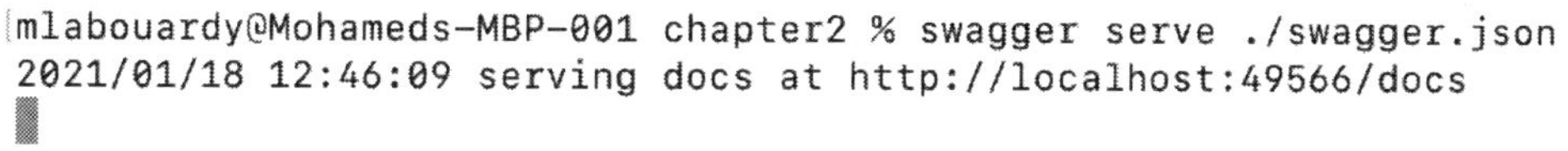

```
mlabouardy@Mohameds-MBP-001 chapter2 % swagger serve ./swagger.json
2021/01/18 12:46:09 serving docs at http://localhost:49566/docs
```

Figure 2.23 – Loading the Swagger specs in the UI

If you point your browser to that URL, you should see the UI based on the Redoc template. The UI comes in two two flavors – Redoc and the Swagger UI:

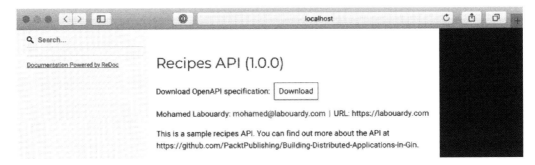

Figure 2.24 – Swagger with a Redoc flavor

If you're a fan of the Swagger UI, you can set the flavor flag to `swagger` with the following command:

```
swagger serve -F swagger ./swagger.json
```

This time, the API specification will be served from the Swagger UI:

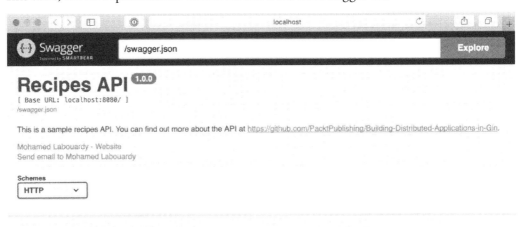

Figure 2.25 – Swagger UI mode

> **Note**
>
> You can also use the Swagger Online Editor (`https://editor.swagger.io/`) to edit and load your OpenAPI Specification file.

Next, we will define a `swagger:operation` for listing recipe endpoints. The annotation has the following attributes:

Property	Description
Summary	A short description of what the operation does
Responses	The list of possible responses when they are returned from executing the operation
Parameters	A list of parameters that can be applied to the operation
Consumes	A list of default MIME type values, one per line for the content the operation receives (for example, `application/json`)
Produces	A list of default MIME type values, one per line for the content the operation sends

You can find all the properties at `https://github.com/OAI/OpenAPI-Specification/blob/master/versions/2.0.md#operationObject`.

Annotate the `ListRecipesHandler` function, as shown here. The annotation takes the HTTP method, path pattern, and operation ID as parameters:

```
// swagger:operation GET /recipes recipes listRecipes
// Returns list of recipes
// ---
// produces:
// - application/json
// responses:
//     '200':
//         description: Successful operation
func ListRecipesHandler(c *gin.Context) {
    c.JSON(http.StatusOK, recipes)
}
```

For each operation, you can describe the HTTP response that matches an HTTP status code (200, 404, and so on) in the `responses` section. For this endpoint, we'll only return a 200 success code when responding to GET `/recipes`. The `description` field explains what this response means.

Generate the specification with the Swagger CLI and reload `swagger.json`. This time, the GET /recipes operation will be added:

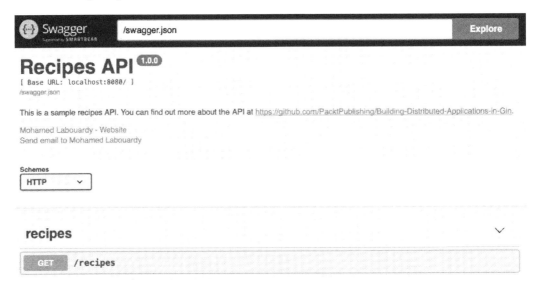

Figure 2.26 – Adding a new Swagger operation

Define another Swagger operation for the PUT /recipes/{id} endpoint. Similar to the previous operation, we can define responses based on the handled response code. We can also define the ID as a `path` parameter in the `parameters` section. As well as provide an optional description, as follows:

```
// swagger:operation PUT /recipes/{id} recipes updateRecipe
// Update an existing recipe
// ---
// parameters:
// - name: id
//    in: path
//    description: ID of the recipe
//    required: true
//    type: string
// produces:
// - application/json
// responses:
//      '200':
//          description: Successful operation
```

```
//        '400':
//            description: Invalid input
//        '404':
//            description: Invalid recipe ID
func UpdateRecipeHandler(c *gin.Context) {}
```

Regenerate the `swagger.json` file and reload the Swagger UI:

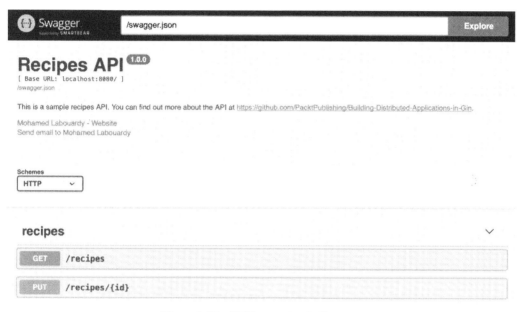

Figure 2.27 – PUT operation in Swagger

Define the rest of the operations. You should have something similar to the following:

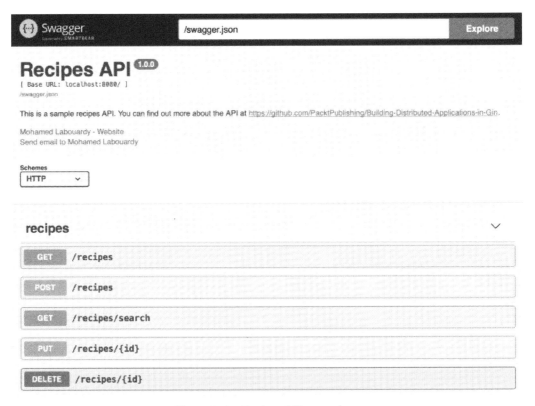

Figure 2.28 – Recipes API operations

With that, you have learned the basics of the OpenAPI Specification.

Being a simple JSON file, the OpenAPI Specification file can be shared and managed within any SCM, just like the application source code. Commit the spec file to GitHub with the following commands:

```
git checkout -b feature/openapi
git add .
git commit -m "added openapi specs"
git push origin feature/openapi
```

The updated repository will look as follows:

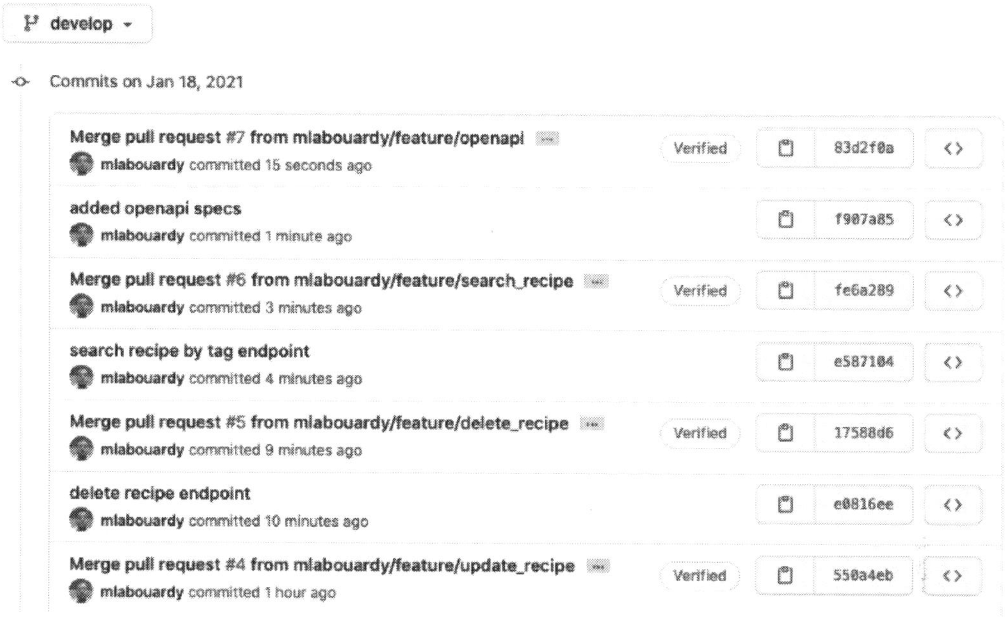

Figure 2.29 – Storing the OpenAPI Specification on GitHub

Summary

In this chapter, you learned how to build a RESTful API from scratch with the Gin framework. We also covered how to validate incoming HTTP requests with Gin data binding and validation methods. Then, we provided an introduction to the OpenAPI Specification and learned how to generate it from an existing API. You should now be familiar with exposing HTTP methods (GET, POST, DELETE, PUT, and so on) to handle HTTP requests.

In the next chapter, we will use MongoDB as a NoSQL database to manage data persistency for our API.

Questions

1. What's the GitFlow strategy?

2. How can we define a data model in Go?

3. How can we validate a POST request body in Gin?

4. Define an API endpoint that can get one recipe by ID.

5. Define a body parameter of the new recipe endpoint with OpenAPI.

Further reading

*   *Hands-On RESTful API Design Patterns and Best Practices*, by Harihara Subramanian, Pethuru Raj, Packt Publishing

*   *DevOps with GIT(Flow) Jenkins, Artifactory, Sonar, ELK, JIRA [Video]*, by Nand Venegalla, Packt Publishing

3
Managing Data Persistence with MongoDB

In the previous chapter, we learned how to build a RESTful API with the Gin web framework. In this one, we will integrate MongoDB into the backend for data storage, and we will also cover how to optimize database queries with Redis as a caching layer.

In this chapter, we will cover the following topics:

- Setting up MongoDB with Docker
- Configuring Go MongoDB driver
- Implementing MongoDB queries & and CRUD operations
- Standard Go project layout
- Deploying Redis with Docker
- Optimizing API response time with caching
- Performance benchmark with Apache Benchmark

By the end of this chapter, you will be able to perform CRUD operations on a MongoDB database using Go.

Technical requirements

To follow the content in this chapter, you will need the following:

- You must have a complete understanding of the previous chapter since this chapter is a follow-up of the previous one; it will use the same source code. Hence, some snippets won't be explained to avoid repetition.

- Some knowledge of NoSQL concepts and MongoDB basic queries.

The code bundle for this chapter is hosted on GitHub at `https://github.com/ PacktPublishing/Building-Distributed-Applications-in-Gin/tree/ main/chapter03`.

Running a MongoDB Server

The API we've built so far is not connected to a database. For a real-world application, we need to use a form of data storage; otherwise, data will be lost if the API crashes or the server hosting the API goes down. MongoDB is one of the most popular NoSQL databases.

The following schema shows how MongoDB will be integrated into the API architecture:

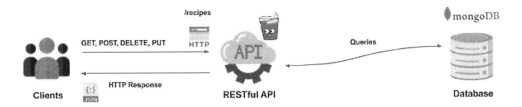

Figure 3.1 – API architecture

Before we get started, we need to deploy a MongoDB server. There are plenty of deployment options:

- You can download the MongoDB Community Edition binary from the following URL: `https://www.mongodb.com/try/download/community`. Select a package based on your OS:

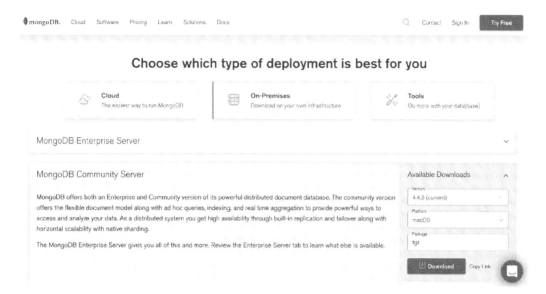

Figure 3.2 – MongoDB Community Server

- You can use the MongoDB as a Service solution, known as MongoDB Atlas (`https://www.mongodb.com/cloud/atlas`), to run a free 500 MB database on the cloud. You can deploy a fully managed MongoDB server on AWS, Google Cloud Platform, or Microsoft Azure.

- You can run MongoDB locally with a containerization solution such as Docker. Multiple Docker images are available on DockerHub with a MongoDB server configured and ready to use out of the box.

I opted to go with Docker due to its popularity and simplicity in running ephemeral environments.

Installing Docker CE

Docker (`https://www.docker.com/get-started`) is an open source project that allows you to run, build, and manage containers. A container is like a separate OS, but not virtualized; it only contains the dependencies needed for that one application, which makes the container portable and deployable on-premises or on the cloud.

The following diagram shows the main difference between containers and virtual machines in their architecture approach:

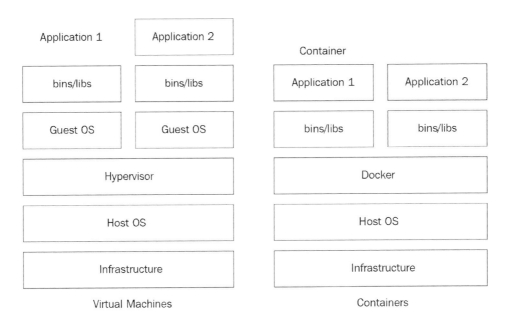

Figure 3.3 – Virtual machines versus containers

Virtualization happens at the hardware level for virtual machines, while for containers, it happens at the application layer. Therefore, containers can share the OS kernel and libraries, which makes them very lightweight and resource-efficient (CPU, RAM, disk, and so on).

To get started, you need to install Docker Engine on your machine. Navigate to `https://docs.docker.com/get-docker/` and install Docker for your platform:

Figure 3.4 – Docker installation

> **Note**
>
> Mac users can also use the Homebrew utility to install Docker with the `brew install docker` command.

Follow the installation wizard and, once completed, verify that everything works fine by executing the following command:

```
docker version
```

At the time of writing this book, I'm using Docker **Community Edition** (**CE**) version 20.10.2, as shown in the following screenshot:

```
Client: Docker Engine - Community
 Cloud integration: 1.0.7
 Version:           20.10.2
 API version:       1.41
 Go version:        go1.13.15
 Git commit:        2291f61
 Built:             Mon Dec 28 16:12:42 2020
 OS/Arch:           darwin/amd64
 Context:           default
 Experimental:      true

Server: Docker Engine - Community
 Engine:
  Version:          20.10.2
  API version:      1.41 (minimum version 1.12)
  Go version:       go1.13.15
  Git commit:       8891c58
  Built:            Mon Dec 28 16:15:28 2020
  OS/Arch:          linux/amd64
  Experimental:     false
 containerd:
  Version:          1.4.3
  GitCommit:        269548fa27e0089a8b8278fc4fc781d7f65a939b
 runc:
  Version:          1.0.0-rc92
  GitCommit:        ff819c7e9184c13b7c2607fe6c30ae19403a7aff
 docker-init:
  Version:          0.19.0
  GitCommit:        de40ad0
```

Figure 3.5 – Docker Community Edition (CE) version

With Docker installed, you can deploy your first container. Issue the following command in your terminal session:

```
docker run hello-world
```

The preceding command will deploy a container based on the `hello-world` image. When the container runs, it will print a *Hello from Docker*! message and exit:

```
mlabouardy@Mohameds-MBP-001 chapter3 % docker run hello-world
Unable to find image 'hello-world:latest' locally
latest: Pulling from library/hello-world
0e03bdcc26d7: Pull complete
Digest: sha256:31b9c7d48790f0d8c50ab433d9c3b7e17666d6993084c002c2ff1ca09b96391d
Status: Downloaded newer image for hello-world:latest

Hello from Docker!
This message shows that your installation appears to be working correctly.

To generate this message, Docker took the following steps:
 1. The Docker client contacted the Docker daemon.
 2. The Docker daemon pulled the "hello-world" image from the Docker Hub.
    (amd64)
 3. The Docker daemon created a new container from that image which runs the
    executable that produces the output you are currently reading.
 4. The Docker daemon streamed that output to the Docker client, which sent it
    to your terminal.

To try something more ambitious, you can run an Ubuntu container with:
 $ docker run -it ubuntu bash

Share images, automate workflows, and more with a free Docker ID:
 https://hub.docker.com/

For more examples and ideas, visit:
 https://docs.docker.com/get-started/
```

Figure 3.6 – Docker hello-world container

Congratulations! You are now successfully running Docker.

Running a MongoDB container

MongoDB's official image can be found on DockerHub (`https://hub.docker.com/_/mongo`). There are numerous images available, each representing different versions of MongoDB. You can use the `latest` tag to find them; however, it's recommended to specify the target version. At the time of writing this book, MongoDB 4.4.3 is the latest stable version. Execute the following command to deploy a container based on that version:

```
docker run -d --name mongodb -e MONGO_INITDB_ROOT_
USERNAME=admin -e MONGO_INITDB_ROOT_PASSWORD=password -p
27017:27017 mongo:4.4.3
```

This command will run a MongoDB container in detached mode (the -d flag). We're also mapping the container port to the host port so that we can access the database from the host level. Finally, we must create a new user and set that user's password through the MONGO_INITDB_ROOT_USERNAME and MONGO_INITDB_ROOT_PASSWORD environment variables.

For now, the MongoDB credentials are in plain text. Another way of passing sensitive information via environment variables is by using Docker Secrets. If you're running in Swarm mode, you can execute the following command:

```
openssl rand -base64 12 | docker secret create mongodb_password
-
```

> **Note**
> Docker Swarm mode is natively integrated in Docker engine. It's a container orchestration platform used to build, deploy, and scale containers across a cluster of nodes.

This command will generate a random password for a MongoDB user and set it as a Docker secret.

Next, update the docker run command so that it uses the Docker Secret instead of the password in plain text:

```
-e MONGO_INITDB_ROOT_PASSWORD_FILE=/run/secrets/mongodb_
password
```

The `docker run` command's output is as follows. It downloads the image from DockerHub and creates an instance (container) from it:

```
Unable to find image 'mongo:4.4.3' locally
4.4.3: Pulling from library/mongo
d519e2592276: Pull complete
d22d2dfcfa9c: Pull complete
b3afe92c540b: Pull complete
a2c1234bf134: Pull complete
05bf57f3b398: Pull complete
4737ab85f84c: Pull complete
6165557c172c: Pull complete
c2ca70046d29: Pull complete
b80a541da2a8: Pull complete
18edd0c32639: Pull complete
86830e28cf71: Pull complete
71e1d772417d: Pull complete
Digest: sha256:88e0308671a06d4ee7da41f87944ba66355b4ee3d57d57caf92f5e1938736abd
Status: Downloaded newer image for mongo:4.4.3
d860b80b1f9c56617bb0a5eddf9748ee97a642cc887187bffaf3514af2720fe7
```

Figure 3.7 – Pulling a MongoDB image from DockerHub

It's worth mentioning that if you're already running the MongoDB container, make sure that you remove it before executing the previous command; otherwise, you'll receive a "Container already exists" error. To remove an existing container, issue the following command:

```
docker rm -f container_name || true
```

Once the container has been created, check the logs by typing the following:

```
docker logs -f CONTAINER_ID
```

The logs should display the MongoDB server's health check:

```
mlabouardy@Mohameds-MBP-001 crew-crm % docker logs -f d860b80b1f9c56617bb0a5eddf9748ee97a642cc887187bffaf3514af2720fe7
about to fork child process, waiting until server is ready for connections.
forked process: 29

{"t":{"$date":"2021-01-23T22:06:08.123+00:00"},"s":"I",  "c":"CONTROL",  "id":20698,   "ctx":"main","msg":"***** SERVER RESTARTED *****"}
{"t":{"$date":"2021-01-23T22:06:08.131+00:00"},"s":"I",  "c":"CONTROL",  "id":23285,   "ctx":"main","msg":"Automatically disabling TLS 1.0, to force-enable
TLS 1.0 specify --sslDisabledProtocols 'none'"}
{"t":{"$date":"2021-01-23T22:06:08.133+00:00"},"s":"W",  "c":"ASIO",     "id":22601,   "ctx":"main","msg":"No TransportLayer configured during NetworkInterf
ace startup"}
{"t":{"$date":"2021-01-23T22:06:08.133+00:00"},"s":"I",  "c":"NETWORK",  "id":4648601, "ctx":"main","msg":"Implicit TCP FastOpen unavailable. If TCP FastOpe
n is required, set tcpFastOpenServer, tcpFastOpenClient, and tcpFastOpenQueueSize."}
{"t":{"$date":"2021-01-23T22:06:08.134+00:00"},"s":"I",  "c":"STORAGE",  "id":4615611, "ctx":"initandlisten","msg":"MongoDB starting","attr":{"pid":29,"port
":27017,"dbPath":"/data/db","architecture":"64-bit","host":"d860b80b1f9c"}}
{"t":{"$date":"2021-01-23T22:06:08.134+00:00"},"s":"I",  "c":"CONTROL",  "id":23403,   "ctx":"initandlisten","msg":"Build Info","attr":{"buildInfo":{"versio
n":"4.4.3","gitVersion":"913d6b62acfbb344dde1b116f4161360acd8fd13","openSSLVersion":"OpenSSL 1.1.1  11 Sep 2018","modules":[],"allocator":"tcmalloc","enviro
nment":{"distmod":"ubuntu1804","distarch":"x86_64","target_arch":"x86_64"}}}}
{"t":{"$date":"2021-01-23T22:06:08.134+00:00"},"s":"I",  "c":"CONTROL",  "id":51765,   "ctx":"initandlisten","msg":"Operating System","attr":{"os":{"name":"
Ubuntu","version":"18.04"}}}
```

Figure 3.8 – MongoDB container runtime logs

> **Note**
>
> It's recommended that you use Docker volumes to map the `/data/db` directory within the container with the underlying host system. That way, if the MongoDB server fails or your laptop restarts, the data won't be lost (data persistency). Create a data directory on the host system and mount the directory to the `/data/db` directory with the following commands:
>
> ```
> mkdir /home/data
>
> docker run -d --name mongodb -v /home/data:/
> data/db -e MONGO_INITDB_ROOT_USERNAME=admin -e
> MONGO_INITDB_ROOT_PASSWORD=password -p 27017:27017
> mongo:4.4.3
> ```

To interact with the MongoDB server, you can use the MongoDB shell to issue queries and view data on the command line. However, there is a better alternative: MongoDB Compass.

Installing MongoDB Compass

MongoDB Compass is a GUI tool that allows you to easily build queries, understand your database schema, and analyze your indexes, all without having to know MongoDB's query syntax.

Download Compass from `https://www.mongodb.com/try/download/compass?tck=docs_compass` based on your OS:

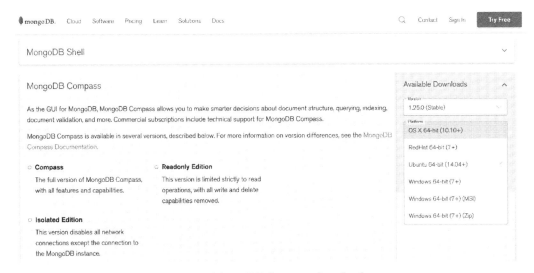

Figure 3.9 – MongoDB Compass download page

Once you've downloaded the package relevant to your OS, run the installer and follow the steps that come after it. Once installed, open Compass, click on **New Connection**, then enter the following URI in the input field (replace the given credentials with your own): `mongodb://admin:password@localhost:27017/test`.

MongoDB is running locally, so the hostname will be localhost and the port will be 27017:

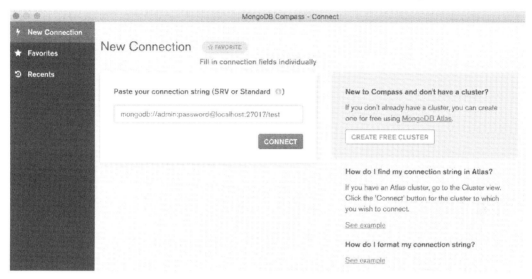

Figure 3.10 – MongoDB Compass – New Connection

Click on the **CONNECT** button. Now, you are connected to your MongoDB server. You will see a list of databases that are available:

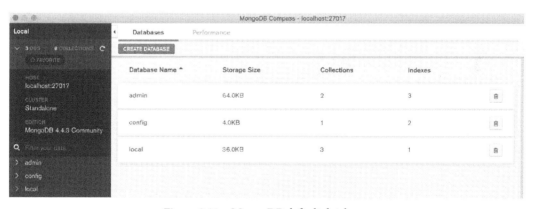

Figure 3.11 – MongoDB default databases

At this point, we have a functional MongoDB deployment. In the next section, we're going to interact with the database using the Recipes API we built in the previous chapter.

> **Note**
>
> To stop MongoDB server, run `docker ps` command to see the list of the running containers and `docker stop CONTAINER_ID` to stop the container.

Configuring Go's MongoDB driver

The Recipes API we implemented in the previous chapter is written in Golang. Therefore, we need to install the official MongoDB Go driver (`https://github.com/mongodb/mongo-go-driver`) to interact with the MongoDB server. The driver fully integrates with the MongoDB API and supports all the main queries and aggregation features of the API.

Issue the following command to install the package from GitHub:

```
go get go.mongodb.org/mongo-driver/mongo
```

This will add the package as a dependency in the `require` section, under the `go.mod` file:

```
module github.com/mlabouardy/recipes-api

go 1.15

require (
    github.com/gin-gonic/gin v1.6.3
    github.com/rs/xid v1.2.1
    go.mongodb.org/mongo-driver v1.4.5
)
```

To get started, import the following packages in the `main.go` file:

```
package main

import (
    "go.mongodb.org/mongo-driver/mongo"
    "go.mongodb.org/mongo-driver/mongo/options"
    "go.mongodb.org/mongo-driver/mongo/readpref"
)
```

In the `init()` method, create a `mongo.Client` with the `Connect` function. This function takes a context as a parameter and the connection string, which is provided with an environment variable called `MONGO_URI`. Also, create the following global variables; they will be used across all the CRUD operation functions:

```
var ctx context.Context
var err error
var client *mongo.Client

func init() {
    ...
    ctx = context.Background()
    client, err = mongo.Connect(ctx,
        options.Client().ApplyURI(os.Getenv("MONGO_URI")))
    if err = client.Ping(context.TODO(),
            readpref.Primary()); err != nil {
        log.Fatal(err)
    }
    log.Println("Connected to MongoDB")
}
```

> **Note**
> I have omitted some of the code to make the example readable and easy to follow. The full source code is available in this book's GitHub repository, under the `chapter03` folder.

Once the `Connect` method returns the client object, we can use the `Ping` method to check whether the connection was successful or not.

Pass the `MONGO_URI` environment variable to the `go run` command and check if the application can successfully connect to your MongoDB server:

```
MONGO_URI="mongodb://admin:password@localhost:27017/
test?authSource=admin" go run main.go
```

If successful, a **Connected to MongoDB** message will be shown:

```
mlabouardy@Mohameds-MBP-001 chapter3 % MONGO_URI="mongodb://admin:password@localhost:27017/test?authSource=admin" go run main.go
2021/01/24 18:39:37 Connected to MongoDB
[GIN-debug] [WARNING] Creating an Engine instance with the Logger and Recovery middleware already attached.

[GIN-debug] [WARNING] Running in "debug" mode. Switch to "release" mode in production.
 - using env:   export GIN_MODE=release
 - using code:  gin.SetMode(gin.ReleaseMode)

[GIN-debug] POST   /recipes                  --> main.NewRecipeHandler (3 handlers)
[GIN-debug] GET    /recipes                  --> main.ListRecipesHandler (3 handlers)
[GIN-debug] PUT    /recipes/:id              --> main.UpdateRecipeHandler (3 handlers)
[GIN-debug] DELETE /recipes/:id              --> main.DeleteRecipeHandler (3 handlers)
[GIN-debug] GET    /recipes/search           --> main.SearchRecipesHandler (3 handlers)
[GIN-debug] Environment variable PORT is undefined. Using port :8080 by default
[GIN-debug] Listening and serving HTTP on :8080
```

Figure 3.12 – MongoDB connection with the Go driver

Now, let's populate a fresh database with some data.

Exploring MongoDB queries

In this section, we will interact with the MongoDB server using CRUD operations, but first, let's create a database where the API data will be stored.

> **Note**
>
> You can view the full documentation for the MongoDB Go driver on the GoDoc website (https://godoc.org/go.mongodb.org/mongo-driver).

The InsertMany operation

Let's initialize the database with the recipes.json file we created in the previous chapter. First, retrieve a Database and then a Collection instance from Client. The Collection instance will be used to insert documents:

```go
func init() {
    recipes = make([]Recipe, 0)
    file, _ := ioutil.ReadFile("recipes.json")
    _ = json.Unmarshal([]byte(file), &recipes)

    ctx = context.Background()
    client, err = mongo.Connect(ctx,
        options.Client().ApplyURI(os.Getenv("MONGO_URI")))
    if err = client.Ping(context.TODO(),
            readpref.Primary()); err != nil {
```

```
        log.Fatal(err)
    }
    log.Println("Connected to MongoDB")


    var listOfRecipes []interface{}
    for _, recipe := range recipes {
        listOfRecipes = append(listOfRecipes, recipe)
    }
    collection := client.Database(os.Getenv(
        "MONGO_DATABASE")).Collection("recipes")
    insertManyResult, err := collection.InsertMany(
        ctx, listOfRecipes)
    if err != nil {
        log.Fatal(err)
    }
    log.Println("Inserted recipes: ",
            len(insertManyResult.InsertedIDs))
}
```

The preceding code reads a JSON file (`https://github.com/PacktPublishing/`
`Building-Distributed-Applications-in-Gin/blob/main/chapter03/`
`recipes.json`), which contains a list of recipes, and encodes it into an array of the
`Recipe` struct. Then, it establishes a connection with the MongoDB server and inserts
the recipes into the `recipes` collection.

To insert multiple documents at a time, we can use the `InsertMany()` method. This
method accepts an interface slice as a parameter. Therefore, we must map the `Recipes`
struct slice to the interface slice.

Rerun the application, but this time, set the `MONGO_URI` and `MONGO_DATABASE`
variables as follows:

```
MONGO_URI="mongodb://USER:PASSWORD@localhost:27017/
 test?authSource=admin" MONGO_DATABASE=demo go run main.go
```

Make sure to replace `USER` with your database user and `PASSWORD` with the user
password we created while deploying the MongoDB container.

The application will be launched; the `init()` method will be executed first and the recipes items will be inserted into the MongoDB collection:

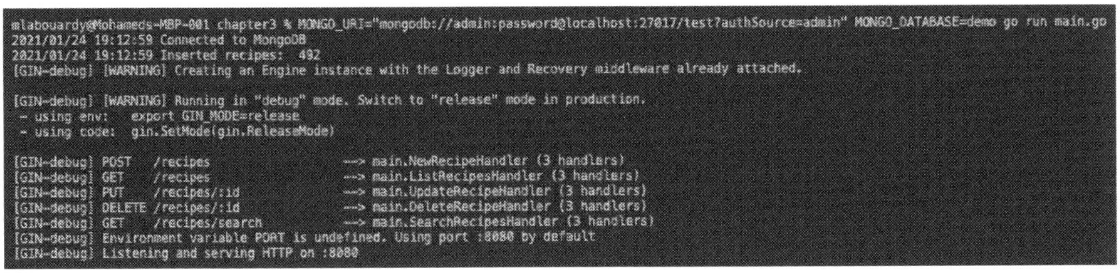

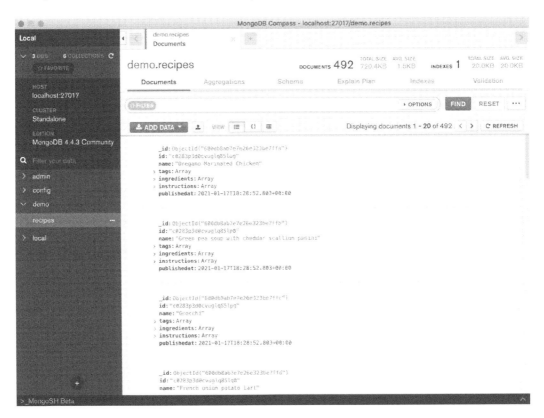

Figure 3.13 – Inserting recipes during startup

To verify that the data has been loaded into the recipes collection, refresh MongoDB Compass. You should see the entries that you created:

Figure 3.14 – Recipes collection

Now that the `recipes` collection has been prepared, we need to update each API endpoint's code so that they use the collection instead of the hardcoded recipes list. But first, we need to update the `init()` method to remove the loading and encoding of the `recipes.json` file:

```go
func init() {
    ctx = context.Background()
    client, err = mongo.Connect(ctx,
        options.Client().ApplyURI(os.Getenv("MONGO_URI")))
    if err = client.Ping(context.TODO(),
                          readpref.Primary()); err != nil {
        log.Fatal(err)
    }
    log.Println("Connected to MongoDB")
}
```

It's worth mentioning that you can use the `mongoimport` utility to load the `recipe.json` file directly into the `recipes` collection without writing a single line of code in Golang. The command for this is as follows:

```
mongoimport --username admin --password password
--authenticationDatabase admin --db demo --collection recipes
--file recipes.json --jsonArray
```

This command will import the content from the JSON file into the `recipes` collection:

```
mlabouardy@Mohameds-MBP-001 chapter3 % mongoimport --username admin --password password --authenticationDatabase admin
--db demo --collection recipes --file recipes.json --jsonArray
2021-01-24T19:19:09.536+0100    connected to: mongodb://localhost/
2021-01-24T19:19:09.592+0100    492 document(s) imported successfully. 0 document(s) failed to import.
mlabouardy@Mohameds-MBP-001 chapter3 %
```

Figure 3.15 – Importing data with mongoimport

In the next section, we will update the existing function handlers to read and write from/to the `recipes` collection.

The Find operation

To get started, we need to implement the function responsible for returning a list of recipes. Update `ListRecipesHandler` so that it uses the `Find()` method to fetch all the items from the `recipes` collection:

```go
func ListRecipesHandler(c *gin.Context) {
    cur, err := collection.Find(ctx, bson.M{})
    if err != nil {
        c.JSON(http.StatusInternalServerError,
            gin.H{"error": err.Error()})
        return
    }
    defer cur.Close(ctx)

    recipes := make([]Recipe, 0)
    for cur.Next(ctx) {
        var recipe Recipe
        cur.Decode(&recipe)
        recipes = append(recipes, recipe)
    }

    c.JSON(http.StatusOK, recipes)
}
```

The `Find()` method returns a cursor, which is a stream of documents. We must go through the stream of documents and decode one at a time into the `Recipe` struct. Then, we must append the document to a list of recipes.

Run the application, then issue a GET request on the /recipes endpoint; a find()
operation will be executed on the recipes collection. As a result, a list of recipes will
be returned:

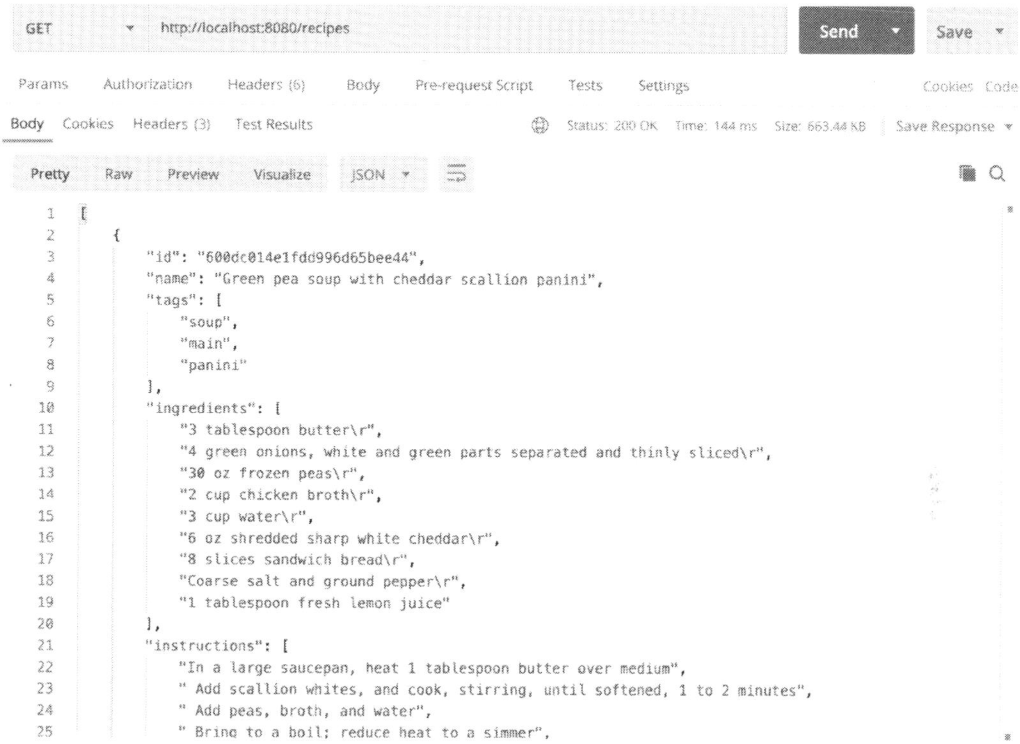

Figure 3.16 – Getting all the recipes

The endpoint is working and fetching the recipe's items from the collection.

The InsertOne operation

The second function to be implemented will be responsible for saving a new recipe.
Update the NewRecipeHandler function so that it calls the InsertOne() method
on the recipes collection:

```
func NewRecipeHandler(c *gin.Context) {
    var recipe Recipe
    if err := c.ShouldBindJSON(&recipe); err != nil {
        c.JSON(http.StatusBadRequest, gin.H{"error":
            err.Error()})
```

```
        return
    }


    recipe.ID = primitive.NewObjectID()
    recipe.PublishedAt = time.Now()
    _, err = collection.InsertOne(ctx, recipe)
    if err != nil {
        fmt.Println(err)
        c.JSON(http.StatusInternalServerError,
            gin.H{"error": "Error while inserting
                a new recipe"})
        return
    }


    c.JSON(http.StatusOK, recipe)
}
```

Here, we set a unique identifier using the `primitive.NewObjectID()` method ahead of saving the item in the collection. Therefore, we need to change the ID type of the `Recipe` struct. Also, note the usage of the `bson` tags to map a `struct` field to the `document` attribute in the MongoDB collection:

```
// swagger:parameters recipes newRecipe
type Recipe struct {
    //swagger:ignore
    ID primitive.ObjectID `json:"id" bson:"_id"`
    Name string `json:"name" bson:"name"`
    Tags []string `json:"tags" bson:"tags"`
    Ingredients []string `json:"ingredients" bson:"ingredients"`
    Instructions []string `json:"instructions"
                            bson:"instructions"`
    PublishedAt time.Time `json:"publishedAt"
                            bson:"publishedAt"`
}
```

> **Note**
>
> By default, Go lowercases the struct field names when encoding struct values. If a different name is needed, you can override the default mechanism with `bson` tags.

Insert a new recipe by calling the following POST request with the Postman client:

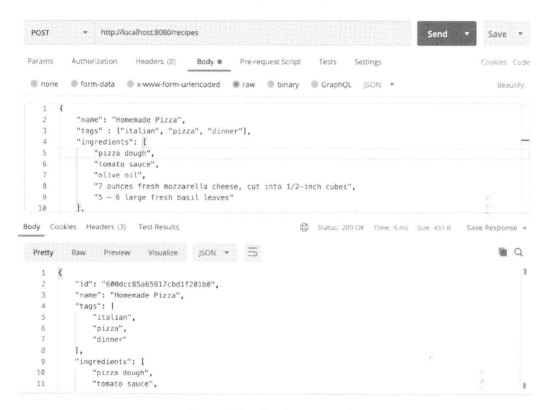

Figure 3.17 – Creating a new recipe

Verify that the recipe has been inserted into the MongoDB collection, as shown in the following screenshot:

Figure 3.18 – Getting the last inserted recipe

To get the last inserted recipe, we use the sort() operation.

The UpdateOne operation

Finally, in order to update an item from the collection, update the UpdateRecipeHandler function so that it calls the UpdateOne() method. This method requires a filter document to match documents in the database and an updater document to describe the update operation. You can build a filter using bson.D{} – a **Binary-encoded JSON (BSON)** document:

```go
func UpdateRecipeHandler(c *gin.Context) {
    id := c.Param("id")
    var recipe Recipe
    if err := c.ShouldBindJSON(&recipe); err != nil {
        c.JSON(http.StatusBadRequest, gin.H{"error":
                                        err.Error()})
        return
    }
```

```go
    objectId, _ := primitive.ObjectIDFromHex(id)
    _, err = collection.UpdateOne(ctx, bson.M{
        "_id": objectId,
    }, bson.D{{"$set", bson.D{
        {"name", recipe.Name},
        {"instructions", recipe.Instructions},
        {"ingredients", recipe.Ingredients},
        {"tags", recipe.Tags},
    }}})
    if err != nil {
        fmt.Println(err)
        c.JSON(http.StatusInternalServerError,
            gin.H{"error": err.Error()})
        return
    }

    c.JSON(http.StatusOK, gin.H{"message": "Recipe
                        has been updated"})
}
```

This method filters documents by their Object ID. We get the Object ID by applying `ObjectIDFromHex` to the route parameter ID. This updates the matched recipe's fields with the new values coming from the request body.

Verify the endpoint is working by calling a PUT request on an existing recipe:

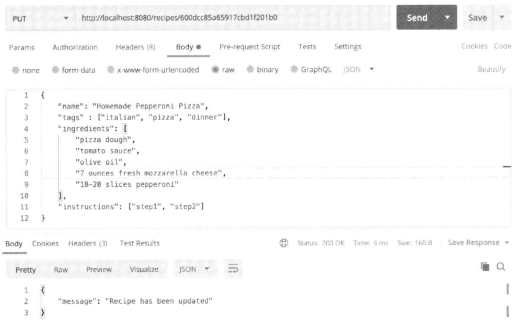

Figure 3.19 – Updating a recipe

The request will match the recipe where ID is 600dcc85a65917cbd1f201b0 and will update its name from "Homemade Pizza" to "Homemade Pepperoni Pizza", and the instructions field with additional steps to make a "Pepperoni Pizza".

With that, the recipe has been successfully updated. You can confirm these changes with MongoDB Compass:

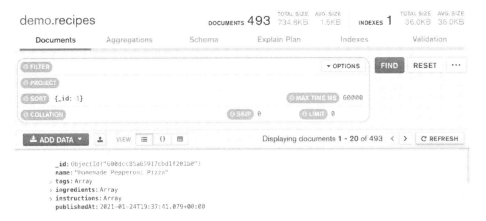

Figure 3.20 – UpdateOne operation results

You should now be familiar with the basic MongoDB queries. Go ahead and implement the remaining CRUD operations.

Finally, make sure that you push the changes to the remote repository with the following commands:

```
git checkout -b feature/mongo_integration
git add .
git commit -m "added mongodb integration"
git push origin feature/mongo_integration
```

Then, create a pull request to merge the `feature` branch into `develop`:

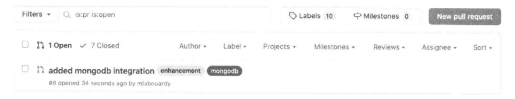

Figure 3.21 – New pull request

> **Note**
> A full implementation of the endpoints can be found in this book's GitHub repository (`https://github.com/PacktPublishing/Building-Distributed-Applications-in-Gin/blob/main/chapter03/main.go`).

You just saw how to integrate MongoDB into the application architecture. In the next section, we will cover how to refactor the source code of our application so that it's maintainable, scalable, and extendable in the long run.

Designing the project's layout

So far, all the code we've written is in the `main.go` file. While this works fine, it's important to make sure the code is well structured; otherwise, you'll end up with a lot of hidden dependencies and messy code (spaghetti code) when the project grows.

We will start with the data model. Let's create a `models` folder so that we can store all the models structs. For now, we have one model, which is the `Recipe` struct. Create a `recipe.go` file under the `models` folder and paste the following content:

```
package models
```

```go
import (
    "time"

    "go.mongodb.org/mongo-driver/bson/primitive"
)

// swagger:parameters recipes newRecipe
type Recipe struct {
    //swagger:ignore
    ID            primitive.ObjectID `json:"id" bson:"_id"`
    Name          string             `json:"name"
                                      bson:"name"`
    Tags          []string           `json:"tags"
                                      bson:"tags"`
    Ingredients   []string           `json:"ingredients"
                                       bson:"ingredients"`
    Instructions  []string           `json:"instructions"
                                       bson:"instructions"`
    PublishedAt   time.Time          `json:"publishedAt"
                                       bson:"publishedAt"`
}
```

Then, create a `handlers` folder with the `handler.go` file. This folder, as its name indicts, handles any incoming HTTP requests by exposing the right function to be called for each HTTP request:

```go
package handlers

import (
    "fmt"
    "net/http"
    "time"

    "github.com/gin-gonic/gin"
    "github.com/mlabouardy/recipes-api/models"
```

```
    "go.mongodb.org/mongo-driver/bson"
    "go.mongodb.org/mongo-driver/bson/primitive"
    "go.mongodb.org/mongo-driver/mongo"
    "golang.org/x/net/context"
)


type RecipesHandler struct {
    collection *mongo.Collection
    ctx        context.Context
}


func NewRecipesHandler(ctx context.Context, collection *mongo.
Collection) *RecipesHandler {
    return &RecipesHandler{
        collection: collection,
        ctx:        ctx,
    }
}
```

This code creates a RecipesHandler struct with the MongoDB collection and context instances encapsulated. In our early simple implementations, we tended to keep these variables global within the main package. Here, we are keeping these variables in the struct. Next, we must define a NewRecipesHandler so that we can create an instance from the RecipesHandler struct.

Now, we can define the endpoints handlers of the RecipesHandler type. The handlers can access all the variables of the struct such as the database connection because it is a method of the RecipesHandler type:

```
func (handler *RecipesHandler) ListRecipesHandler(c *gin.
Context) {
    cur, err := handler.collection.Find(handler.ctx, bson.M{})
    if err != nil {
        c.JSON(http.StatusInternalServerError,
            gin.H{"error": err.Error()})
        return
    }
    defer cur.Close(handler.ctx)
```

```
    recipes := make([]models.Recipe, 0)
    for cur.Next(handler.ctx) {
        var recipe models.Recipe
        cur.Decode(&recipe)
        recipes = append(recipes, recipe)
    }

    c.JSON(http.StatusOK, recipes)
}
```

From our `main.go` file, we'll provide all the database credentials and connect to the MongoDB server:

```
package main

import (
    "context"
    "log"
    "os"

    "github.com/gin-gonic/gin"
    handlers "github.com/mlabouardy/recipes-api/handlers"
    "go.mongodb.org/mongo-driver/mongo"
    "go.mongodb.org/mongo-driver/mongo/options"
    "go.mongodb.org/mongo-driver/mongo/readpref"
)
```

Then, we must create a global variable to access the endpoints handlers. Update the `init()` method, as follows:

```
var recipesHandler *handlers.RecipesHandler

func init() {
    ctx := context.Background()
    client, err := mongo.Connect(ctx,
        options.Client().ApplyURI(os.Getenv("MONGO_URI")))
    if err = client.Ping(context.TODO(),
            readpref.Primary()); err != nil {
```

```
        log.Fatal(err)
    }
    log.Println("Connected to MongoDB")
    collection := client.Database(os.Getenv(
        "MONGO_DATABASE")).Collection("recipes")
    recipesHandler = handlers.NewRecipesHandler(ctx,
        collection)
}
```

Finally, use the `recipesHandler` variable to access the handler for each HTTP endpoint:

```
func main() {
    router := gin.Default()
    router.POST("/recipes", recipesHandler.NewRecipeHandler)
    router.GET("/recipes",
        recipesHandler.ListRecipesHandler)
    router.PUT("/recipes/:id",
        recipesHandler.UpdateRecipeHandler)
    router.Run()
}
```

Run the application. This time, run all the `.go` files within the current directory:

```
MONGO_URI="mongodb://admin:password@localhost:27017/
test?authSource=admin" MONGO_DATABASE=demo go run *.go
```

The application will be working as expected. The server logs are as follows:

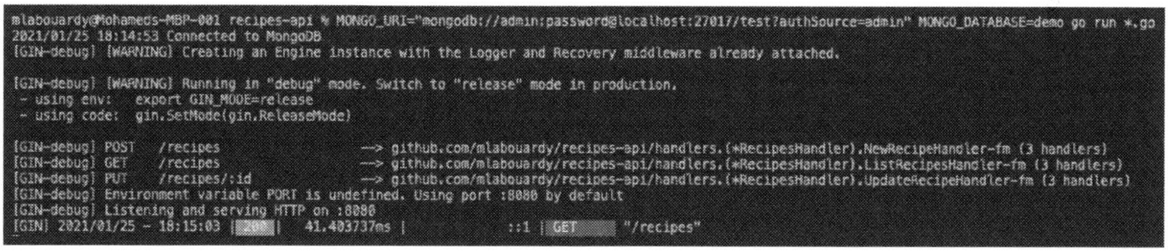

Figure 3.22 – Gin debug logs

Now, your project structure should look like this:

```
.
├── go.mod
├── go.sum
├── handlers
│   └── handler.go
├── main.go
├── models
│   └── recipe.go
├── recipes.json
└── swagger.json
```

This is a basic layout for a Go application project. There are Go directories that we will cover in upcoming chapters.

Push the changes to GitHub on a feature branch and merge the branch into `develop`:

```
git checkout -b fix/code_refactoring
git add .
git commit -m "code refactoring"
git push origin fix/code_refactoring
```

When running a service that interacts with a database, its operations may become bottlenecks, thus degrading the user experience and impacting your business. That is why response time is one of the most important metrics to evaluate when developing a RESTful API.

Luckily, we can add a cache layer to store frequently accessed data in memory to speed things up, thus reducing the number of operations/queries on the database.

Caching an API with Redis

In this section, we will cover how to add a caching mechanism to our API. Let's imagine that we have a tremendous number of recipes in our MongoDB database. Every time we try to query a list of recipes, we struggle with performance issues. What we can do instead is use an in-memory database, such as Redis, to reuse previously retrieved recipes and avoiding hitting the MongoDB database on each request.

Redis is consistently faster at retrieving data because it is always in RAM – that's why it's an excellent choice for caching. On the other hand, MongoDB might have to retrieve data from disk for advancing queries.

According to the official documentation (`https://redis.io/`), Redis is an open source, distributed, in-memory, key-value database, cache, and message broker. The following diagram illustrates how Redis fits in our API architecture:

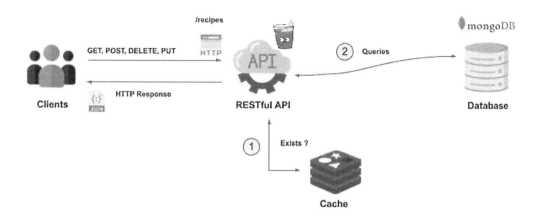

Figure 3.23 – API new architecture

Let's say we want to get a list of recipes. First, the API will look around in Redis. If a list of recipes exists, it will be returned (this is called a **cache hit**). If the cache is empty (this is called a **cache miss**), then a MongoDB `find({})` query will be issued, and the results will be returned and also saved in the cache for future requests.

Running Redis in Docker

The easiest way to set up Redis is through Docker. We will use the Redis official image available at DockerHub for this (`https://hub.docker.com/_/redis`). At the time of writing this book, the latest stable version is 6.0. Run a container based on that image:

```
docker run -d --name redis -p 6379:6379 redis:6.0
```

This command does the following two main things:

- The `-d` flag runs the Redis container as a daemon.
- The `-p` flag maps port 6379 of the container to port 6379 of the host. Port 6379 is the port where the Redis server is exposed.

The command's output is as follows:

```
mlabouardy@Mohameds-MBP-001 recipes-api % docker run -d --name redis -p 6379:6379 redis
Unable to find image 'redis:latest' locally
latest: Pulling from library/redis
a076a628af6f: Pull complete
f40dd07fe7be: Pull complete
ce21c8a3dbee: Pull complete
ee99c35818f8: Pull complete
56b9a72e68ff: Pull complete
3f703e7f380f: Pull complete
Digest: sha256:0f97c1c9daf5b69b93390ccbe8d3e2971617ec4801fd0882c72bf7cad3a13494
Status: Downloaded newer image for redis:latest
9c89f27d6fa076f74aab6e28eceb19f30e717e27ffe934df4a8bcd427e00fc8a
mlabouardy@Mohameds-MBP-001 recipes-api % ▌
```

Figure 3.24 – Pulling a Redis image from DockerHub

Always check the Docker log to see the chain of events:

```
docker logs -f CONTAINER_ID
```

The logs provide a wealth of useful information, such as the default configuration and the exposed server port:

```
mlabouardy@Mohameds-MBP-001 recipes-api % docker logs -f 9c89f27d6fa076f74aab6e28eceb19f30e717e27ffe934df4a8bcd427e00fc8a
1:C 25 Jan 2021 17:26:45.043 # oO0OoO0OoO0Oo Redis is starting oO0OoO0OoO0Oo
1:C 25 Jan 2021 17:26:45.043 # Redis version=6.0.10, bits=64, commit=00000000, modified=0, pid=1, just started
1:C 25 Jan 2021 17:26:45.043 # Warning: no config file specified, using the default config. In order to specify a config file use
redis-server /path/to/redis.conf
1:M 25 Jan 2021 17:26:45.047 * Running mode=standalone, port=6379.
1:M 25 Jan 2021 17:26:45.047 # WARNING: The TCP backlog setting of 511 cannot be enforced because /proc/sys/net/core/somaxconn is
set to the lower value of 128.
1:M 25 Jan 2021 17:26:45.047 # Server initialized
1:M 25 Jan 2021 17:26:45.048 * Ready to accept connections
▌
```

Figure 3.25 – Redis server logs

The Redis container uses the basic caching policy. For production usage, it's recommended to configure an eviction policy. You can configure the policy with a `redis.conf` file:

```
maxmemory-policy allkeys-lru
```
```
maxmemory 512mb
```

This config allocates 512 MB of memory for Redis and sets the eviction policy to the **Least Recently Used (LRU)** algorithm, which deletes the cache items that were the least recently used. As a result, we only keep the items with the highest chances of getting read again.

You can then pass the config at the runtime of the container with the following command:

```
docker run -d -v $PWD/conf:/usr/local/etc/redis --name redis -p
6379:6379 redis:6.0
```

Here, `$PWD/conf` is the folder containing the `redis.conf` file.

Now that Redis is running, we can use it to cache API data. But first, let's install the official Redis Go driver (`https://github.com/go-redis/redis`) by executing the following command:

```
go get github.com/go-redis/redis/v8
```

Import the following package in the `main.go` file:

```
import "github.com/go-redis/redis"
```

Now, on the `init()` method, initialize the Redis client with `redis.NewClient()`. This method takes the server address, password, and database as parameters. Next, we will call the `Ping()` method on the Redis client to check the connection status to the Redis server:

```
redisClient := redis.NewClient(&redis.Options{
        Addr:     "localhost:6379",
        Password: "",
        DB:       0,
})
status := redisClient.Ping()
fmt.Println(status)
```

This code will set up a connection with the Redis server after deployment:

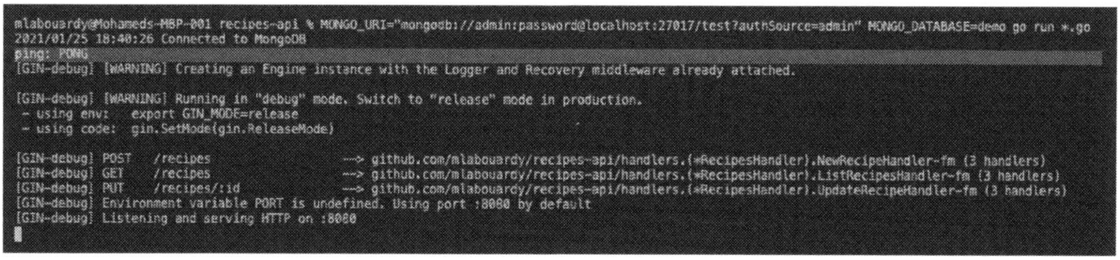

Figure 3.26 – Checking the connection with the Redis server

If the connection is successful, a `ping: PONG` message will be displayed, as shown in the preceding screenshot.

Optimizing MongoDB queries

With a connection being established with the Redis server, we can update the `RecipesHandler` struct to store an instance of the Redis client so that the handlers can interact with Redis:

```
type RecipesHandler struct {
    collection   *mongo.Collection
    ctx          context.Context
    redisClient  *redis.Client
}

func NewRecipesHandler(ctx context.Context, collection
    *mongo.Collection, redisClient *redis.Client)
    *RecipesHandler {
    return &RecipesHandler{
        collection:  collection,
        ctx:         ctx,
        redisClient: redisClient,
    }
}
```

Make sure that you pass the Redis client instance to the `RecipesHandler` instance in the `init()` method:

```
recipesHandler = handlers.NewRecipesHandler(ctx, collection,
                                            redisClient)
```

Next, we must update `ListRecipesHandler` to check if the recipes have been cached in Redis. If they are, we return a list. If not, we will retrieve the data from MongoDB and cache it in Redis. The new changes we must make to the code are as follows:

```
func (handler *RecipesHandler) ListRecipesHandler(c
    *gin.Context) {
    val, err := handler.redisClient.Get("recipes").Result()
    if err == redis.Nil {
        log.Printf("Request to MongoDB")
```

```
        cur, err := handler.collection.Find(handler.ctx,
                                       bson.M{})
        if err != nil {
            c.JSON(http.StatusInternalServerError,
                gin.H{"error": err.Error()})
            return
        }
        defer cur.Close(handler.ctx)

        recipes := make([]models.Recipe, 0)
        for cur.Next(handler.ctx) {
            var recipe models.Recipe
            cur.Decode(&recipe)
            recipes = append(recipes, recipe)
        }

        data, _ := json.Marshal(recipes)
        handler.redisClient.Set("recipes", string(data), 0)
        c.JSON(http.StatusOK, recipes)
    } else if err != nil {
        c.JSON(http.StatusInternalServerError,
            gin.H{"error": err.Error()})
        return
    } else {
        log.Printf("Request to Redis")
        recipes := make([]models.Recipe, 0)
        json.Unmarshal([]byte(val), &recipes)
        c.JSON(http.StatusOK, recipes)
    }
}
```

It's worth mentioning that the Redis value has to be a string, so we had to encode the recipes slice into a string with the json.Marshal() method.

To test out the new changes, run the application. Then, issue a GET request on the /recipes endpoint with Postman client or with a cURL command. Flip back to your Terminal and view the Gin logs. You should see a message in the console for the first request corresponding to getting data from MongoDB:

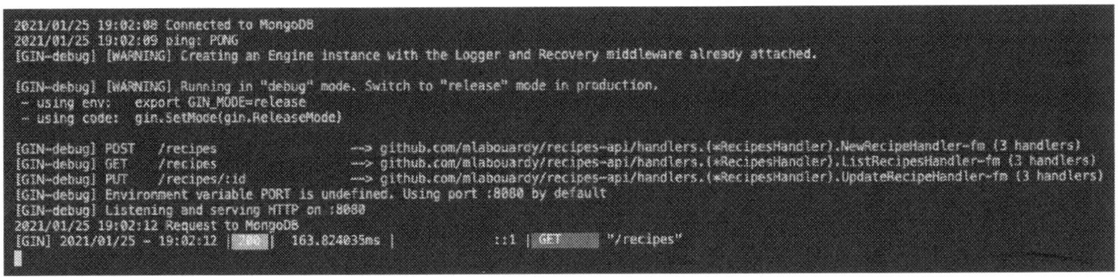

Figure 3.27 – Getting data from MongoDB

> **Note**
>
> For a step-by-step guide on how to use the Postman client or cURL command, check out *Chapter 1, Getting Started with Gin.*

If you hit a second HTTP request, this time, data will be returned from Redis because it was cached in the first request:

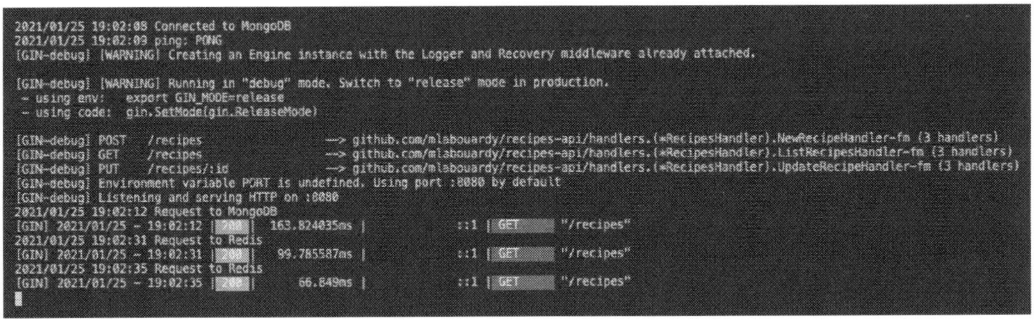

Figure 3.28 – Getting data from Redis

As we can see, retrieving data from memory (Redis) is wicked fast compared to retrieving data from disk (MongoDB).

We can verify that data is being cached in Redis by running the Redis CLI from the container. Run the following commands:

```
docker ps
docker exec -it CONTAINER_ID bash
```

These commands will connect to the Redis container using the interactive terminal and start the bash shell. You'll notice that you're now using your terminal as if you were inside your container, as shown in the following screenshot:

```
mlabouardy@Mohameds-MBP-001 recipes-api % docker exec -it 9c89f27d6fa0 bas
mlabouardy@Mohameds-MBP-001 recipes-api %
mlabouardy@Mohameds-MBP-001 recipes-api %
mlabouardy@Mohameds-MBP-001 recipes-api %
mlabouardy@Mohameds-MBP-001 recipes-api % docker ps
CONTAINER ID   IMAGE        COMMAND                 CREATED        STATUS         PORTS                       NAMES
9c89f27d6fa0   redis        "docker-entrypoint.s…"  37 minutes ago Up 37 minutes  0.0.0.0:6379->6379/tcp      redis
d860b80b1f9c   mongo:4.4.3  "docker-entrypoint.s…"  44 hours ago   Up 44 hours    0.0.0.0:27017->27017/tcp    mongodb
mlabouardy@Mohameds-MBP-001 recipes-api % docker exec -it 9c89f27d6fa0 bash
root@9c89f27d6fa0:/data# []
```

Figure 3.29 – Running an interactive session inside a Redis container

Now that we're attached to the Redis container, we can use the Redis command line:

```
redis-cli
```

From there, we can use the EXISTS command to check if the recipes key exists:

```
EXISTS recipes
```

This command will return 1 (if the key exists) or 0 (if the key doesn't exist). In our case, the list of recipes has been cached in Redis:

```
root@9c89f27d6fa0:/data# redis-cli
127.0.0.1:6379> EXISTS recipes
(integer) 1
127.0.0.1:6379>
```

Figure 3.30 – Checking if a key exists in Redis

There is a lot that you can accomplish with the shell client, but you've got the general idea. Type exit to leave the MongoDB shell and then exit once again to leave the interactive shell.

For GUI fans, you can use Redis Insights (https://redislabs.com/fr/redis-enterprise/redis-insight/). It provides an intuitive interface to explore Redis and interact with its data. Similar to the Redis server, you can deploy Redis Insights with Docker:

```
docker run -d --name redisinsight --link redis -p 8001:8001
redislabs/redisinsight
```

This command will run a container based on the Redis Insight official image and expose the interface on port 8001.

Navigate with your browser to `http://localhost:8081`. The Redis Insights home page should appear. Click on **I already have a database** and then on the **Connect to Redis database** button:

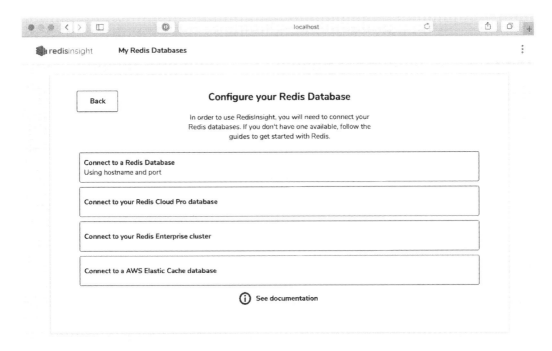

Figure 3.31 – Configuring the Redis database

Set the **Host** to `redis`, **port** to `6379`, and name the database. The settings are as follows:

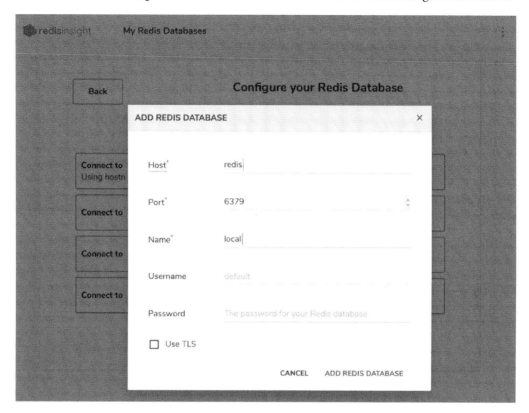

Figure 3.32 – New Redis settings

Next, click on **ADD REDIS DATABASE**. The **local** database will be saved; click on it:

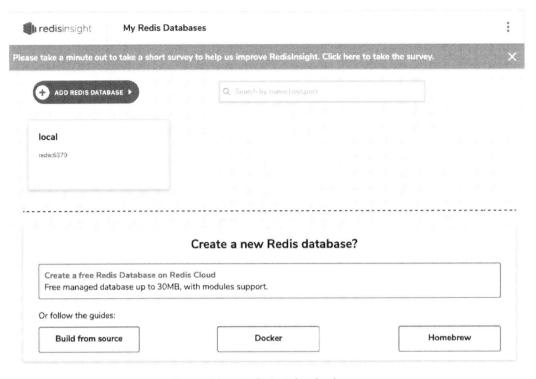

Figure 3.33 – Redis Insights databases

You will be redirected to the **Summary** page, which contains real metrics and stats about the Redis server:

Figure 3.34 – Redis server metrics

If you click on **BROWSE**, you will see a list of all the keys that have been stored in Redis. As shown in the following screenshot, the recipes key has been cached:

Figure 3.35 – Redis list of keys

Now, you can use the interface to explore, manipulate, and visualize data within Redis.

So far, the API we've built is working as a charm, right? Not really; imagine that you add a new recipe to the database:

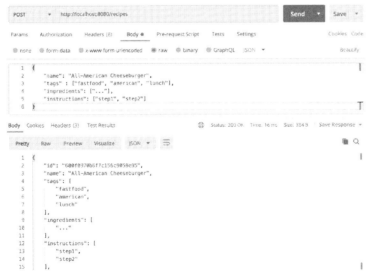

Figure 3.36 – Creating a new recipe

Now, if you issue a GET /recipes request, the new recipe won't be found. This is because the data is being returned from the cache:

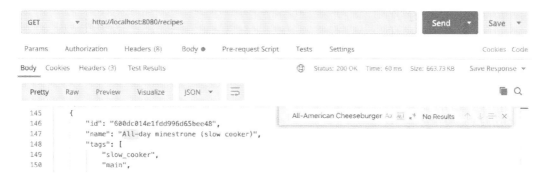

Figure 3.37 – Recipe not found

One of the issues that caching introduces is that of keeping the cache up to date when data changes:

```
2021/01/25 19:02:12 Request to MongoDB
[GIN] 2021/01/25 - 19:02:12 | 200 |   163.824035ms |       ::1 | GET      "/recipes"
2021/01/25 19:02:31 Request to Redis
[GIN] 2021/01/25 - 19:02:31 | 200 |    99.785587ms |       ::1 | GET      "/recipes"
2021/01/25 19:02:35 Request to Redis
[GIN] 2021/01/25 - 19:02:35 | 200 |      66.849ms  |       ::1 | GET      "/recipes"
[GIN] 2021/01/25 - 19:09:52 | 200 |     5.688538ms |       ::1 | POST     "/recipes"
2021/01/25 19:11:02 Request to Redis
[GIN] 2021/01/25 - 19:11:02 | 200 |     55.21406ms |       ::1 | GET      "/recipes"
```

Figure 3.38 – All future requests are hitting Redis

There are two group rules in this case to fix inconsistencies. First, we can add a **Time to Live (TTL)** field for the recipes key in Redis. Second we can clear the **recipes** key in Redis each time a new recipe is inserted or updated.

> **Note**
>
> The time to retain the cache's TTL depends on your application logic. You may need to save it for an hour or days, depending on how often the data gets updated.

We can implement the second solution by updating the `NewRecipeHandler` function so that it deletes the `recipes` key when a new recipe is being inserted. In this case, the implementation will be as follows:

```go
func (handler *RecipesHandler) NewRecipeHandler(c *gin.Context)
{
    var recipe models.Recipe
    if err := c.ShouldBindJSON(&recipe); err != nil {
        c.JSON(http.StatusBadRequest,
            gin.H{"error":err.Error()})
        return
    }

    recipe.ID = primitive.NewObjectID()
    recipe.PublishedAt = time.Now()
    _, err := handler.collection.InsertOne(handler.ctx,
                                        recipe)
    if err != nil {
        c.JSON(http.StatusInternalServerError,
        gin.H{"error": "Error while inserting
            a new recipe"})
        return
    }

    log.Println("Remove data from Redis")
    handler.redisClient.Del("recipes")

    c.JSON(http.StatusOK, recipe)
}
```

Redeploy the application. Now, if you hit a GET /recipes request, the data will be returned from MongoDB as expected; then, it will be cached in Redis. The second GET request will return data from Redis. However, now, if we issue a POST /recipes request to insert a new recipe, the recipes key in Redis will be cleared, as confirmed by the Remove data from Redis message. This means that the next GET /recipes request will fetch data from MongoDB:

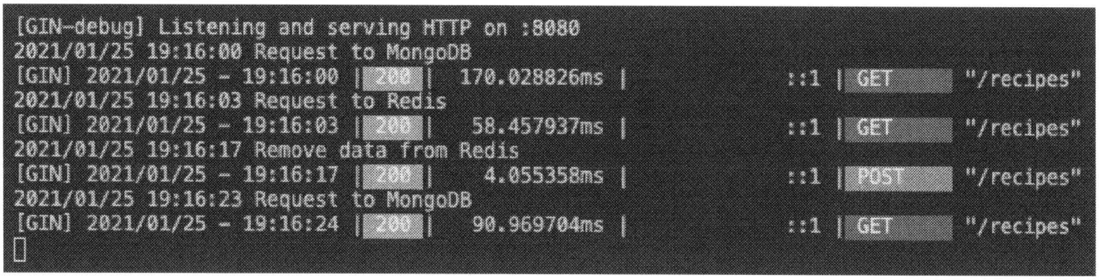

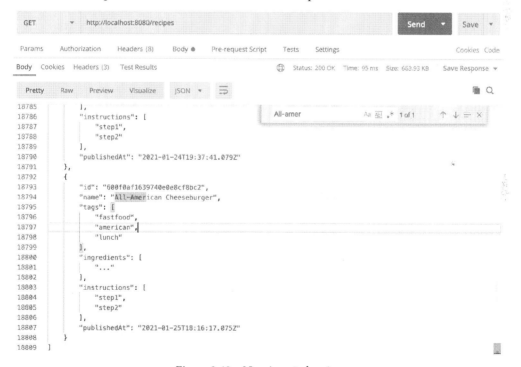

Figure 3.39 – Clearing the cache upon inserting a request

Now, the new recipe will be returned in the list of recipes:

Figure 3.40 – New inserted recipe

> **Note**
>
> Update `UpdateRecipeHandler` to clear the cache when a PUT request is occurring on the `/recipes/{id}` endpoint.

While caching offers great benefits for applications with heavy reads, it may not be as beneficial for applications that perform a lot of database updates and can slow down writes.

Performance benchmark

We can take this further and see how the API will behave under a huge volume of requests. We can simulate multiple requests with Apache Benchmark (`https://httpd.apache.org/docs/2.4/programs/ab.html`).

First, let's test the API without the caching layer. You can run 2,000 GET requests in total on the `/recipes` endpoint with 100 concurrent requests with the following command:

```
ab -n 2000 -c 100 -g without-cache.data http://localhost:8080/
recipes
```

It should take a few minutes for all the requests to be completed. Once done, you should see the following results:

```
Server Software:
Server Hostname:        localhost
Server Port:            8080

Document Path:          /recipes
Document Length:        679730 bytes

Concurrency Level:      100
Time taken for tests:   91.192 seconds
Complete requests:      2000
Failed requests:        0
Total transferred:      1359666000 bytes
HTML transferred:       1359460000 bytes
Requests per second:    21.93 [#/sec] (mean)
Time per request:       4559.585 [ms] (mean)
Time per request:       45.596 [ms] (mean, across all concurrent requests)
Transfer rate:          14560.52 [Kbytes/sec] received
```

Figure 3.41 – API without a caching layer

The important thing to take from this output is as follows:

- **Time taken for tests**: This means the total time to complete the 2,000 requests.

- **Time per request**: This means how many milliseconds it takes to complete one request.

Next, we will issue the same requests but this time on the API with caching (Redis):

```
ab -n 2000 -c 100 -g with-cache.data http://localhost:8080/
recipes
```

It should take a few seconds for the 2,000 requests to be completed:

```
Server Software:
Server Hostname:        localhost
Server Port:            8080

Document Path:          /recipes
Document Length:        679730 bytes

Concurrency Level:      100
Time taken for tests:   40.347 seconds
Complete requests:      2000
Failed requests:        2
    (Connect: 0, Receive: 0, Length: 2, Exceptions: 0)
Non-2xx responses:      2
Total transferred:      1358306742 bytes
HTML transferred:       1358100664 bytes
Requests per second:    49.57 [#/sec] (mean)
Time per request:       2017.342 [ms] (mean)
Time per request:       20.173 [ms] (mean, across all concurrent requests)
Transfer rate:          32876.71 [Kbytes/sec] received
```

Figure 3.42 – API with a caching layer

To compare both results, we can use the `gnuplot` utility to plot a chart based on the `without-cache.data` and `with-cache.data` files. But first, create an `apache-benchmark.p` file to render data into a graph:

```
set terminal png
set output "benchmark.png"
set title "Cache benchmark"
set size 1,0.7
set grid y
set xlabel "request"
```

```
set ylabel "response time (ms)"

plot "with-cache.data" using 9 smooth sbezier with lines title
"with cache", "without-cache.data" using 9 smooth sbezier with
lines title "without cache"
```

These commands will draw two plots on the same graph based on the .data files and save the output as a PNG image. Next, run the gnuplot command to create the image:

```
gnuplot apache-benchmark.p
```

A benchmark.png image will be created, as follows:

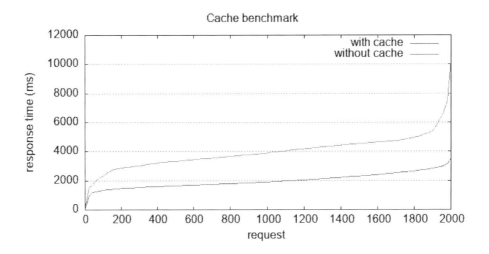

Figure 3.43 – Benchmark of APIs with and without caches

The API's response time with the caching mechanism enabled is wicked fast compared to API's response time without caching.

Make sure that you push the changes to GitHub with a feature branch. Then, create a pull request to merge into develop:

```
git checkout -b feature/redis_integration
git add .
git commit -m "added redis integration"
git push origin feature/redis_integration
```

By the end of this chapter, your GitHub repository should look like this:

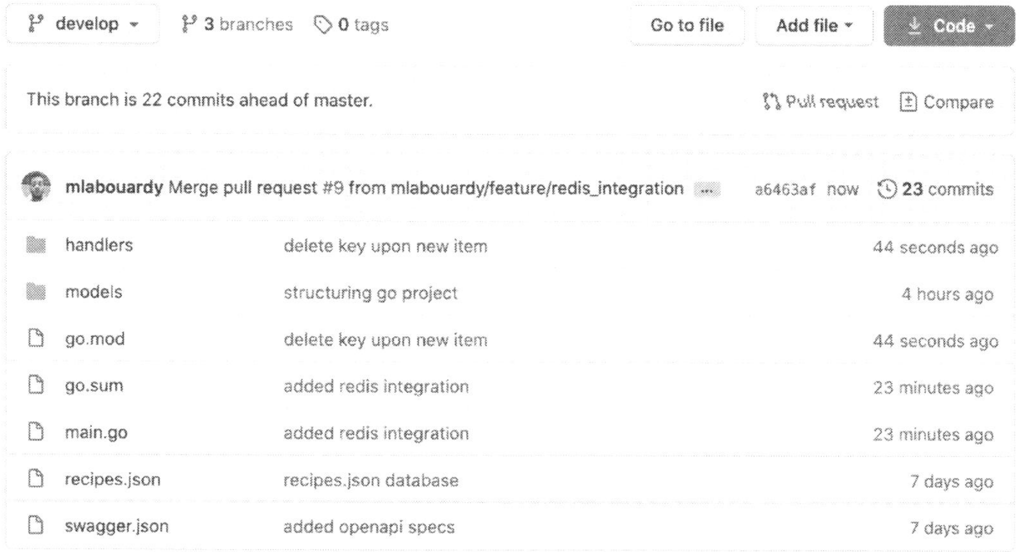

Figure 3.44 – Project's GitHub repository

Great! Now, you should be able to integrate a MongoDB database into your API architecture to manage data persistency.

Summary

In this chapter, we learned how to build a RESTful API that leverages the Gin framework and Go driver for creating queries and querying in a NoSQL database such as MongoDB.

We also explored how to speed up the API by caching the data it accesses with Redis. It is definitely a great addition to your application if your data is mostly static and does not change constantly. Finally, we covered how to run performance benchmarks with Apache Benchmark.

The RESTful API we have built so far works like a charm and is open to the public (if deployed on a remote server). If you leave the API unauthenticated, then anybody can hit any endpoint, which may very undesirable as your data could be damaged by users. Even worse, you might expose sensitive information from your database to the whole internet. That's why, in the next chapter, we will cover how to secure the API with authentication, such as JWT.

Questions

1. Implement a delete recipe operation when a `DELETE` request occurs.

2. Implement a GET `/recipes/{id}` endpoint using the `FindOne` operation.

3. How are JSON documents stored in MongoDB?

4. How does the LRU eviction policy work in Redis?

Further reading

- *MongoDB Fundamentals*, by Amit Phaltankar, Juned Ahsan, Michael Harrison, and Liviu Nedov, Packt Publishing

- *Learn MongoDB 4.x*, by Doug Bierer, Packt Publishing

- *Hands-On RESTful Web Services with Go – Second Edition*, by Naren Yellavula, Packt Publishing

4

Building API Authentication

This chapter is dedicated to the best practices and recommendations to follow while building a public **REpresentational State Transfer (REST) application programming interface (API)**. It explores how to write an authentication middleware to secure the access to the API endpoints and how to serve them through **HyperText Transfer Protocol Secure (HTTPS)**.

In this chapter, we will focus on the following main topics:

- Exploring authentication
- Introducing **JavaScript Object Notation (JSON) Web Tokens (JWTs)**
- Persisting client sessions and cookies
- Authenticating with Auth0
- Building an HTTPS server

By the end of this chapter, you will be able to build a RESTful API with both private and public endpoints.

Technical requirements

To follow the instructions in this chapter, you will need the following:

- A complete understanding of the previous chapter—this chapter is a follow-up of the previous one and it will use the same source code. Hence, some snippets won't be explained, to avoid repetition.

- A basic understanding of API authentication concepts and the HTTPS protocol.

The code bundle for this chapter is hosted on GitHub at `https://github.com/ PacktPublishing/Building-Distributed-Applications-in-Gin/tree/ main/chapter04`.

Exploring authentication

In the previous chapter, the API we built exposed multiple endpoints. For now, those endpoints are public and don't require any authentication. In a real-world scenario, you would need to secure those endpoints.

The following diagram illustrates the endpoints to be secured by the end of this chapter:

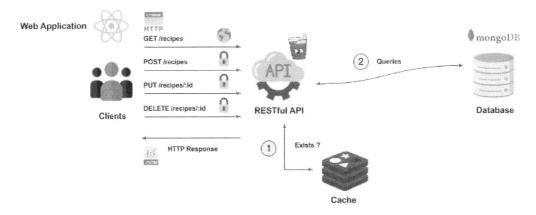

Figure 4.1 – Securing RESTful API endpoints

Listing recipes will require no authentication, while the endpoints responsible for **adding**, **updating**, or **deleting** a recipe will require authentication.

Multiple methods can be used to secure the preceding endpoints—here are a few of the methods we could use: API keys, Basic Auth, client sessions, OpenID Connect, **Open Authorization** (**OAuth**) 2.0, and so on. The most basic authentication mechanism is the usage of API keys.

Using API keys

In this method, the client provides a secret, called an **API key**, in the request header. The key is then verified at the endpoint handler when an HTTP request is being issued. The following is an implementation of API key authentication. The HTTP handler checks for the X-API-KEY header in the HTTP request; if the key is wrong or not found in the request header, then an unauthorized error (401) is thrown, as illustrated in the following code snippet (the full code has been cropped for brevity):

```
func (handler *RecipesHandler) NewRecipeHandler(
             c *gin.Context) {
   if c.GetHeader("X-API-KEY") != os.Getenv("X_API_KEY") {
       c.JSON(http.StatusUnauthorized, gin.H{
          "error": "API key not provided or invalid"})
       return
   }
}
```

Run the application after running the MongoDB and Redis containers, but this time set the X-API-KEY environment variable as follows:

```
X_API_KEY=eUbP9shywUygMx7u  MONGO_URI="mongodb://
admin:password@localhost:27017/test?authSource=admin" MONGO_
DATABASE=demo go run *.go
```

> **Note**
>
> You can use OpenSSL to generate a random secret string with the following command: openssl rand -base64 16.

If you try to add a new recipe, a `401` error message will be returned, as shown in the following screenshot:

Figure 4.2 – New recipe

However, if you include a valid `X-API-KEY` header in the `POST` request, the recipe will be inserted, as shown in the following screenshot:

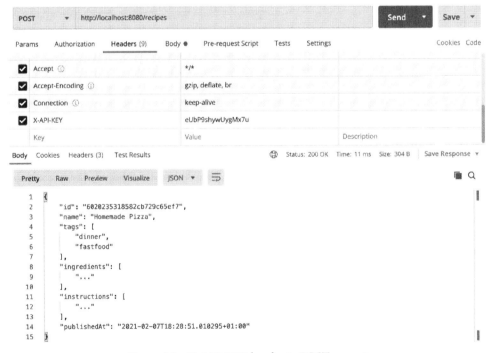

Figure 4.3 – X-API-KEY header in POST request

If you're not a fan of Postman as an HTTP/s client, you can execute the following cURL command on your terminal:

```
curl --location --request POST 'http://localhost:8080/recipes' \
--header 'X-API-KEY: eUbP9shywUygMx7u' \
--header 'Content-Type: application/json' \
--data-raw '{
    "name": "Homemade Pizza",
    "ingredients": ["..."],
    "instructions": ["..."],
    "tags": ["dinner", "fastfood"]
}'
```

For now, only the POST /recipes request is secured. To avoid repeating the same code snippet in other HTTP endpoints, create an authentication middleware by writing the following code:

```
func AuthMiddleware() gin.HandlerFunc {
    return func(c *gin.Context) {
        if c.GetHeader("X-API-KEY") !=
                os.Getenv("X_API_KEY") {
            c.AbortWithStatus(401)
        }
        c.Next()
    }
}
```

In the router definition, use the authentication middleware. Lastly, regroup the endpoints in a single group, as follows:

```
authorized := router.Group("/")
authorized.Use(AuthMiddleware()){
        authorized.POST("/recipes",
                        recipesHandler.NewRecipeHandler)
        authorized.GET("/recipes",
                        recipesHandler.ListRecipesHandler)
        authorized.PUT("/recipes/:id",
                        recipesHandler.UpdateRecipeHandler)
```

```
    authorized.DELETE("/recipes/:id",
                            recipesHandler.DeleteRecipeHandler)
}
```

At this stage, rerun the application. If you issue a GET /recipes request, a 401 error
will be returned, as illustrated in the following screenshot. This is normal because the
route handler for list recipes is behind the authentication middleware:

Figure 4.4 – API key required on GET /recipes

You want the GET /recipes request to be public, therefore register the endpoint
outside of the group router, as follows:

```
func main() {
    router := gin.Default()

    router.GET("/recipes",
                recipesHandler.ListRecipesHandler)

    authorized := router.Group("/")
    authorized.Use(AuthMiddleware())
    {
        authorized.POST("/recipes",
                            recipesHandler.NewRecipeHandler)
        authorized.PUT("/recipes/:id",
                            recipesHandler.UpdateRecipeHandler)
        authorized.DELETE("/recipes/:id",
                            recipesHandler.DeleteRecipeHandler)
        authorized.GET("/recipes/:id",
                            recipesHandler.GetOneRecipeHandler)
    }

    router.Run()
}
```

If you test it out, this time the endpoint will return a list of recipes, as illustrated in the following screenshot:

Figure 4.5 – List of recipes

API keys are simple; however, anyone who makes a request to an API transmits their key, and in theory, the key can be picked up easily with a **man-in-the-middle** (**MITM**) attack when no encryption is in use. That's why, in the next section, we will cover a more secure authentication mechanism known as JWTs.

> **Note**
>
> MITM refers to a situation where an attacker positions themself in a conversation between two parties in order to steal their credentials. For more details, check out the following link: `https://snyk.io/learn/man-in-the-middle-attack/`.

Introducing JWTs

According to **Request for Comments** (**RFC**) *7519* (`https://tools.ietf.org/html/rfc7519`):

> *"A JSON Web Token (JWT) is an open standard that defines a compact and self-contained way for securely transmitting information between parties as a JSON object. This information can be verified and trusted because it is digitally signed. JWTs can be signed using a secret or a public/private key pair."*

A JWT token consists of three parts separated by dots, as depicted in the following screenshot:

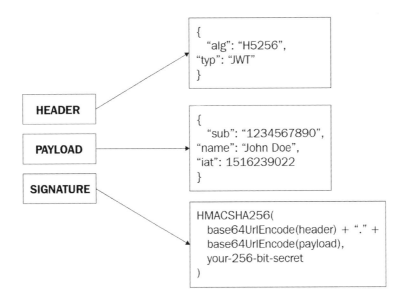

Figure 4.6 – JWT parts

The **header** indicates the algorithm used to generate the signature. The **payload** contains information about the user, along with the token expiration date. Finally, the **signature** is the result of hashing the header and payload parts with a secret key.

Now that we've seen how JWT works, let's integrate it into our API. To get started, install the JWT Go implementation with the following command:

```
go get github.com/dgrijalva/jwt-go
```

The package will be automatically added to the go.mod file, as follows:

```
module github.com/mlabouardy/recipes-api

go 1.15

require (
    github.com/dgrijalva/jwt-go v3.2.0+incompatible
    // indirect
    github.com/gin-gonic/gin v1.6.3
    github.com/go-redis/redis v6.15.9+incompatible
```

```
    github.com/go-redis/redis/v8 v8.4.10
    go.mongodb.org/mongo-driver v1.4.5
    golang.org/x/net v0.0.0-20201202161906-c7110b5ffcbb
)
```

Before getting your hands dirty, let me explain how the JWT authentication will be implemented. Basically, the client will need to sign in using a username and password. If those credentials are valid, a JWT token will be generated and returned. The client will use the token in future requests by including an `Authorization` header. If a request is issued to the API, the token will be verified by comparing its signature against a signature generated with the secret key, and the API will return the target response. Otherwise, a `401` error will be returned.

The following sequence diagram illustrates the communication between the client and the API:

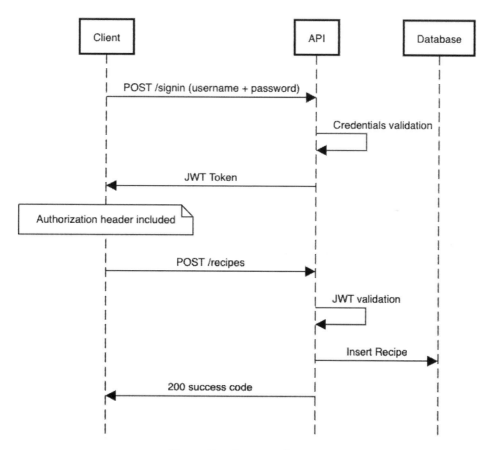

Figure 4.7 – Sequence diagram

With that being said, create an auth.go file under the handlers folder. This file will expose the functions that will handle the authentication workflow. Here is the code to do this (the full code has been cropped for brevity):

```
package handlers

import (
    "net/http"
    "os"
    "time"

    "github.com/dgrijalva/jwt-go"
)

type AuthHandler struct{}

type Claims struct {
    Username string `json:"username"`
    jwt.StandardClaims
}

type JWTOutput struct {
    Token   string    `json:"token"`
    Expires time.Time `json:"expires"`
}

func (handler *AuthHandler) SignInHandler(c *gin.Context) {}
```

Next, you need to define an entity model for user credentials. In the models folder, create a user.go struct with username and password attributes, as follows:

```
package models

type User struct {
    Password string `json:"password"`
    Username string `json:"username"`
}
```

With the model being defined, we can go ahead and implement the authentication handler.

Sign-in HTTP handler

SignInHandler will encode the request body into a User struct and verify the credentials are correct. Then, it will issue a JWT token with an expiration time of 10 minutes. The signature of the JWT is the output of combining the Base64 representation of the header and payload along with a secret key (notice the usage of the JWT_SECRET environment variable). The combination is then passed to an HS256 hashing algorithm. It's worth mentioning that you must keep your credentials out of the source code as a security measure. The implementation is shown here:

```
func (handler *AuthHandler) SignInHandler(c *gin.Context) {
    var user models.User
    if err := c.ShouldBindJSON(&user); err != nil {
        c.JSON(http.StatusBadRequest, gin.H{"error":
            err.Error()})
        return
    }

    if user.Username != "admin" || user.Password !=
            "password" {
        c.JSON(http.StatusUnauthorized, gin.H{"error":
            "Invalid username or password"})
        return
    }

    expirationTime := time.Now().Add(10 * time.Minute)
    claims := &Claims{
        Username: user.Username,
        StandardClaims: jwt.StandardClaims{
            ExpiresAt: expirationTime.Unix(),
        },
    }

    token := jwt.NewWithClaims(jwt.SigningMethodHS256,
                        claims)
```

```
    tokenString, err := token.SignedString([]byte(
                    os.Getenv("JWT_SECRET")))
    if err != nil {
        c.JSON(http.StatusInternalServerError,
                gin.H{"error": err.Error()})
        return
    }

    jwtOutput := JWTOutput{
        Token:    tokenString,
        Expires:  expirationTime,
    }
    c.JSON(http.StatusOK, jwtOutput)
}
```

> **Note**
> For more information on how the hashing algorithm works, check out the
> official RFC: https://tools.ietf.org/html/rfc7518.

With the `SignInHandler` handler created, let's register this handler on the POST /
signin endpoint by updating the main.go file, as follows (the code has been cropped
for brevity):

```
package main

import (
    ...
)
var authHandler *handlers.AuthHandler
var recipesHandler *handlers.RecipesHandler

func init() {
    ...
    recipesHandler = handlers.NewRecipesHandler(ctx,
        collection, redisClient)
    authHandler = &handlers.AuthHandler{}
}
```

```
func main() {
    router := gin.Default()
    router.GET("/recipes",
               recipesHandler.ListRecipesHandler)
    router.POST("/signin", authHandler.SignInHandler)
    ...
}
```

Next, we update the authentication middleware in `handler/auth.go` to check for the `Authorization` header instead of the `X-API-KEY` attribute. The header is then passed to the `ParseWithClaims` method. It generates a signature using the header and payload from the `Authorization` header and the secret key. Then, it verifies if the signature matches the one on the JWT. If not, the JWT is not considered valid, and a `401` status code is returned. The Go implementation is shown here:

```
func (handler *AuthHandler) AuthMiddleware() gin.HandlerFunc {
    return func(c *gin.Context) {
        tokenValue := c.GetHeader("Authorization")
        claims := &Claims{}

        tkn, err := jwt.ParseWithClaims(tokenValue, claims,
                func(token *jwt.Token) (interface{}, error) {
            return []byte(os.Getenv("JWT_SECRET")), nil
        })
        if err != nil {
            c.AbortWithStatus(http.StatusUnauthorized)
        }
        if tkn == nil ||!tkn.Valid {
            c.AbortWithStatus(http.StatusUnauthorized)
        }
        c.Next()
    }
}
```

Rerun the application with the following command:

```
JWT_SECRET=eUbP9shywUygMx7u MONGO_URI="mongodb://
admin:password@localhost:27017/test?authSource=admin" MONGO_
DATABASE=demo go run *.go
```

The server logs are shown in the following screenshot:

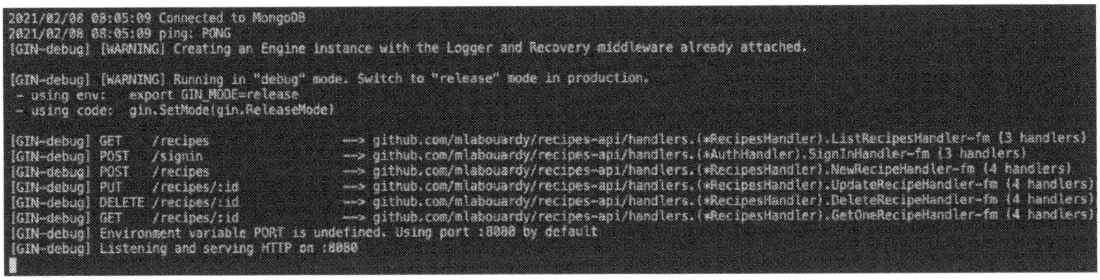

Figure 4.8 – Application logs

Now, if you try to insert a new recipe, a 401 error will be returned, as follows:

Figure 4.9 – Unauthorized endpoint

You need to sign in first using the admin/password credentials by executing a POST request on the /signin endpoint. Once successful, the endpoint will return a token that looks like this:

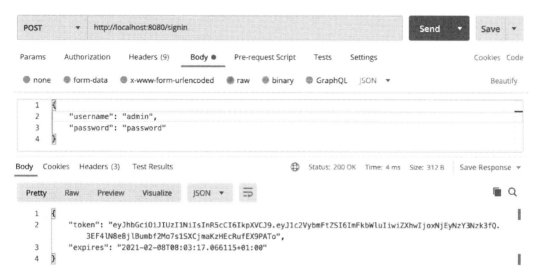

Figure 4.10 – Sign-in endpoint

The token consists of three parts separated by a dot. You can decode the token by going to `https://jwt.io/` to return the following output (your results might look different):

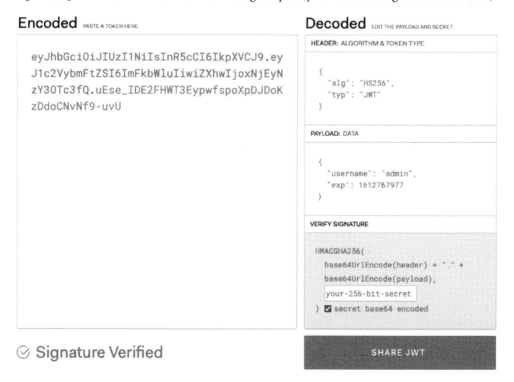

Figure 4.11 – Decoding a JWT token

> **Note**
>
> The header and payload parts are Base64-encoded, but you can use the `base64` command to decode their value.

Now, for further requests, you need to include the token in the `Authorization` header to be able to access secured endpoints such as posting a new recipe, as illustrated in the following screenshot:

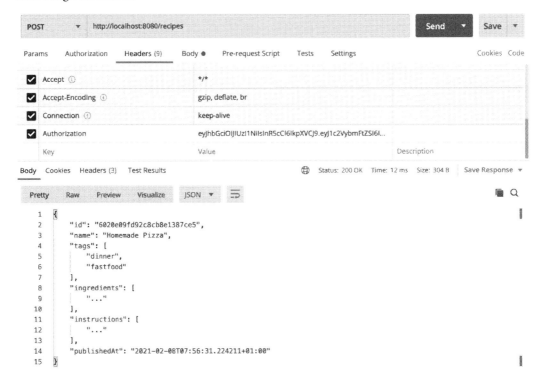

Figure 4.12 – Posting a new recipe

So far, everything is going well—however, in 10 minutes, the token will expire. If, for instance, you try to post a new recipe, a `401` unauthorized message will be thrown even though you have included the `Authorization` header, as we can see in the following screenshot:

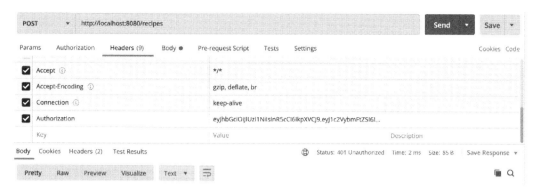

Figure 4.13 – Expired JWT

So, let's check out how you can renew this token after it expires.

Renewing a JWT

You can increase the expiration time to make a JWT token last; however, this is not a permanent solution. What you can do instead is to expose an endpoint to allow the user to refresh a token, which will let the client application refresh the token without asking the user for the username and password again. The function handler is shown in the following code snippet—it takes the previous token and returns a new token with a renewed expiry time:

```go
func (handler *AuthHandler) RefreshHandler(c *gin.Context) {
    tokenValue := c.GetHeader("Authorization")
    claims := &Claims{}
    tkn, err := jwt.ParseWithClaims(tokenValue, claims,
            func(token *jwt.Token) (interface{}, error) {
        return []byte(os.Getenv("JWT_SECRET")), nil
    })
    if err != nil {
        c.JSON(http.StatusUnauthorized, gin.H{"error":
            err.Error()})
        return
    }
    if tkn == nil ||!tkn.Valid {
        c.JSON(http.StatusUnauthorized, gin.H{"error": "Invalid
                                    token"})
        return
    }
```

```go
    if time.Unix(claims.ExpiresAt, 0).Sub(time.Now()) >
            30*time.Second {
        c.JSON(http.StatusBadRequest, gin.H{"error":
            "Token is not expired yet"})
        return
    }

    expirationTime := time.Now().Add(5 * time.Minute)
    claims.ExpiresAt = expirationTime.Unix()
    token := jwt.NewWithClaims(jwt.SigningMethodHS256,
                            claims)
    tokenString, err := token.SignedString(os.Getenv(
                    "JWT_SECRET"))
    if err != nil {
        c.JSON(http.StatusInternalServerError,
            gin.H{"error": err.Error()})
        return
    }

    jwtOutput := JWTOutput{
        Token:    tokenString,
        Expires: expirationTime,
    }
    c.JSON(http.StatusOK, jwtOutput)
}
```

> **Note**
>
> In a web application, the `/refresh` endpoint can be used to refresh the JWT token in the background without asking the user to sign in every couple of minutes.

Register the `RefreshHandler` handler on the `POST /refresh` endpoint with the following code:

```go
router.POST("/refresh", authHandler.RefreshHandler)
```

If you rerun the app, the /refresh endpoint will be exposed, as shown in the following screenshot:

```
[GIN-debug] GET    /recipes                 ---> github.com/mlabouardy/recipes-api/handlers.(*RecipesHandler).ListRecipesHandler-fm (3 handlers)
[GIN-debug] POST   /signin                  ---> github.com/mlabouardy/recipes-api/handlers.(*AuthHandler).SignInHandler-fm (3 handlers)
[GIN-debug] POST   /refresh                 ---> github.com/mlabouardy/recipes-api/handlers.(*AuthHandler).RefreshHandler-fm (3 handlers)
[GIN-debug] POST   /recipes                 ---> github.com/mlabouardy/recipes-api/handlers.(*RecipesHandler).NewRecipeHandler-fm (4 handlers)
[GIN-debug] PUT    /recipes/:id             ---> github.com/mlabouardy/recipes-api/handlers.(*RecipesHandler).UpdateRecipeHandler-fm (4 handlers)
[GIN-debug] DELETE /recipes/:id             ---> github.com/mlabouardy/recipes-api/handlers.(*RecipesHandler).DeleteRecipeHandler-fm (4 handlers)
[GIN-debug] GET    /recipes/:id             ---> github.com/mlabouardy/recipes-api/handlers.(*RecipesHandler).GetOneRecipeHandler-fm (4 handlers)
[GIN-debug] Environment variable PORT is undefined. Using port :8080 by default
[GIN-debug] Listening and serving HTTP on :8080
```

Figure 4.14 – /refresh endpoint

You can now issue a POST request on the /refresh endpoint, and a new token will be generated and returned.

Awesome—you now have a working authentication workflow! However, the user credentials are still hardcoded in the application code source. You can improve this by storing them in your **MongoDB** server. An updated sequence diagram is provided here:

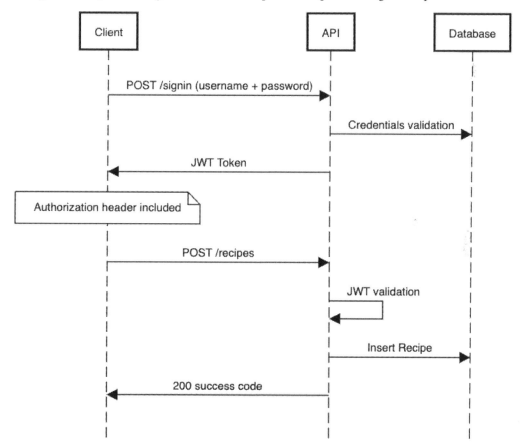

Figure 4.15 – Storing credentials in MongoDB

To be able to interact with the MongoDB server, you need to add the MongoDB collection to the `AuthHandler` struct in the `auth.go` file, as illustrated in the following code snippet. Then, you can issue a `FindOne` operation on the `users` collection to verify if the given credentials exist:

```
type AuthHandler struct {
    collection *mongo.Collection
    ctx        context.Context
}

func NewAuthHandler(ctx context.Context, collection
        *mongo.Collection) *AuthHandler {
    return &AuthHandler{
        collection: collection,
        ctx:        ctx,
    }
}
```

Next, update the `SignInHandler` method to verify if the user credentials are valid by comparing them with entries in the database. Here is how it should be done:

```
func (handler *AuthHandler) SignInHandler(c *gin.Context) {



    h := sha256.New()

    cur := handler.collection.FindOne(handler.ctx, bson.M{
        "username": user.Username,
        "password": string(h.Sum([]byte(user.Password))),
    })
    if cur.Err() != nil {
        c.JSON(http.StatusUnauthorized, gin.H{"error":
            "Invalid username or password"})
        return
    }

    ...
}
```

In the `init()` method, you need to set up a connection to the `users` collection then pass the collection instance to the `AuthHandler` instance, as follows:

```
collectionUsers := client.Database(os.Getenv(
            "MONGO_DATABASE")).Collection("users")
authHandler = handlers.NewAuthHandler(ctx, collectionUsers)
```

Make sure to save the `main.go` changes, and the API is then ready!

Hashing and salting passwords

Before running the app, we need to initialize the *users* collection with some users. Create a new project in **Visual Studio Code** (**VSCode**), and then define a `main.go` file with the following content:

```
func main() {
    users := map[string]string{
        "admin":       "fCRmh4Q2J7Rseqkz",
        "packt":       "RE4zfHB35VPtTkbT",
        "mlabouardy": "L3nSFRcZzNQ67bcc",
    }

    ctx := context.Background()
    client, err := mongo.Connect(ctx,
        options.Client().ApplyURI(os.Getenv("MONGO_URI")))
    if err = client.Ping(context.TODO(),
            readpref.Primary()); err != nil {
        log.Fatal(err)
    }

    collection := client.Database(os.Getenv(
        "MONGO_DATABASE")).Collection("users")
    h := sha256.New()

    for username, password := range users {
        collection.InsertOne(ctx, bson.M{
            "username": username,
            "password": string(h.Sum([]byte(password))),
```

```
        })
    }
}
```

The preceding code will insert three users (`admin`, `packt`, `mlabouardy`) into the `users` collection. The passwords are **hashed** and **salted** before they are saved into MongoDB using the *SHA256* algorithm for security purposes. The algorithm generates a unique 256-bit signature for the password that can be decrypted back to the original password. That way, sensitive information can remain secure.

> **Note**
>
> Storing plaintext passwords in the database is not recommended. By hashing and salting users' passwords, we make sure that hackers are not able to sign in, as the stolen data won't contain the credentials.

You can run the code with the `MONGO_URI="mongodb://admin:password@ localhost:27017/test?authSource=admin" MONGO_DATABASE=demo go run main.go` command. Check if the users have been inserted using MongoDB Compass (for a step-by-step guide on how to use MongoDB Compass, head back to *Chapter 3, Managing Data Persistence with MongoDB*), as illustrated in the following screenshot:

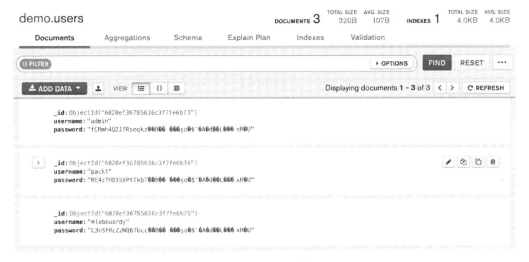

Figure 4.16 – Users collection

As you might notice, the passwords are hashed and salted. With the users being inserted into MongoDB, we can test out the sign-in endpoint by issuing a POST request with the following payload:

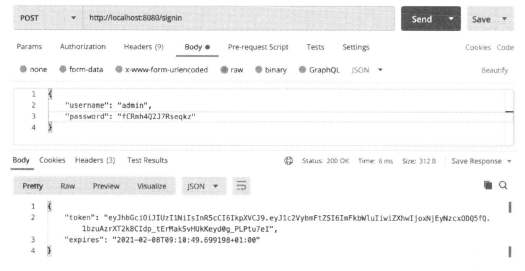

Figure 4.17 – Sign-in endpoint

> **Note**
>
> We can improve the JWT implementation by setting a cookie on the client side with the JWT value. That way, the cookie is sent along with the request.

You can take this further and create a sign-up endpoint to create a new user and save it to the MongoDB database. You should now be familiar with how to implement an authentication mechanism with JWT.

Persisting client sessions and cookies

Up to now, you had to include the Authorization header on each request. A better solution is to generate a **session cookie**. Session cookies allow users to be recognized within an application without having to authenticate every time. Without a cookie, every time you issue an API request, the server will treat you like a completely new visitor.

To generate a session cookie, proceed as follows:

1. Install *Gin middleware* for session management with the following command:

```
go get github.com/gin-contrib/sessions
```

2. Configure *Redis* as a store for users' sessions with the following code:

```
store, _ := redisStore.NewStore(10, "tcp",
        "localhost:6379", "", []byte("secret"))
router.Use(sessions.Sessions("recipes_api", store))
```

> **Note**
>
> Instead of hardcoding the Redis **Uniform Resource Identifier** (**URI**), you can use an environment variable. That way, you can keep configuration out of the API source code.

3. Then, update `SignInHandler` to generate a session with a unique ID, as illustrated in the following code snippet. The session starts once a user logs in and expires sometime after that. The session information of the logged-in user will be stored in the Redis cache:

```
func (handler *AuthHandler) SignInHandler(c *gin.Context)
{
    var user models.User
    if err := c.ShouldBindJSON(&user); err != nil {
        c.JSON(http.StatusBadRequest, gin.H{"error":
            err.Error()})
        return
    }

    h := sha256.New()

    cur := handler.collection.FindOne(handler.ctx, bson.M{
        "username": user.Username,
        "password": string(h.Sum([]byte(user.Password))),
    })
    if cur.Err() != nil {
        c.JSON(http.StatusUnauthorized, gin.H{"error":
```

```
            "Invalid username or password"})
        return
    }


    sessionToken := xid.New().String()
    session := sessions.Default(c)
    session.Set("username", user.Username)
    session.Set("token", sessionToken)
    session.Save()


    c.JSON(http.StatusOK, gin.H{"message":
                                "User signed in"})
}
```

4. Next, update AuthMiddleware to obtain the token from the request cookie. If the cookie is not set, we return a 403 code (Forbidden) by returning an http. StatusForbidden response, as illustrated in the following code snippet:

```
func (handler *AuthHandler) AuthMiddleware() gin.
    HandlerFunc {
    return func(c *gin.Context) {
        session := sessions.Default(c)
        sessionToken := session.Get("token")
        if sessionToken == nil {
            c.JSON(http.StatusForbidden, gin.H{
                "message": "Not logged",
            })
            c.Abort()
        }
        c.Next()
    }
}
```

5. Start the server on port 8080, and issue a POST request on the /signin endpoint with a valid username and password. A cookie should be generated, like the one shown in the following screenshot:

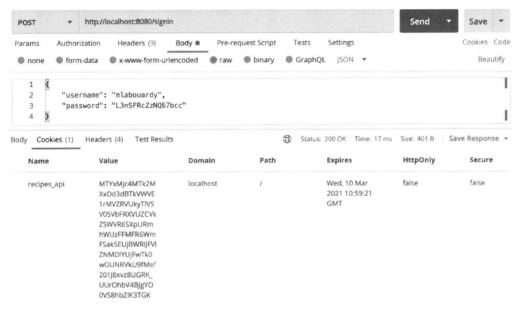

Figure 4.18 – Session cookie

Now the session will be persisted across all other API routes. Therefore, you can interact with API endpoints without including any authorization header, as illustrated in the following screenshot:

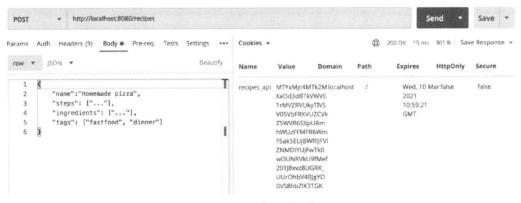

Figure 4.19 – Session-based authentication

The previous example uses the Postman client, but if you're a cURL fan, do the following:

1. Use the following command to store the generated cookie in a text file:

```
curl -c cookies.txt -X POST http://localhost:8080/signin
-d '{"username":"admin", "password":"fCRmh4Q2J7Rseqkz"}'
```

2. Then, inject the cookies.txt file in future requests, like this:

```
curl -b cookies.txt -X POST http://localhost:8080/
recipes -d '{"name":"Homemade Pizza", "steps":[],
"instructions":[]}'
```

> **Note**
>
> You can implement a refresh route to generate a new session cookie with a renewed expiry time.

All the sessions generated by the API will be persisted in Redis. You can use the Redis Insight **user interface** (**UI**) (hosted on a Docker container) to browse the saved session, as illustrated in the following screenshot:

Figure 4.20 – List of sessions stored in Redis

3. To log out, you can implement the SignOutHandler handler to clear the session cookie with the following command:

```
func (handler *AuthHandler) SignOutHandler(c
      *gin.Context) {
    session := sessions.Default(c)
    session.Clear()
    session.Save()
    c.JSON(http.StatusOK, gin.H{"message":
                             "Signed out..."})
}
```

4. Remember to register the handler on the `main.go` file, like so:

```
router.POST("/signout", authHandler.SignOutHandler)
```

5. Run the application, and a sign-out endpoint should be exposed, as illustrated in the following screenshot:

```
[GIN-debug] GET    /recipes         --> github.com/mlabouardy/recipes-api/handlers.(*RecipesHandler).ListRecipesHandler-fm (4 handlers)
[GIN-debug] POST   /signin          --> github.com/mlabouardy/recipes-api/handlers.(*AuthHandler).SignInHandler-fm (4 handlers)
[GIN-debug] POST   /refresh         --> github.com/mlabouardy/recipes-api/handlers.(*AuthHandler).RefreshHandler-fm (4 handlers)
[GIN-debug] POST   /signout         --> github.com/mlabouardy/recipes-api/handlers.(*AuthHandler).SignOutHandler-fm (4 handlers)
[GIN-debug] POST   /recipes         --> github.com/mlabouardy/recipes-api/handlers.(*RecipesHandler).NewRecipeHandler-fm (5 handlers)
[GIN-debug] PUT    /recipes/:id     --> github.com/mlabouardy/recipes-api/handlers.(*RecipesHandler).UpdateRecipeHandler-fm (5 handlers)
[GIN-debug] DELETE /recipes/:id     --> github.com/mlabouardy/recipes-api/handlers.(*RecipesHandler).DeleteRecipeHandler-fm (5 handlers)
[GIN-debug] GET    /recipes/:id     --> github.com/mlabouardy/recipes-api/handlers.(*RecipesHandler).GetOneRecipeHandler-fm (5 handlers)
[GIN-debug] Environment variable PORT is undefined. Using port :8080 by default
[GIN-debug] Listening and serving HTTP on :8080
```

Figure 4.21 – Sign-out handler

6. Now, test it out with the Postman client by executing a `POST` request, like so:

Figure 4.22 – Signing out

The session cookie will be deleted, and if you now try to add a new recipe, a `403` error will be returned, as illustrated in the following screenshot:

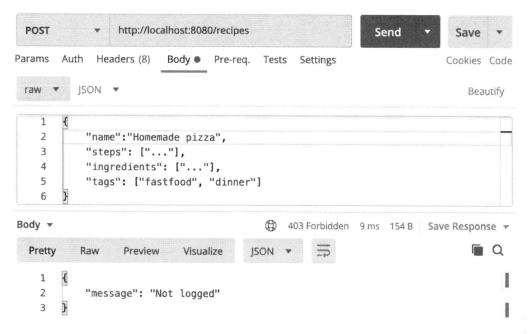

Figure 4.23 – Adding a new recipe

7. Make sure to commit the changes to GitHub by creating a new feature branch. Then, merge the branch into development mode, as follows:

```
git add .
git commit -m "session based authentication"
git checkout -b feature/session
git push origin feature/session
```

The following screenshot shows the pull requests containing the JWT and cookie authentication features:

Figure 4.24 – Pull requests on GitHub

Awesome! The API endpoints are now secured and can be served to the public.

Authenticating with Auth0

So far, the authentication mechanism is built in within the application. Maintaining such a system might be a bottleneck in the long run, which is why you might need to consider an external service such as **Auth0**. This is an all-in-one authentication solution that gives you access to powerful reporting and analytics as well as a **role-based access control** (**RBAC**) system.

To get started, follow these steps:

1. Create a free account (`https://auth0.com/signup`). Once created, set up a tenant domain in the region where you're located, as illustrated in the following screenshot:

Figure 4.25 – Auth0 tenant domain

2. Then, create a new API called `Recipes API`. Set the identifier to `https://api.recipes.io` and the signing algorithm to `RS256`, as illustrated in the following screenshot:

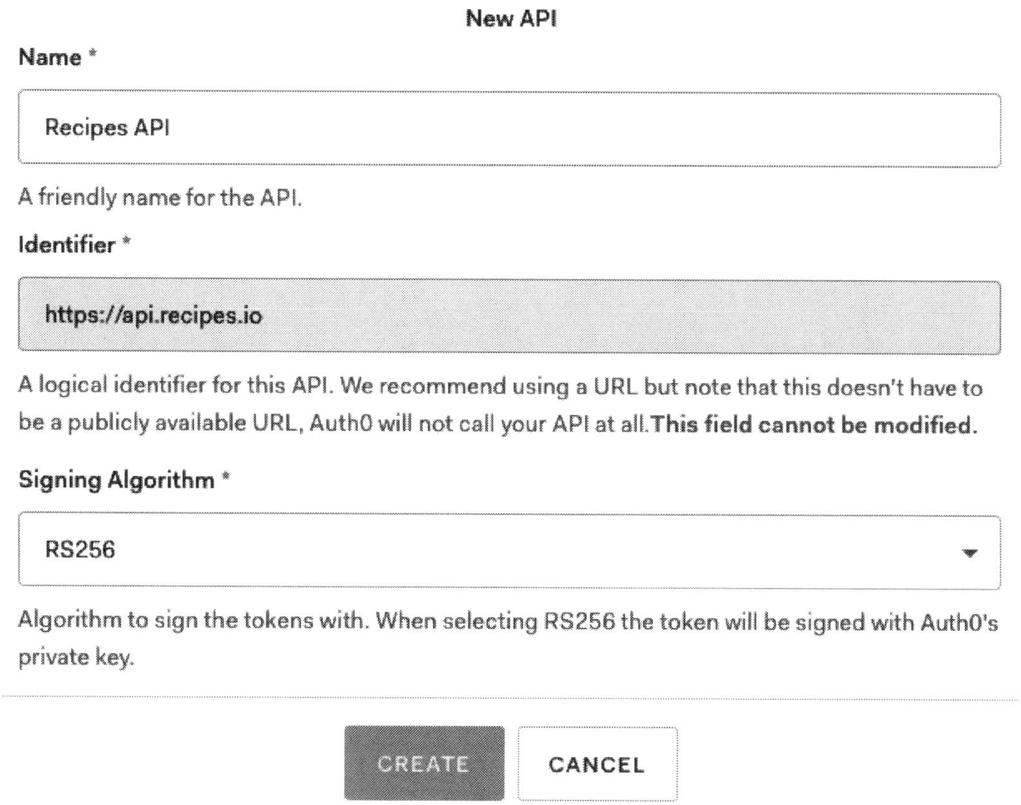

New API

Name *

> Recipes API

A friendly name for the API.

Identifier *

> https://api.recipes.io

A logical identifier for this API. We recommend using a URL but note that this doesn't have to be a publicly available URL, Auth0 will not call your API at all. **This field cannot be modified.**

Signing Algorithm *

> RS256   ▼

Algorithm to sign the tokens with. When selecting RS256 the token will be signed with Auth0's private key.

CREATE   CANCEL

Figure 4.26 – Auth0 new API

3. Once the API is created, you need to integrate the Auth0 service into the API. Download the following Go packages:

```
go get -v gopkg.in/square/go-jose.v2
go get -v github.com/auth0-community/go-auth0
```

4. Next, update AuthMiddleware, as illustrated in the following code snippet. The middleware will check if an access token exists and if this is valid. If it passes the checks, the request will proceed. If not, a 401 Authorization error is returned:

```
func (handler *AuthHandler) AuthMiddleware() gin.
HandlerFunc {
    return func(c *gin.Context) {
        var auth0Domain = "https://" + os.Getenv(
            "AUTH0_DOMAIN") + "/"
        client := auth0.NewJWKClient(auth0.
```

```
JWKClientOptions{
        URI: auth0Domain + ".well-known/jwks.json"},
        nil)
    configuration := auth0.NewConfiguration(client,
        []string{os.Getenv("AUTH0_API_IDENTIFIER")},
        auth0Domain, jose.RS256)
    validator := auth0.NewValidator(configuration,
                                    nil)


    _, err := validator.ValidateRequest(c.Request)


    if err != nil {
        c.JSON(http.StatusUnauthorized,
            gin.H{"message": "Invalid token"})
        c.Abort()
        return
    }
    c.Next()
    }
}
```

Auth0 uses RS256 algorithm-signing access tokens. The verification process uses a public key (located at AUTH0_DOMAIN/.well-known/jwks.json) in **JSON Web Key Set (JWKS)** format to verify the given token.

5. Run the application with AUTH0_DOMAIN and AUTH0_API_IDENTIFIER, as illustrated in the following code snippet. Make sure to replace those variables with the values you copied from your Auth0 dashboard:

```
AUTH0_DOMAIN=DOMAIN.eu.auth0.com  AUTH0_API_
IDENTIFIER="https://api.recipes.io" MONGO_URI="mongodb://
admin:password@localhost:27017/test?authSource=admin"
MONGO_DATABASE=demo go run *.go
```

Now, if you try to issue a request to your API without sending an access token, you will see this message:

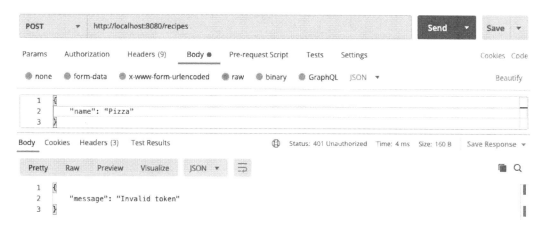

Figure 4.27 – Unauthorized access

6. To generate an access token. Head back to the **Auth0** dashboard, click on **APIs**, then select **Recipes API**. From there, click on the **Test** tab and copy the cURL command shown in the following screenshot:

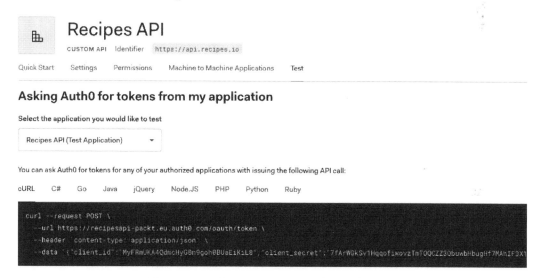

Figure 4.28 – Generating access token with cURL

7. Execute the following command on your terminal session to generate an access token that you can use to communicate with your backend API:

```
curl --request POST \
    --url https://recipesapi-packt.eu.auth0.com/oauth/token
\
    --data '{"client_id":"MyFRmUZS","client_
```

```
secret":"7fArWGkSva","audience":"https://api.recipes.
io","grant_type":"client_credentials"}'
```

An access token will be generated, as follows (you should have a different value):

```
{
  "access_token":"eyJhbGciOiJSUzI1NiIsInR5cCI
6IkpXVCIsImtpZCI6IkZ5T19SN2dScDdPakp3RmJQRVB3dCDz",
    "expires_in":86400,
    "token_type":"Bearer"
}
```

8. Now, update your API request to include the access token, as shown in the following screenshot:

Figure 4.29 – Authorized access

9. This can also be tested straight from the command line with cURL. Just replace the ACCESS_TOKEN value shown in the following code snippet with your test token and then paste it into your terminal:

```
curl --request POST \
  --url http://localhost:8080/recipes \
  --header 'Authorization: Bearer ACCESS_TOKEN'\
  --data '{"name":"Pizza "}'
```

Awesome! You just developed a secure API with Go and the Gin framework.

Building an HTTPS server

So far, the API is served locally through HTTP, but for a real-world application, it should be served under a domain name through HTTPS.

To set this up, proceed as follows:

1. Use the `ngrok` solution to serve our local web API with a public **Uniform Resource Locator** (**URL**) that supports both HTTP and HTTPS.

   > **Note**
   > In advanced chapters, we will explore how to purchase a domain name and set up HTTPS for free on a cloud provider such as **Amazon Web Services** (**AWS**).

2. Download the ZIP file based on your **operating system** (**OS**) from the official Ngrok page at `https://ngrok.com/download`. In this book, we will work with version 2.3.35. Once downloaded, unzip Ngrok from a terminal with the following commands:

   ```
   unzip ngrok-stable-darwin-amd64.zip
   cp ngrok /usr/local/bin/
   chmod +x /usr/local/bin/ngrok
   ```

3. Verify if it's properly installed by executing the following command:

   ```
   ngrok version
   ```

   It should output the following message:

   ```
   mlabouardy@Mohameds-MBP-001 chapter4 % ngrok version
   ngrok version 2.3.35
   mlabouardy@Mohameds-MBP-001 chapter4 %
   ```

   Figure 4.30 – Ngrok version

4. Configure Ngrok to listen and forward requests into port 8080, which is the port where the RESTful API is exposed, by running the following command:

   ```
   ngrok http 8080
   ```

A public URL will be generated that can be used as a proxy to interact with the API from the internet, as illustrated here:

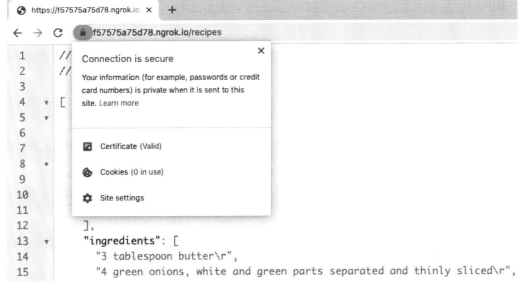

Figure 4.31 – Ngrok forwarding

5. Navigate to the forwarding URL using the HTTPS protocol. A **Connection is secure** message should be displayed next to the URL, as illustrated in the following screenshot:

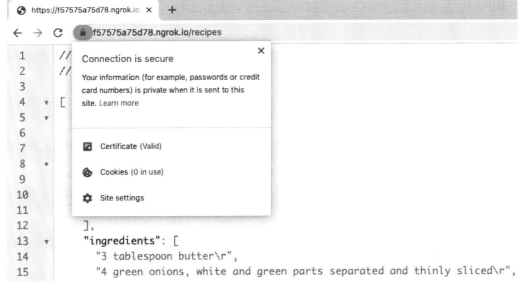

Figure 4.32 – Serving through HTTPS

You can now access the API from another machine or device or share it with others. In the next section, we will cover how to create your own **Secure Sockets Layer** (**SSL**) certificates to secure a domain name running locally.

Self-signed certificates

SSL certificates are what websites use to move from HTTP and HTTPS. The certificate uses SSL/**Transport Layer Security (TLS)** encryption to keep user data secure, verify ownership of the website, prevent attackers from creating a fake version of the site, and gain user trust.

To create self-signed certificates, proceed as follows:

1. Create a directory where the certificates will be stored and use the OpenSSL command line to generate public and private keys, as follows:

    ```
    mkdir certs
    openssl req -x509 -nodes -days 365 -newkey rsa:2048
    -keyout certs/localhost.key -out certs/localhost.crt
    ```

2. You'll need to fill a simple questionnaire—make sure to set the fully qualified hostname to `localhost`, as shown here:

```
Generating a 2048 bit RSA private key
...............+++
...............+++
writing new private key to 'certs/localhost.key'
-----
You are about to be asked to enter information that will be incorporated
into your certificate request.
What you are about to enter is what is called a Distinguished Name or a DN.
There are quite a few fields but you can leave some blank
For some fields there will be a default value,
If you enter '.', the field will be left blank.
-----
Country Name (2 letter code) []:FR
State or Province Name (full name) []:Paris
Locality Name (eg, city) []:Ile de France
Organization Name (eg, company) []:Packt
Organizational Unit Name (eg, section) []:Development
Common Name (eg, fully qualified host name) []:localhost
Email Address []:mohamed@labouardy.com
```

Figure 4.33 – Generating self-signed certificates

In doing so, two files will be generated, as follows:

`localhost.crt`: Self-signed certificate

`localhost.key`: Private key

> **Note**
> In advanced chapters, we will cover how to retrieve a valid certificate for production with Let's Encrypt (`https://letsencrypt.org`) for free.

3. Update `main.go` to run the server on HTTPS by utilizing the self-signed certificates, as follows (note that we use port 443 now, which is the default HTTPS port):

```
router.RunTLS(":443", "certs/localhost.crt", "certs/
localhost.key")
```

4. Run the application, and the logs will confirm the API is served through HTTPS, as illustrated here:

Figure 4.34 – Listening and serving HTTPS

5. Head to your browser, and then navigate to `https://localhost/recipes`. A secure-website icon will be shown on the left side of the URL bar, as illustrated in the following screenshot:

Figure 4.35 – Encrypted connection to localhost

> **Note**
>
> If you're using Google Chrome as your default browser, you need to enable the `allow-insecure-localhost` option for the browser to accept the self-signed certificates.

If you're using cURL to interact with the API, skip certificate verification, otherwise you'll get the following error message:

```
mlabouardy@Mohameds-MBP-001 chapter4 % curl  https://localhost/recipes
curl: (60) SSL certificate problem: self signed certificate
More details here: https://curl.haxx.se/docs/sslcerts.html

curl failed to verify the legitimacy of the server and therefore could not
establish a secure connection to it. To learn more about this situation and
how to fix it, please visit the web page mentioned above.
mlabouardy@Mohameds-MBP-001 chapter4 %
```

Figure 4.36 – Self-signed certificate verification

You can fix the preceding error by specifying a certificate bundle on the **command-line interface (CLI)** with the following command:

```
curl --cacert certs/localhost.crt https://localhost/
recipes
```

Or, you can use a `-k` flag to skip the SSL verification, as follows (not recommended if interacting with external websites):

```
curl -k https://localhost/recipes
```

6. For development, simply keep using the localhost, or access the API from a custom domain. You can create an alias with a domain name locally by adding the following entry to your `/etc/hosts` file:

```
127.0.0.1 api.recipes.io
```

7. Once the changes are saved, you can test it out by executing a `ping` command on `api.recipes.io`, as follows:

```
mlabouardy@Mohameds-MBP-001 recipes-api % ping api.recipes.io
PING localhost (127.0.0.1): 56 data bytes
64 bytes from 127.0.0.1: icmp_seq=0 ttl=64 time=0.048 ms
64 bytes from 127.0.0.1: icmp_seq=1 ttl=64 time=0.088 ms
64 bytes from 127.0.0.1: icmp_seq=2 ttl=64 time=0.045 ms
64 bytes from 127.0.0.1: icmp_seq=3 ttl=64 time=0.105 ms
64 bytes from 127.0.0.1: icmp_seq=4 ttl=64 time=0.078 ms
```

Figure 4.37 – ping output

The domain name is reachable and points to `127.0.0.1`. You can now access the RESTful API by navigating to `https://api.recipes.io:8080`, as illustrated in the following screenshot:

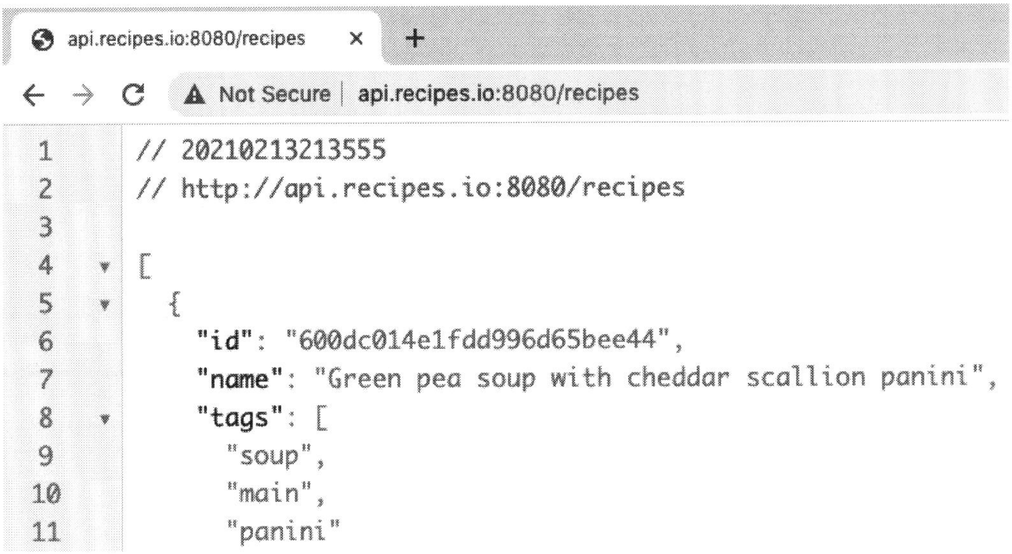

Figure 4.38 – Alias domain name

Great! You will now be able to secure your API endpoints with authentication and serve your API through a custom domain name locally.

Before we wrap up this chapter, you need to update the API documentation to include the authentication endpoints we implemented throughout the chapter, as follows:

1. First, update the general metadata to include an `Authorization` header in the API requests, as follows:

```
// Recipes API
//
// This is a sample recipes API. You can find out more
   about the API at
   https://github.com/PacktPublishing/Building-
   Distributed-Applications-in-Gin.
//
//    Schemes: http
//    Host: api.recipes.io:8080
//    BasePath: /
//    Version: 1.0.0
```

```
//   Contact: Mohamed Labouardy
//   <mohamed@labouardy.com> https://labouardy.com
//   SecurityDefinitions:
//   api_key:
//     type: apiKey
//     name: Authorization
//    in: header
//
//   Consumes:
//   - application/json
//
//   Produces:
//   - application/json
// swagger:meta
package main
```

2. Then, write a `swagger:operation` annotation on top of the `SignInHandler` handler, as follows:

```
// swagger:operation POST /signin auth signIn
// Login with username and password
// ---
// produces:
// - application/json
// responses:
//     '200':
//         description: Successful operation
//     '401':
//         description: Invalid credentials
func (handler *AuthHandler) SignInHandler(c *gin.Context)
{}
```

3. Write a `swagger:operation` annotation on top of the `RefreshHandler` handler, as follows:

```
// swagger:operation POST /refresh auth refresh
// Get new token in exchange for an old one
// ---
```

```
// produces:
// - application/json
// responses:
//       '200':
//           description: Successful operation
//       '400':
//           description: Token is new and doesn't need
//                           a refresh
//       '401':
//           description: Invalid credentials
func (handler *AuthHandler) RefreshHandler(c *gin.
Context)
{}
```

4. The operation expects a request body with the following attributes:

```
// API user credentials
// It is used to sign in
//
// swagger:model user
type User struct {
  // User's password
  //
  // required: true
  Password string `json:"password"`
  // User's login
  //
  // required: true
  Username string `json:"username"`
}
```

5. Generate the OpenAPI specification, then serve the JSON file with the Swagger UI by executing the following commands:

```
swagger generate spec -o ./swagger.json
swagger serve --flavor=swagger ./swagger.json
```

The authentication endpoints (/refresh and /signin) should be added to the list of operations, as shown in the following screenshot:

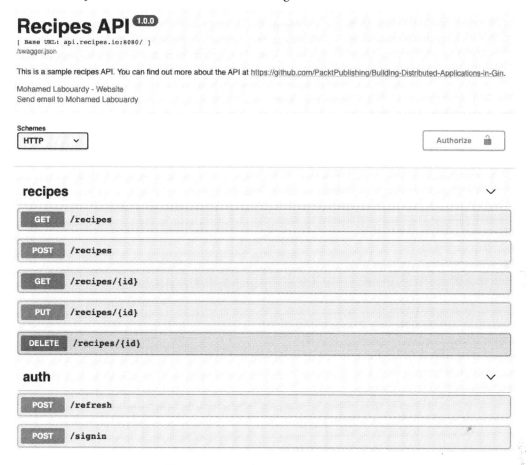

Figure 4.39 – Authentication operations

6. Now, click on the `signin` endpoint, and you will be able to fill the username and password attributes directly from the Swagger UI, as illustrated in the following screenshot:

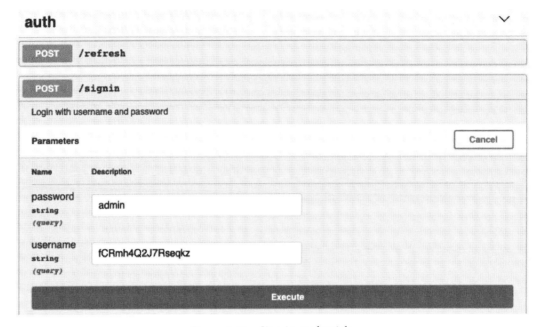

Figure 4.40 – Sign-in credentials

7. Next, click on **Execute** and a token should be generated that you can include in the `Authorization` header to interact with endpoints that require authorization, as illustrated in the following screenshot:

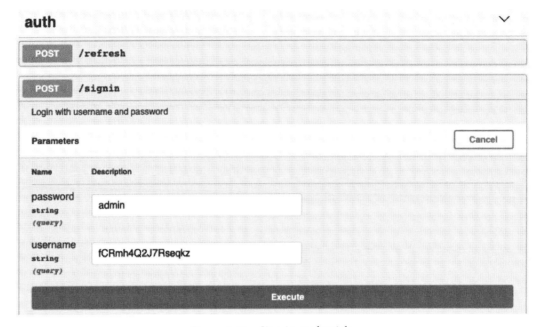

Figure 4.41 – Authorization header

You now are able to build a secure Gin RESTful API and serve it through the HTTPS protocol.

Summary

In this chapter, you learned a few of the best practices and recommendations for building a secure RESTful API based on the Gin web framework. You also covered how to implement JWT in Golang and how to persist session cookies across API requests.

You have also explored how a third-party solution such as Auth0 can be used as an authentication provider and how it can be integrated with Golang to secure API endpoints. Finally, you learned how to serve an API through the HTTPS protocol.

In the next chapter, we will build a user-friendly UI (also known as a frontend) on top of the RESTful API with the React web framework.

Questions

1. How would you implement a sign-up endpoint to create a new user account?

2. How would you implement a profile endpoint to return a user profile?

3. How would you generate a Swagger specification for a sign-out endpoint?

Further reading

- *OAuth 2.0 Cookbook* by Adolfo Eloy Nascimento, Packt Publishing
- *SSL Complete Guide* - HTTP to HTTPS by Bogdan Stashchuk, Packt Publishing

5
Serving Static HTML in Gin

In this chapter, you will learn how to build a **static web application** that consumes Gin-based **API** responses. Along the way, you will learn how to serve web assets (JavaScript, **Cascading Style Sheets** (**CSS**), and images) and render **HTML** templates with Gin. Finally, you will cover how to build a self-contained web application with Go and resolve **cross-origin resource sharing** (**CORS**) policy errors with a Gin middleware.

In this chapter, we will focus on the following topics:

- Serving static files
- Rendering HTML templates
- Building a self-contained web application
- Building a **Single-Page Application** (**SPA**)

By the end of this chapter, you will be able to build a SPA with React to consume your RESTful API endpoints.

Technical requirements

To follow the instructions in this chapter, you will need the following:

- A complete understanding of the previous chapter—this chapter is a follow-up of the previous one and it will use the same source code. Hence, some snippets won't be explained, to avoid repetition.

- Previous experience with a frontend development, and ideally knowledge of a web framework such as Angular, React, or Vue.js.

The code bundle for this chapter is hosted on GitHub at `https://github.com/ PacktPublishing/Building-Distributed-Applications-in-Gin/tree/ main/chapter05`.

Serving static files

In the previous chapters, you have seen how to render API responses in **JSON** and **XML** formats. In this chapter, you will learn how you can render different types of responses. We will start by serving a basic `index.html` file and then move on to serving static files, such as JavaScript, CSS files, and images from a filesystem, and eventually render HTML templates.

To start serving static files, follow these steps:

1. Create a new project folder and open it with the **VSCode IDE**. Then, create an `index.html` file to display a `Hello world` message with an `<h2>` tag, as follows:

```
<html>
<head>
    <title>Recipes Platform</title>
</head>
<body>
    <h2>Hello world</h2>
</body>
</html>
```

2. Next, with the go get command, install github.com/gin-gonic/gin, write a main.go file, and define a router with the gin.Default() method. Then, define a route for the index page and register an IndexHandler handler on it. The route handler will serve the index.html file using the c.File method. The complete main.go file looks like this:

```
package main

import "github.com/gin-gonic/gin"

func IndexHandler(c *gin.Context) {
    c.File("index.html")
}

func main() {
    router := gin.Default()
    router.GET("/", IndexHandler)
    router.Run()
}
```

3. Run the application with the following command:

```
go run main.go
```

The server will run on localhost and serves on port 8080 by default, as illustrated in the following screenshot:

```
[GIN-debug] [WARNING] Creating an Engine instance with the Logger and Recovery middleware already attached.

[GIN-debug] [WARNING] Running in "debug" mode. Switch to "release" mode in production.
 - using env:   export GIN_MODE=release
 - using code:  gin.SetMode(gin.ReleaseMode)

[GIN-debug] GET    /                         --> main.IndexHandler (3 handlers)
[GIN-debug] Environment variable PORT is undefined. Using port :8080 by default
[GIN-debug] Listening and serving HTTP on :8080
```

Figure 5.1 – Server logs

4.   Using your favorite browser, head to `http://localhost:8080`, and you should see a **Hello world** message, as follows:

Hello world

Figure 5.2 – Serving index.html

5.   Next, update the `index.html` file to display some recipes using the following code. It references static assets for page styling (`app.css`) and recipes' images (`burger.jpg` and `pizza.jpg`):

```html
<html>
<head>
    <title>Recipes Platform</title>
    <link rel="stylesheet" href="assets/css/app.css">
</head>
<body>
    <div class="recipes">
        <div class="recipe">
            <h2>Pizza</h2>
            <img src="assets/images/pizza.jpg" />
        </div>
        <div class="recipe">
            <h2>Burger</h2>
            <img src="assets/images/burger.jpg" />
        </div>
    </div>
</body>
</html>
```

6.   The static files are stored under an `assets` folder in the project root repository. Create an `assets` folder with the following structure:

```
.
├── css
│   └── app.css
└── images
```

```
├── burger.jpg
└── pizza.jpg
```

> **Note**
>
> The recipe images can be downloaded from the following **URL**: `https://github.com/PacktPublishing/Building-Distributed-Applications-in-Gin/tree/main/chapter05/go-assets/assets/images`.

The `app.css` file defines CSS classes to control the alignments of `div` elements holding the recipe title as well as the recipe image size, as illustrated in the following code snippet:

```css
.recipes {
    width: 100%;
}

.recipe {
    width: 50%;
    float: left;
}

.recipe img {
    height: 320px;
}
```

7. To be able to load those assets from `index.html`, the server should serve them as well. That's where the `router.Static` method comes into play. Add the following instruction to serve the `assets` folder under the `/assets` route:

```
router.Static("/assets", "./assets")
```

8. Rerun the application—the images and CSS file should now be accessible from `http://localhost:8080/assets/PATH`, as illustrated in the following screenshot:

```
[GIN-debug] [WARNING] Creating an Engine instance with the Logger and Recovery middleware already attached.

[GIN-debug] [WARNING] Running in "debug" mode. Switch to "release" mode in production.
 - using env:   export GIN_MODE=release
 - using code:  gin.SetMode(gin.ReleaseMode)

[GIN-debug] GET    /assets/*filepath         --> github.com/gin-gonic/gin.(*RouterGroup).createStaticHandler.func1 (3 handlers)
[GIN-debug] HEAD   /assets/*filepath         --> github.com/gin-gonic/gin.(*RouterGroup).createStaticHandler.func1 (3 handlers)
[GIN-debug] GET    /                         --> main.IndexHandler (3 handlers)
[GIN-debug] Environment variable PORT is undefined. Using port :8080 by default
[GIN-debug] Listening and serving HTTP on :8080
```

Figure 5.3 – Serving assets

9. Head back to your browser and refresh the page—it should now display the following results:

Figure 5.4 – Serving CSS and images with Gin

The page is pretty basic, as you can tell! You now can serve static assets with Gin.

So far, you have seen how to serve HTML and static files from a Gin application. In the following section, we will cover how to create HTML templates and render dynamic content.

Rendering HTML templates

In this section, you will add the functionality to display a list of recipes dynamically by generating an `index.html` file from the server side. The Gin framework uses the Go standard `text/template` and `html/template` packages in the background to generate text and HTML outputs.

To get started, proceed as follows:

1. Create a `Recipe` struct. The structure will hold just two fields: a name and picture. This can be represented as follows:

```
type Recipe struct {
    Name    string `json:"name"`
    Picture string `json:"picture"`
}
```

2. Next, update the `IndexHandler` handler to create a `recipes` slice. Then, call the `c.HTML` method to render the `index.tmpl` file by passing the `recipes` slice. To keep things simple, the list of recipes is kept in memory, which is why we will initialize the `recipes` slice with two hardcoded recipes, as follows:

```
func IndexHandler(c *gin.Context) {
    recipes := make([]Recipe, 0)
    recipes = append(recipes, Recipe{
        Name:    "Burger",
        Picture: "/assets/images/burger.jpg",
    })
    recipes = append(recipes, Recipe{
        Name:    "Pizza",
        Picture: "/assets/images/pizza.jpg",
    })
    recipes = append(recipes, Recipe{
        Name:    "Tacos",
        Picture: "/assets/images/tacos.jpg",
    })

    c.HTML(http.StatusOK, "index.tmpl", gin.H{
        "recipes": recipes,
```

```
        })
    }
```

> **Note**
>
> The `.tmpl` extension is not required; however, it's recommended to be consistent within a project for clarity.

3. Create a `templates` folder in the root of the project folder, and write an `index.tmpl` file with the following content:

```
<html>
<head>
    <title>Recipes</title>
    <link rel="stylesheet" href="assets/css/app.css">
</head>
<body>
    <div class="recipes">
        {{range .recipes}}
        <div class="recipe">
            <h2>{{ .Name }}</h2>
            <img src="{{ .Picture }}" />
        </div>
        {{end}}
    </div>
</body>
</html>
```

4. The `range` keyword is used to iterate over all recipes in the `recipes` slice. For each recipe in the range of recipes, display its picture and name. Within a range, each recipe becomes `{{ . }}` and the recipe properties therefore become `{{.Name}}` or `{{.Picture}}`.

5. Next, tell Gin to load templates from the `templates` directory. The templates will be loaded once from disk at server startup; therefore, the application will serve the HTML pages faster. The code is illustrated in the following snippet:

```
router.LoadHTMLGlob("templates/*")
```

6. Rerun the application, and head once again to `localhost:8080`. A list of recipes will be displayed, as illustrated in the following screenshot:

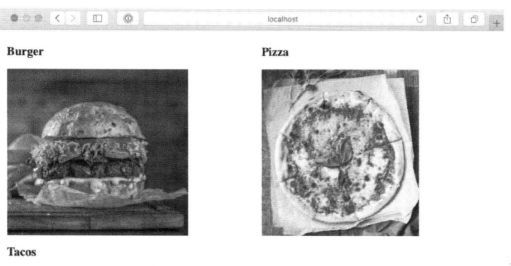

Tacos

Figure 5.5 – Iterating over items with range

You can take this further, and load the `recipes.json` file used in *Chapter 2, Setting up API Endpoints*. Later in this chapter, you'll see how to fetch a list of recipes from the API built in previous chapters. The file contains an array of recipes with the following structure:

```
[
    {
        "name": "Crock Pot Roast",
        "ingredients": [
            {
                "quantity": "1",
```

```
                "name": "beef roast",
                "type": "Meat"
            },
            {
                "quantity": "1 package",
                "name": "brown gravy mix",
                "type": "Baking"
            },
            {
                "quantity": "1 package",
                "name": "dried Italian salad
                        dressing mix",
                "type": "Condiments"
            },
            {
                "quantity": "1 package",
                "name": "dry ranch dressing mix",
                "type": "Condiments"
            },
            {
                "quantity": "1/2 cup",
                "name": "water",
                "type": "Drinks"
            }
        ],
        "steps": [
            "Place beef roast in crock pot.",
            "Mix the dried mixes together in a bowl
                and sprinkle over the roast.",
            "Pour the water around the roast.",
            "Cook on low for 7-9 hours."
        ],
        "imageURL": "/assets/images/
                crock-pot-roast.jpg"
    }
]
```

7. Update the `Recipe` struct to mirror the `recipe` fields, as follows:

```
type Recipe struct {
    Name         string         `json:"name"`
    Ingredients  []Ingredient   `json:"ingredients"`
    Steps        []string       `json:"steps"`
    Picture      string         `json:"imageURL"`
}

type Ingredient struct {
    Quantity string `json:"quantity"`
    Name     string `json:"name"`
    Type     string `json:"type"`
}

var recipes []Recipe
```

8. In the `init()` method, read the JSON file and encode its content to the `recipes` slice using the `json.Unmarshal` method, as follows:

```
func init() {
    recipes = make([]Recipe, 0)
    file, _ := ioutil.ReadFile("recipes.json")
    _ = json.Unmarshal([]byte(file), &recipes)
}
```

9. Then, update the `IndexHandler` handler to pass the `recipes` slice to the `index.tmpl` template in a variable named `recipes`, as follows:

```
func IndexHandler(c *gin.Context) {
    c.HTML(http.StatusOK, "index.tmpl", gin.H{
        "recipes": recipes,
    })
}
```

10. Finally, customize the template file to display the recipe ingredients and steps using the `range` keyword. The recipe attributes are accessed using a *dot* with the field name (`{{ .FieldName }}`), as illustrated in the following code snippet:

```html
<html>

<head>
    <title>Recipes</title>
    <link rel="stylesheet" href="assets/css/app.css">
    <link href="https://cdn.jsdelivr.net/npm/
bootstrap@5.0.0-beta2/dist/css/bootstrap.min.css"
rel="stylesheet">
</head>

<body class="container">
    <div class="row">
        {{range .recipes}}
        <div class="col-md-3">
            <div class="card" style="width: 18rem;">
                <img src="{{ .Picture }}" class="
                    card-img-top" alt="...">
                <div class="card-body">
                    <h5 class="card-title">{{
                        .Name }}</h5>
                    {{range $ingredient :=
                        .Ingredients}}
                    <span class="badge bg-danger
                        ingredient">
                        {{$ingredient.Name}}
```

```
                    </span>
                  {{end}}
                  <ul class="steps">
                      {{range $step := .Steps}}
                      <li>{{$step}}</li>
                      {{end}}
                  </ul>
              </div>
          </div>
      </div>
      {{end}}
    </div>
  </body>
  <script src="https://cdn.jsdelivr.net/npm/
  bootstrap@5.0.0-beta2/dist/js/bootstrap.bundle.min.js"></
  script>
  </html>
```

> **Note**
>
> For further explanation about advanced template actions and operators, refer to the Go official documentation at `https://golang.org/pkg/text/template/`.

11. Rerun the application, and refresh the page on your browser. This time, an aesthetically pleasing **user interface (UI)** will be displayed, as illustrated in the following screenshot:

Figure 5.6 – Rendering data with Go templates

As you can see, your application looks much nicer. All you did was add some CSS with the Bootstrap framework (to know more about the framework, refer https://getbootstrap.com/); so, from a functionality point of view, nothing has changed.

If you go back to the terminal, you will notice that the images and other assets were served from the HTTP server, as we can see here:

```
[GIN-debug] Loaded HTML Templates (2):
	-
	- index.tmpl

[GIN-debug] GET    /assets/*filepath          --> github.com/gin-gonic/gin.(*RouterGroup).createStaticHandler.func1 (3 handlers)
[GIN-debug] HEAD   /assets/*filepath          --> github.com/gin-gonic/gin.(*RouterGroup).createStaticHandler.func1 (3 handlers)
[GIN-debug] GET    /                          --> main.IndexHandler (3 handlers)
[GIN-debug] Environment variable PORT is undefined. Using port :8080 by default
[GIN-debug] Listening and serving HTTP on :8080
[GIN] 2021/03/03 - 14:45:34 | 200 |   1.210981ms |       ::1 | GET     "/"
[GIN] 2021/03/03 - 14:45:35 | 304 |    129.124µs |       ::1 | GET     "/assets/css/app.css"
[GIN] 2021/03/03 - 14:45:35 | 304 |     85.98µs  |       ::1 | GET     "/assets/images/crock-pot-roast.jpg"
[GIN] 2021/03/03 - 14:45:35 | 304 |    103.844µs |       ::1 | GET     "/assets/images/curried-chicken-lentils-and-rice.jpeg"
[GIN] 2021/03/03 - 14:45:35 | 304 |     83.766µs |       ::1 | GET     "/assets/images/yorkshire_pudding.jpg"
[GIN] 2021/03/03 - 14:45:35 | 304 |     93.793µs |       ::1 | GET     "/assets/images/oatmeal-cookies.jpg"
[GIN] 2021/03/03 - 14:45:35 | 304 |     95.288µs |       ::1 | GET     "/assets/images/blueberry-crumb-bars.jpg"
[GIN] 2021/03/03 - 14:45:35 | 304 |    123.296µs |       ::1 | GET     "/assets/images/curry-chicken-salad.jpg"
```

Figure 5.7 – Serving images

Great! The assets are served from the Gin server, and you can now build a dynamic web page.

Creating the view templates

For now, the application we have built displays a list of recipes. You can take this further and create a recipe page where users can see the full recipe. To do so, you need to create a unique identifier for each recipe; that way, you can have a unique URL to access each recipe.

To get started, proceed as follows:

1. Add an `id` attribute to the recipe's items in the `recipes.json` file as follows, or you can download the `recipes.json` file from the `chapter05` folder located in the book's GitHub repository:

```
[
    {
        "id": "603fa0f0b39c47f0e40659c2",
        "name": "Crock Pot Roast",
        "ingredients": [...],
        "steps": [...],
        "imageURL": "/assets/images/
                     crock-pot-roast.jpg"
    }
]
```

2. Then, add the `ID` field to the `Recipe` struct, as follows:

```
type Recipe struct {
    ID              string          `json:"id"`
```

```
Name              string          `json:"name"`
Ingredients []Ingredient `json:"ingredients"`
Steps             []string        `json:"steps"`
Picture           string          `json:"imageURL"`
}
```

3. To be able to navigate to the recipe page, add a button to each recipe item in the
    index.tmpl file. When clicking on the button, the user will be redirected to the
    target recipe page. The {{ .ID }} expression will be evaluated and replaced by
    the recipe ID. The code is illustrated in the following snippet:

```html
<section class="container">
    <div class="row">
        {{range .recipes}}
        <div class="col-md-3">
            <div class="card" style="width:
            18rem;">
                <img src="{{ .Picture }}"
                class="card-img-top" alt="...">
                <div class="card-body">
                    <h5 class="card-title">{{
                    .Name }}</h5>
                    {{range $ingredient :=
                    .Ingredients}}
                    <span class="badge bg-danger
                    ingredient">
                    {{$ingredient.Name}}
                    </span>
                    {{end}}
                    <ul class="steps">
                        {{range $step := .Steps}}
                        <li>{{$step}}</li>
                        {{end}}
                    </ul>
                    <a href="/recipes/{{ .ID }}"
                    class="btn btn-primary btn-
                    sm">See recipe</a>
```

```
                    </div>
                 </div>
              </div>
              {{end}}
           </div>
    </section>
```

4. With that being said, serve the recipe page at /recipes/:id. Take note of the
    :id part in this route. The two *dots* at the beginning indicate that this is a dynamic
    route. The route will store the recipe id attribute in the route parameter named ID,
    which we can access in the RecipeHandler handler. Here's the code you need:

```
router.GET("/recipes/:id", RecipeHandler)
```

The following code snippet contains the route-handler code, and is self-explanatory.
It loops through the recipes slice, looking for a recipe that matches the ID given
in the request parameter. If a match is found, then the recipe.tmpl file will be
rendered with the data of the recipe. If not, the user will be redirected to a **404 – not
found** error page:

```go
func RecipeHandler(c *gin.Context) {
    for _, recipe := range recipes {
        if recipe.ID == c.Param("id") {
            c.HTML(http.StatusOK, "recipe.tmpl", gin.H{
                "recipe": recipe,
            })
            return
        }
    }
    c.File("404.html")
}
```

> **Note**
>
> As the web application grows, it would make sense to move the route handlers
> to a separate file. For Go project structure best practices, head back to *Chapter
> 3, Managing Data Persistence with MongoDB*.

The `recipe.tmpl` template has the same structure as the `index.tmpl` template. However, instead of the `recipes` variable containing a list of recipes, in this case it will contain a single recipe. The template is shown here:

```html
<html>


<head>
    <title>{{ .recipe.Name }} - Recipes</title>
    <link rel="stylesheet" href="/assets/css/app.css">
    <link href="https://cdn.jsdelivr.net/npm/
bootstrap@5.0.0-beta2/dist/css/bootstrap.min.css"
rel="stylesheet">
</head>


<body>
    <section class="container recipe">
        <div class="row">
            <div class="col-md-3">
                <img src="{{ .recipe.Picture }}"
                class="card-img-top">
            </div>
            <div class="col-md-9">
                <h4>{{ .recipe.Name }}</h4>
                <ul class="list-group list-steps">
                    <li class="list-group-item
                        active">Steps</li>
                    {{range $step := .recipe.Steps }}
                    <li class="list-group-
                        item">{{$step}}</li>
                    {{end}}
                </ul>
            </div>
        </div>
    </section>
</body>
<script src="https://cdn.jsdelivr.net/npm/
bootstrap@5.0.0-beta2/dist/js/bootstrap.bundle.min.js"></
script>
```

```
</html>
```

The `404.html` error page will simply display a 404 illustration with a `Recipe not found` message. This can be done using the following code:

```html
<html>

<head>
    <title>Recipe not found</title>
    <link rel="stylesheet" href="/assets/css/app.css">
    <link href="https://cdn.jsdelivr.net/npm/
      bootstrap@5.0.0-beta2/dist/css/bootstrap.min.css"
      rel="stylesheet">
</head>

<body>
    <section class="container not-found">
        <h4>Recipe not found /h4>
        <img src="/assets/images/404.jpg" width="60%">
    </section>
</body>
<script src="https://cdn.jsdelivr.net/npm/
bootstrap@5.0.0-beta2/dist/js/bootstrap.bundle.min.js"></
script>

</html>
```

5. To test out the new changes, rerun the server, and head back to the browser and refresh the page. A list of recipes will be returned, but this time we have a **See recipe** button, as illustrated in the following screenshot:

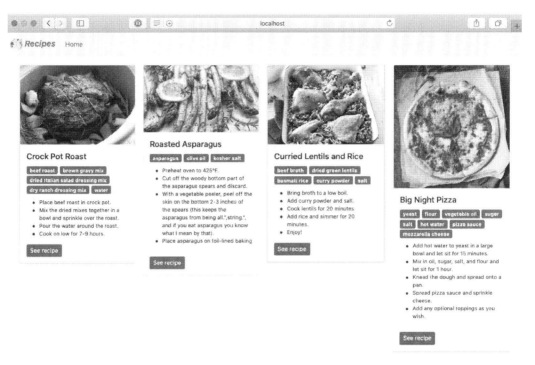

Figure 5.8 – Home page

6. Click on the **See recipe** button.

You'll be redirected to the **Recipe** page, where you can see a complete recipe's ingredients and instructions, as illustrated in the following screenshot:

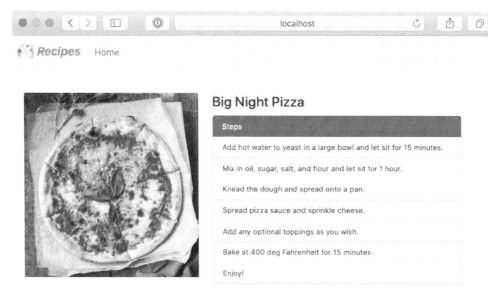

Figure 5.9 – Recipe page

You can also share your favorite recipes by sharing their URLs with your friends. If a particular recipe doesn't exist anymore or you've shared a wrong ID for a recipe, then a 404 page will be displayed, as follows:

Figure 5.10 – 404 error page

You might have noticed that you used a navigation bar to be able to switch easily between the home page (where a list of recipes is being displayed) and the recipe page. The same code is being used in two different template files. To avoid duplicating code, you can create **reusable templates**.

Creating reusable templates

The **navbar** is a common functionality that will be reused across multiple pages of our application. In order to create a reusable template, proceed as follows:

1. Create a `navbar.tmpl` file in the `templates` folder and place the navbar code in it, as follows:

```
<nav class="container-fluid navbar navbar-expand-lg
navbar-light bg-light">
    <a class="navbar-brand" href="#">
        <div class="logo">
            <img src="/assets/images/logo.svg">
            <span>Recipes</span>
        </div>
    </a>
    <button class="navbar-toggler" type="button" data-
toggle="collapse" data-target="#navbarSupportedContent"
        aria-controls="navbarSupportedContent" aria-
expanded="false" aria-label="Toggle navigation">
        <span class="navbar-toggler-icon"></span>
    </button>

    <div class="collapse navbar-collapse"
        id="navbarSupportedContent">
        <ul class="navbar-nav mr-auto">
            <li class="nav-item active">
                <a class="nav-link" href="/">Home</a>
            </li>
        </ul>
    </div>
</nav>
```

2. Next, remove the navbar lines of code from the index.tmpl and recipe.tmpl files and import the navbar template from the navbar.tmpl file with the following instructions:

```
<html>
<head>
    <title>{{ .recipe.Name }} - Recipes</title>
    ...
</head>
<body>
    {{template "navbar.tmpl"}}

    <section class="container recipe">
        <div class="row">
            <div class="col-md-3">
                <img src="{{ .recipe.Picture }}"
                 class="card-img-top">
            </div>
            <div class="col-md-9">
                <h4>{{ .recipe.Name }}</h4>
                <ul class="list-group list-steps">
                    <li class="list-group-item
                     active">Steps</li>
                    {{range $step := .recipe.Steps }}
                    <li class="list-group-
                     item">{{$step}}</li>
                    {{end}}
                </ul>
            </div>
        </div>
    </section>
</body>
...
</html>
```

Your reusable template is created.

The line containing {{template "navbar.tmpl"}} is used to dynamically load the navbar. As with the navbar, you can create reusable templates from common pieces of your application such as header, footer, forms, and so on. The directory structure of your project at this stage should look like this:

```
├── 404.html
├── assets
│   ├── css
│   │   └── app.css
│   └── images
│       ├── 404.jpg
│       ├── blueberry-crumb-bars.jpg
│       ├── burger.jpg
│       ├── crock-pot-roast.jpg
│       ├── curried-chicken-lentils-and-rice.jpeg
│       ├── curry-chicken-salad.jpg
│       ├── logo.svg
│       ├── oatmeal-cookies.jpg
│       ├── pizza.jpg
│       ├── roasted-asparagus.jpg
│       ├── stuffed-cornsquash.jpg
│       ├── tacos.jpg
│       └── yorkshire_pudding.jpg
├── main.go
├── recipes.json
├── templates
│   ├── index.tmpl
│   ├── navbar.tmpl
│   └── recipe.tmpl
└── test.json
```

Figure 5.11 – Project structure

So far, you have seen how to run the application locally by compiling the source code. But what if you wanted to build a binary of our web application so that we can deploy it remotely or share it with others? Let's have a look at how to do this.

Building a self-contained web application

Luckily, Go is a compiled language, which means that you can create an executable or binary with the needed dependencies, all with a single command, as illustrated here:

```
go build -o app main.go
```

> **Note**
> You can build an executable for different architectures or platforms (Windows, macOS, Linux, and so on) with GOOS and GOARCH environment variables.

The command creates an executable called `app` in your current directory. By default, Go uses the name of the application directory for naming the executable. However, you can specify a different name or location for the executable with a `-o` flag.

You can now execute the binary with the following command:

```
./app
```

The server will start on port `8080` as usual, and you can access the web application from `localhost:8080`, as illustrated in the following screenshot:

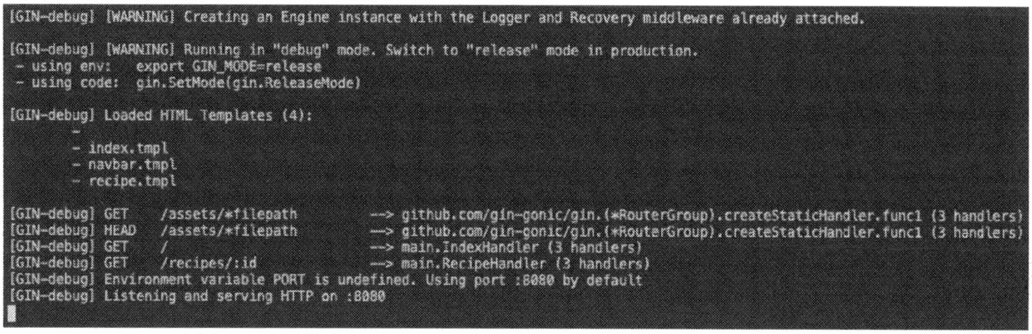

Figure 5.12 – Running an executable

The application is working as expected because the HTML templates and assets are located in the same folder where the executable is being executed.

What if you run the binary from a different directory? In that case, you would need to follow these steps:

1. Copy the executable to your home directory with the following commands:

```
mv app $HOME
cd $HOME
```

2. Rerun the application—it should crash immediately due to the `templates` folder not being found. You will see something that looks like this:

```
[GIN-debug] [WARNING] Creating an Engine instance with the Logger and Recovery middleware already attached.

[GIN-debug] [WARNING] Running in "debug" mode. Switch to "release" mode in production.
 - using env:   export GIN_MODE=release
 - using code:  gin.SetMode(gin.ReleaseMode)

panic: html/template: pattern matches no files: `templates/*`

goroutine 1 [running]:
html/template.Must(...)
        /usr/local/Cellar/go/1.15.6/libexec/src/html/template/template.go:372
github.com/gin-gonic/gin.(*Engine).LoadHTMLGlob(0xc0002f8780, 0x165a865, 0xb)
        /Users/mlabouardy/go/src/github.com/gin-gonic/gin/gin.go:188 +0x36a
main.main()
        /Users/mlabouardy/github/Building-Distributed-Applications-in-Gin/chapter5/main.go:53 +0x49
```

Figure 5.13 – Application stack traces

You can copy the `templates` and `assets` folders to the home directory. However, it's often cumbersome to remember to update all the file references when upgrading or moving a binary to a new location. A better solution is to embed all static files in a single binary.

3. `go-assets-builder` is a tool that converts any text or binary file into Go source code, making it the perfect choice for embedding assets into Go applications. Install the `go-assets-builder` package with the following command:

```
go get github.com/jessevdk/go-assets-builder
```

4. Then, invoke the `go-assets-builder` command to generate Go code from the static files, as follows:

```
go-assets-builder templates assets 404.html recipes.json
-o assets.go
```

The command will generate an `assets.go` source file. The resulting code will look like this:

```
var Assets = assets.NewFileSystem(map[string][]string{
    "/": []string{"assets", "templates", "404.html",
    "recipes.json"}, "/assets/css":
    []string{"app.css"}, "/assets/images":
    []string{"stuffed-cornsquash.jpg", "curry-chicken-
    salad.jpg"}, "/templates": []string{"navbar.tmpl",
    "index.tmpl", "recipe.tmpl"}},
    map[string]*assets.File{
    "/": &assets.File{
```

```go
        Path:      "/",
        FileMode: 0x800001ed,
        Mtime:     time.Unix(1615118299,
                   1615118299722824447),
        Data:      nil,
    }, "/templates/navbar.tmpl": &assets.File{
        Path:      "/templates/navbar.tmpl",
        FileMode: 0x1a4,
        Mtime:     time.Unix(1614862865,
                        1614862865957528581),
        Data:      []byte(_Assets9a0a5c784c66e5609ac
                        d084702e97a6a733e0d56),
    }, "/recipes.json": &assets.File{
        Path:      "/recipes.json",
        FileMode: 0x1a4,
        Mtime:     time.Unix(1614782782,
                        1614782782296236029),
        Data:      []byte(_Assets142ce9f9ba8b43eeb97b8
                        3c79ea872ed40e6cba1),
    }, "")
```

5. Next, update `main.go` to load the HTML files. The templates are accessible via the `Assets.Files` map structure. Make sure to import the `html/template` library. The code is illustrated in the following snippet:

```go
func loadTemplate() (*template.Template, error) {
    t := template.New("")
    for name, file := range Assets.Files {
        if file.IsDir() || !strings.HasSuffix(name,
               ".tmpl") {
            continue
        }
        h, err := ioutil.ReadAll(file)
        if err != nil {
            return nil, err
        }
        t, err = t.New(name).Parse(string(h))
```

```
        if err != nil {
            return nil, err
        }
    }
    return t, nil
}
```

6. Then, update the HTTP router to call the `loadTemplate` method when the server is asked to serve `index.tmpl`, `recipe.tmpl`, or `navbar.tmpl` templates, as follows:

```
func main() {
    t, err := loadTemplate()
    if err != nil {
        panic(err)
    }

    router := gin.Default()
    router.SetHTMLTemplate(t)
    router.GET("/", IndexHandler)
    router.GET("/recipes/:id", RecipeHandler)
    router.GET("/assets/*filepath", StaticHandler)
    router.Run()
}
```

7. For assets files (CSS and images), define a custom HTTP handler to serve the right asset based on the `filepath` parameter, as follows:

```
func StaticHandler(c *gin.Context) {
    filepath := c.Param("filepath")
    data := Assets.Files["/assets"+filepath].Data
    c.Writer.Write(data)
}
```

8. Next, define a route for the `assets` folder with a `filepath` parameter, as follows:

```
router.GET("/assets/*filepath", StaticHandler)
```

9. Update the `recipes.json` file as well, to load it from the `Assets.Files` map instead of the disk, as follows:

```
func init() {
    recipes = make([]Recipe, 0)
    json.Unmarshal(Assets.Files["/recipes.json"].Data,
        &recipes)
}
```

10. Make sure to update the `navbar` reference in `index.tmpl` and `recipe.tmpl` as well, like this:

```
{{template "/templates/navbar.tmpl"}}
```

11. Finally, fix the `templates` path in both `RecipeHandler` and `IndexHandler` handlers.

12. Now, build the application with the new changes. Issue the following command:

```
go build -o app
mv app $HOME
cd $HOME
./app
```

This time, the application will be functional, and all assets will be loaded from the binary. You can see the result here:

Figure 5.14 – Embedding web application assets

You can now share the binary with your friends and deploy it easily on a remote server.

> **Note**
>
> In *Chapter 8, Deploying the Application on AWS*, we will explore how to deploy your distributed web application on the cloud with Docker and Kubernetes.

Bundling static files

In this chapter, we are using Go 1.16, which comes with new features and enhancements such as embedded files being supported without the need for an external package such as `go-assets-builder`.

> **Note**
>
> You can use **Go Version Manager** (**GVM**) to manage multiple Go versions.
> You can install the latest release of Go with the `gvm install go1.16`
> command.

Go 1.16 introduced a `//go:embed` directive that allows you to include contents of files
and directories within a Go application. You can do so by implementing the following:

1. In `main.go`, define an `embed.FS` variable to hold a group of files. Then, define a
    comment just above the variable declaration, as follows:

```
//go:embed assets/* templates/* 404.html recipes.json
var f embed.FS
```

2. Update the `init()` function to read the `recipes.json` file from the `FS` variable,
    as follows:

```
func init() {
    recipes = make([]Recipe, 0)
    data, _ := f.ReadFile("recipes.json")
    json.Unmarshal(data, &recipes)
}
```

3. Then, use the `http.FS` file to create an HTTP filesystem to serve `assets` files, as
    follows:

```
func main() {
    templ := template.Must(template.New("").ParseFS(f,
"templates/*.tmpl"))

    fsys, err := fs.Sub(f, "assets")
    if err != nil {
        panic(err)
    }

    router := gin.Default()
    router.SetHTMLTemplate(templ)
    router.StaticFS("/assets", http.FS(fsys))
    router.GET("/", IndexHandler)
    router.GET("/recipes/:id", RecipeHandler)
```

```
        router.Run()
    }
```

4. Rebuild the binary with the `go build` command.

> **Note**
> Make sure to remove the `/templates` prefixes from the HTTP handlers and template files before building the binary.

The final result is a single web server binary ready for distribution!

Building a SPA

While you can build complete web applications with Gin by rendering HTML templates and serving the static files, as the application grows it becomes hard to maintain it. That's why you can adopt a popular frontend JavaScript framework such as Angular, React, or Vue.js to build your SPA. In this section we will go with React, but you can get the same results with other JavaScript frameworks as well.

The application we'll build will do the following:

- Display the list of all recipes on the home page (for all users).
- Let users sign in with their username and password.
- Let users create new recipes (logged-in users only).

First of all, we will need to make sure that Node.js is installed on your system. You can install the **long-term support** (**LTS**) version (14.16.0) from the official page at `https://nodejs.org/en/download/`, or you can use the **Node Version Manager** (**NVM**) to install Node.js easily, based on your **operating system** (**OS**).

To install NVM, proceed as follows:

1. Run the following script:

```
curl -o- https://raw.githubusercontent.com/nvm-sh/nvm/
v0.37.2/install.sh | bash
```

2. This could take anywhere from a few seconds to a few minutes, but once your installation has completed, issue the following command to install the LTS version of Node.js:

```
nvm install 14.16.0
```

With Node.js installed, we're ready to build our web application with React.

Getting started with React

In this section, you will set up your React environment. To do so, apply the following steps:

1. Open your terminal and navigate to your workspace. Then, install `create react app` with the following command. The **command-line interface (CLI)** simplifies the setup process of a React environment:

   ```
   npm install -g create-react-app
   ```

2. Then, create a React project with the CRA CLI. The project name is `recipes-web`, as we can see here:

   ```
   create-react-app recipes-web
   ```

   Here is the command output:

   ```
   Creating a new React app in /Users/mlabouardy/github/Building-Distributed-Applications-in-Gin/chapter5/recipes-web.

   Installing packages. This might take a couple of minutes.
   Installing react, react-dom, and react-scripts with cra-template...

   added 1947 packages, and audited 1948 packages in 37s

   130 packages are looking for funding
     run `npm fund` for details

   found 0 vulnerabilities

   Installing template dependencies using npm...

   added 32 packages, and audited 1980 packages in 4s

   130 packages are looking for funding
     run `npm fund` for details

   found 0 vulnerabilities
   Removing template package using npm...

   removed 1 package, and audited 1979 packages in 3s

   130 packages are looking for funding
     run `npm fund` for details

   found 0 vulnerabilities

   Success! Created recipes-web at /Users/mlabouardy/github/Building-Distributed-Applications-in-Gin/chapter5/recipes-web
   ```

   Figure 5.15 – Setup of a new React project

After running the preceding command, the project structure will look like this. The project is created with all of the proper behind-the-scenes configurations automatically hooked up:

Figure 5.16 – React project structure

> **Note**
> Make sure to create a GitHub repository for your web application and push all the changes to the remote repository.

3. Navigate to the `recipes-web` folder and enter the following commands to launch the application:

```
cd recipes-web
npm start
```

The project will be built, and a local web server will be exposed on port 3000, as illustrated in the following screenshot:

```
Compiled successfully!

You can now view recipes-web in the browser.

  Local:            http://localhost:3000
  On Your Network:  http://192.168.1.7:3000

Note that the development build is not optimized.
To create a production build, use npm run build.
```

Figure 5.17 – Local development server

4. Head to your browser and navigate to `Localhost:3000. Apart from;` you will see something similar to the following screenshot:

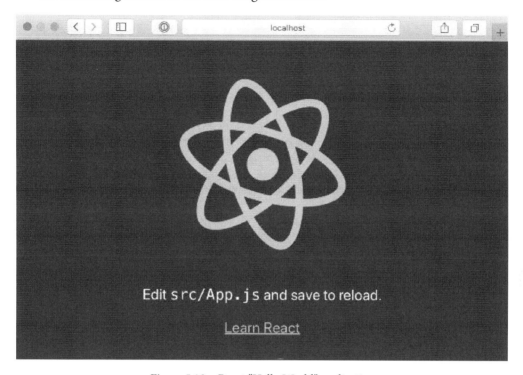

Figure 5.18 – React "Hello World" application

Right now, your application doesn't do a whole lot. It doesn't look like much, either. Let's build the recipe listing, using React components.

Exploring React components

One of the basic foundations when building a SPA is the usage of components. Throughout this section, we'll explore how to build a **Recipes** dashboard based on React components.

The first thing you're going to do is create an App component to list the `recipes` array by referencing a `Recipe` element. To do so, proceed as follows:

1. Update the `App.js` file with the following content:

```
import React from 'react';
import './App.css';
```

```
import Recipe from './Recipe';

class App extends React.Component {
 constructor(props) {
   super(props)

   this.state = {
     recipes: [
       {
         "name": "Oregano Marinated Chicken",
         "tags": [
           "main",
           "chicken"
         ],
         "ingredients": [],
         "instructions": []
       },
       {
         "name": "Green pea soup with cheddar
                  scallion panini",
         "tags": [
           "soup",
           "main",
           "panini"
         ],
         "ingredients": [],
         "instructions": []
       }
     ]
   }
 }

 render() {
   return (<div>
     {this.state.recipes.map((recipe, index) => (
       <Recipe recipe={recipe} />
```

```
        ))}
    </div>);
}
```

The component constructor defines a `recipes` array in the `state` object. The array stores a list of hardcoded recipes.

2. Next, create a `Recipe` component to display the recipe properties (name, steps, ingredients, and so on). In the `src` directory, create a new file named `Recipe.js` and add the following content to it:

```
import React from 'react';
import './Recipe.css';

class Recipe extends React.Component {
    render() {
        return (
            <div class="recipe">
                <h4>{this.props.recipe.name}</h4>
                <ul>
                    {this.props.recipe.ingredients &&
                     this.props.recipe.ingredients.map(
                     (ingredient, index) => {
                        return <li>{ingredient}</li>
                    })}
                </ul>
            </div>
        )
    }
}

export default Recipe;
```

3. Create a style sheet called `Recipe.css` and add the appropriate style rules to improve the look and feel of the UI elements. Then, import the style sheet in `Recipe.js`.

4. Once you've done this, save all of your changes and preview it in your browser, and you'll see something that looks like this:

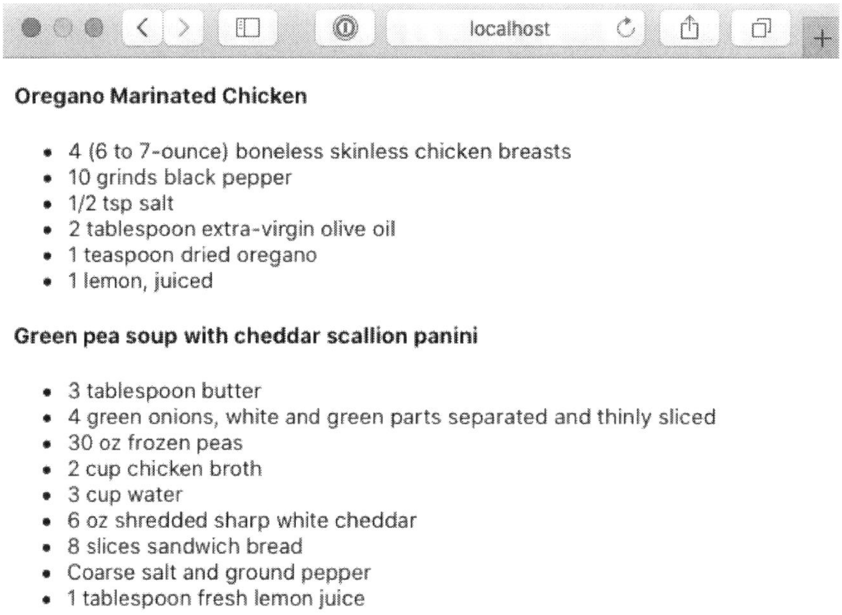

Oregano Marinated Chicken

- 4 (6 to 7-ounce) boneless skinless chicken breasts
- 10 grinds black pepper
- 1/2 tsp salt
- 2 tablespoon extra-virgin olive oil
- 1 teaspoon dried oregano
- 1 lemon, juiced

Green pea soup with cheddar scallion panini

- 3 tablespoon butter
- 4 green onions, white and green parts separated and thinly sliced
- 30 oz frozen peas
- 2 cup chicken broth
- 3 cup water
- 6 oz shredded sharp white cheddar
- 8 slices sandwich bread
- Coarse salt and ground pepper
- 1 tablespoon fresh lemon juice

Figure 5.19 – Rendering the App component

Great! You have successfully built a SPA to list recipes.

Right now, the list of recipes is static. You will fix that by calling the `Recipes` API, built in the previous chapter. To do so, proceed as follows:

1. First, look here at the architecture you're going to build:

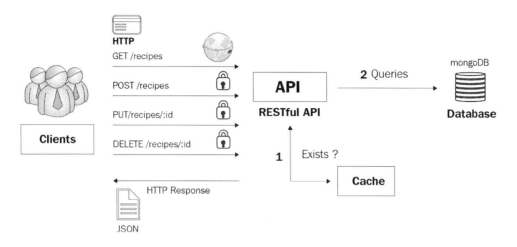

Figure 5.20 – Application architecture

The Recipes API is exposed on port 8080, therefore define a getRecipes method in App.js to call the /recipes endpoint and save the returned results in the recipes array, as follows:

```
getRecipes() {
    fetch('http://localhost:8080/recipes')
        .then(response => response.json())
        .then(data => this.setState({ recipes: data }));
}
```

2. Next, call the method on the App component constructor with the following instruction:

```
constructor(props) {
    super(props)

    this.state = {
        recipes: []
    }

    this.getRecipes();
}
```

3.   Make sure the API is being served on port 8080, as follows:

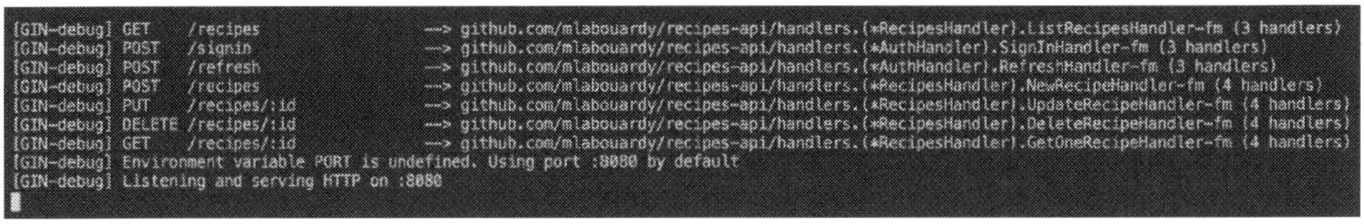

Figure 5.21 – Recipes API logs

4.   Head back to your browser, and you should see a blank page. If you open the browser debugging console, you'll see that the call to the API has been blocked by a CORS policy, as illustrated in the following screenshot:

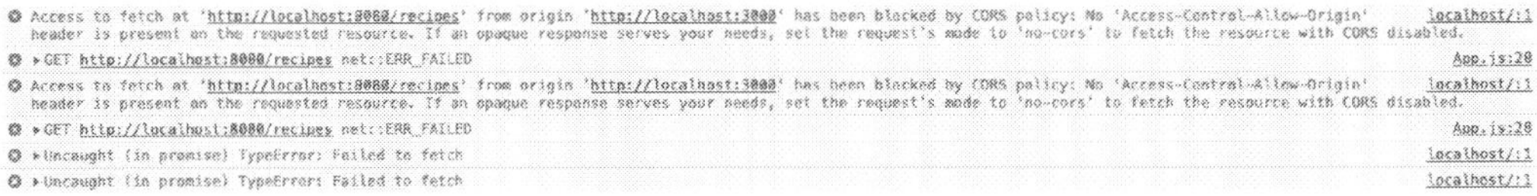

Figure 5.22 – CORS errors

Because the Recipes API and web application are running in different ports, you need to set some headers on the API to allow the **Cross-Origin Resource Sharing (CORS)**.

Resolving cross-origin requests

By default, the API uses a same-origin policy to limit the ability for the API to interact with resources outside of the source domain. We can bypass the same-origin policy with CORS.

To resolve the CORS issues, proceed as follows:

1.   Download the Gin official CORS middleware with the following command:

```
go get github.com/gin-contrib/cors
```

2.   Then, update the main.go file of the Recipes API project to allow all origins by defining the cors.Default() method as a middleware, as follows:

```
router.Use(cors.Default())
```

3. The middleware will be executed before handling the incoming HTTP request. The
   `cors.Default()` method will allow all HTTP methods and origins, but you can
   restrict the requests to trusted origins. Define the origins and allow incoming HTTP
   methods with the following code:

```
router.Use(cors.New(cors.Config{
    AllowOrigins:     []string{"http://localhost
                     :3000"},
    AllowMethods:     []string{"GET", "OPTIONS"},
    AllowHeaders:     []string{"Origin"},
    ExposeHeaders:    []string{"Content-Length"},
    AllowCredentials: true,
    MaxAge: 12 * time.Hour,
}))
```

4. Rerun the API server and head back to your browser, and refresh the web
   application page.

This time, the HTTP request should be successful, and you should see a list of recipes, as follows:

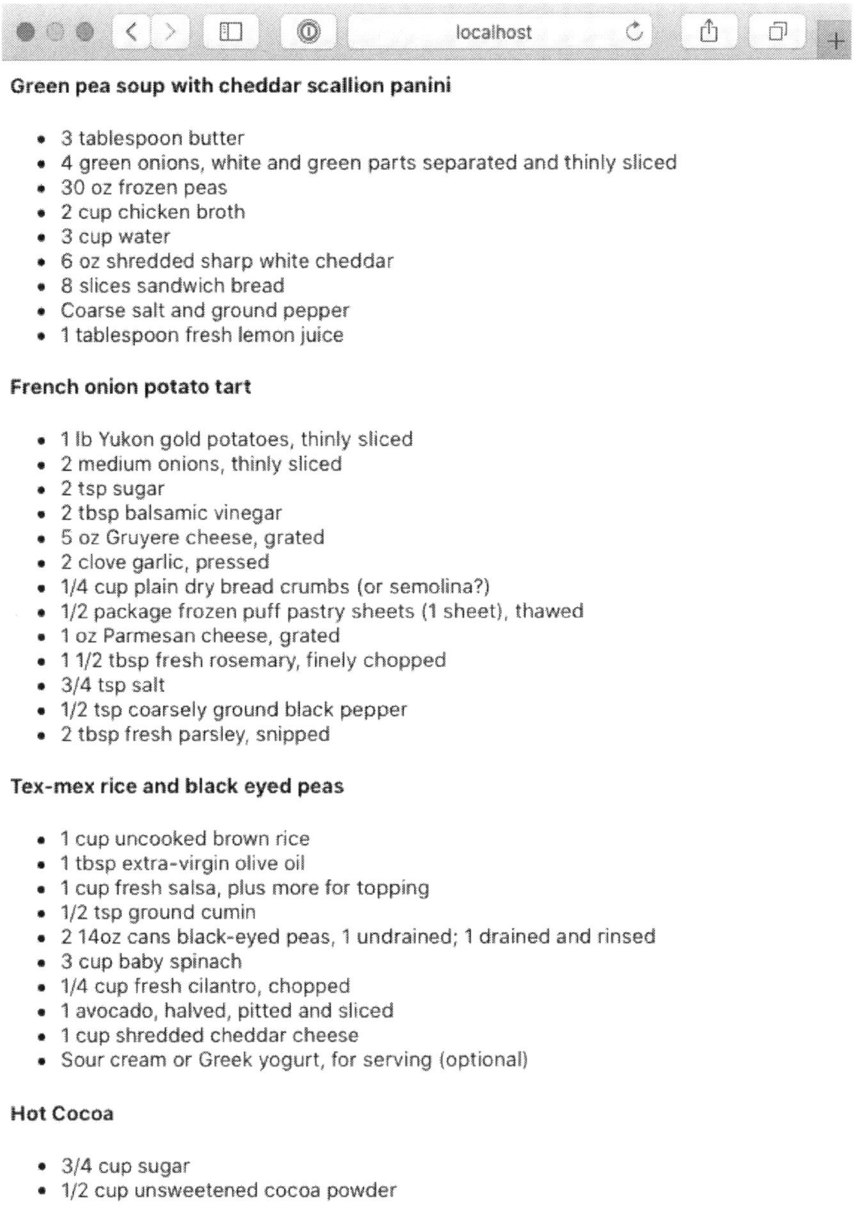

Green pea soup with cheddar scallion panini

- 3 tablespoon butter
- 4 green onions, white and green parts separated and thinly sliced
- 30 oz frozen peas
- 2 cup chicken broth
- 3 cup water
- 6 oz shredded sharp white cheddar
- 8 slices sandwich bread
- Coarse salt and ground pepper
- 1 tablespoon fresh lemon juice

French onion potato tart

- 1 lb Yukon gold potatoes, thinly sliced
- 2 medium onions, thinly sliced
- 2 tsp sugar
- 2 tbsp balsamic vinegar
- 5 oz Gruyere cheese, grated
- 2 clove garlic, pressed
- 1/4 cup plain dry bread crumbs (or semolina?)
- 1/2 package frozen puff pastry sheets (1 sheet), thawed
- 1 oz Parmesan cheese, grated
- 1 1/2 tbsp fresh rosemary, finely chopped
- 3/4 tsp salt
- 1/2 tsp coarsely ground black pepper
- 2 tbsp fresh parsley, snipped

Tex-mex rice and black eyed peas

- 1 cup uncooked brown rice
- 1 tbsp extra-virgin olive oil
- 1 cup fresh salsa, plus more for topping
- 1/2 tsp ground cumin
- 2 14oz cans black-eyed peas, 1 undrained; 1 drained and rinsed
- 3 cup baby spinach
- 1/4 cup fresh cilantro, chopped
- 1 avocado, halved, pitted and sliced
- 1 cup shredded cheddar cheese
- Sour cream or Greek yogurt, for serving (optional)

Hot Cocoa

- 3/4 cup sugar
- 1/2 cup unsweetened cocoa powder

Figure 5.23 – List of recipes

Now, you can take the project further and add an authentication layer with Auth0, as follows:

> **Note**
> For a step-by-step guide on how to enable authentication with Auth0, check the previous chapter.

1. Navigate to the **Auth0 dashboard** (`https://manage.auth0.com/dashboard`), and create an application of type **Single Page Web Applications**, as illustrated in the following screenshot:

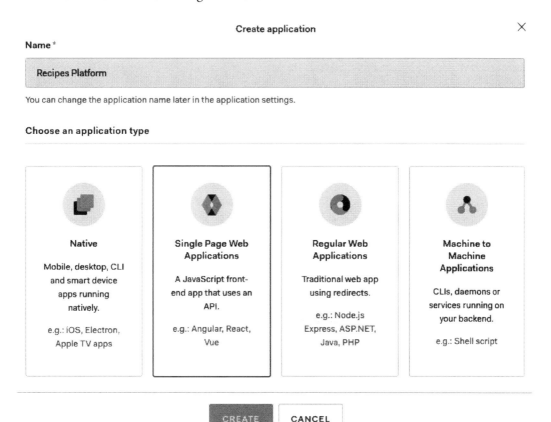

Figure 5.24 – SPA on Auth0

2. Next, click on **Create**, and set the **Allowed Callback URLs** field to `Localhost:3000. Apart from`, as illustrated in the following screenshot. The URL will be used by Auth0 to redirect users after they have authenticated:

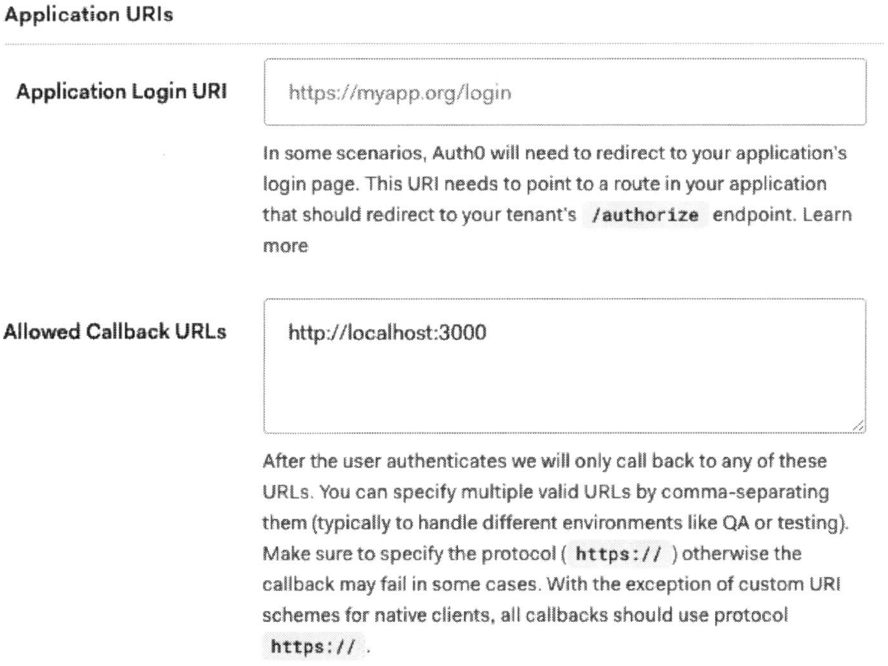

Application URIs

Application Login URI

https://myapp.org/login

In some scenarios, Auth0 will need to redirect to your application's login page. This URI needs to point to a route in your application that should redirect to your tenant's `/authorize` endpoint. Learn more

Allowed Callback URLs

http://localhost:3000

After the user authenticates we will only call back to any of these URLs. You can specify multiple valid URLs by comma-separating them (typically to handle different environments like QA or testing). Make sure to specify the protocol (`https://`) otherwise the callback may fail in some cases. With the exception of custom URI schemes for native clients, all callbacks should use protocol `https://` .

Figure 5.25 – Configuring allowed callback URLs

3. Set the **Allowed Origins** field to `localhost:3000` to authorize the application to make requests to the Auth0 API.

4. Now, to integrate Auth0 into your web application, install the Auth0 React **software development kit** (**SDK**). Run the following command within your project folder to install the SDK:

```
npm install @auth0/auth0-react
```

5. Next, wrap the root component of the application with `Auth0Provider`. Update the `index.js` file, as follows:

```
import { Auth0Provider } from "@auth0/auth0-react";

ReactDOM.render(
  <Auth0Provider
```

```
      domain="AUTH0_DOMAIN"
      clientId="AUTH_CLIENT_ID"
      redirectUri={window.location.origin}
    >
      <App />
    </Auth0Provider>,
    document.getElementById("root")
  );
```

The Auth0 component takes the following properties:

a. `domain`: The Auth0 domain. The value is available under the **Settings** page of the SPA you created earlier.

b. `clientId`: The Auth0 client ID. The value is also available under the **Settings** page.

c. `redirectUri`: The **Uniform Resource Identifier** (**URI**) where you would like to redirect users after they authenticate with Auth0.

The `ReactDOM.render` method looks for the root element defined in `index.html` (located inside the `public` folder) and loads the Auth0 component on it.

6. Then, create a `Navbar` component with a login button. When the user clicks on the login button, the `loginWithRedirect` method from the `useAuth0()` hook will be called. The method will redirect the user to the Auth0 login page, where they can authenticate. Upon successful authentication, Auth0 will redirect the user back to the application based on the redirection URL defined earlier. The code is illustrated in the following snippet:

```
import React from 'react';
import { useAuth0 } from "@auth0/auth0-react";
import Profile from './Profile';

const Navbar = () => {
    const { isAuthenticated, loginWithRedirect, logout,
           user } = useAuth0();
    return (
        <nav class="navbar navbar-expand-lg navbar-
           light bg-light">
            <a class="navbar-brand"
```

```
                    href="#">Recipes</a>
        <button class="navbar-toggler"
        type="button" data-toggle="collapse" data-
        target="#navbarTogglerDemo02" aria-
        controls="navbarTogglerDemo02" aria-
        expanded="false" aria-label="Toggle
        navigation">
            <span class="navbar-toggler-
                    icon"></span>
        </button>

        <div class="collapse navbar-collapse"
                id="navbarTogglerDemo02">
            <ul class="navbar-nav ml-auto">
                <li class="nav-item">
                    {isAuthenticated ? (<Profile
                        />) : (
                        <a class="nav-link active"
                            onClick={() =>
                                loginWithRedirect()}>
                            Login</a>
                    )}
                </li>
            </ul>
        </div>
    </nav >
  )
}

export default Navbar;
```

> **Note**
>
> To prevent any rendering errors, the `isAuthenticated` property is used to check if Auth0 has authenticated the user before displaying the logged-in username and picture using the `Profile` component.

7. In the code, we're using existing UI elements provided by the Bootstrap framework. The framework can be installed with the following command:

```
npm install bootstrap
```

8. Once installed, reference the framework with an `import` statement on top of `index.js`, as follows:

```
import 'bootstrap/dist/css/bootstrap.min.css';
import 'bootstrap/dist/js/bootstrap.min.js';
```

9. Then, add the `Navbar` component to `App.js`, as follows:

```
render() {
   return (<div>
      <Navbar />
      {this.state.recipes.map((recipe, index) => (
         <Recipe recipe={recipe} />
      ))}
   </div>);
}
```

10. Preview your application after this change, and it should look like this:

Recipes   Login

Green pea soup with cheddar scallion panini

- 3 tablespoon butter
- 4 green onions, white and green parts separated and thinly sliced
- 30 oz frozen peas
- 2 cup chicken broth
- 3 cup water
- 6 oz shredded sharp white cheddar
- 8 slices sandwich bread
- Coarse salt and ground pepper
- 1 tablespoon fresh lemon juice

French onion potato tart

- 1 lb Yukon gold potatoes, thinly sliced
- 2 medium onions, thinly sliced
- 2 tsp sugar
- 2 tbsp balsamic vinegar
- 5 oz Gruyere cheese, grated
- 2 clove garlic, pressed
- 1/4 cup plain dry bread crumbs (or semolina?)
- 1/2 package frozen puff pastry sheets (1 sheet), thawed
- 1 oz Parmesan cheese, grated
- 1 1/2 tbsp fresh rosemary, finely chopped
- 3/4 tsp salt
- 1/2 tsp coarsely ground black pepper
- 2 tbsp fresh parsley, snipped

Tex-mex rice and black eyed peas

- 1 cup uncooked brown rice
- 1 tbsp extra-virgin olive oil
- 1 cup fresh salsa, plus more for topping
- 1/2 tsp ground cumin
- 2 14oz cans black-eyed peas, 1 undrained; 1 drained and rinsed
- 3 cup baby spinach

Figure 5.26 – Rendering list of recipes

11. Now, click on **Login**. You'll be redirected to the Auth0 login page, where you can sign up for a new account or sign in with an existing account, as illustrated in the following screenshot:

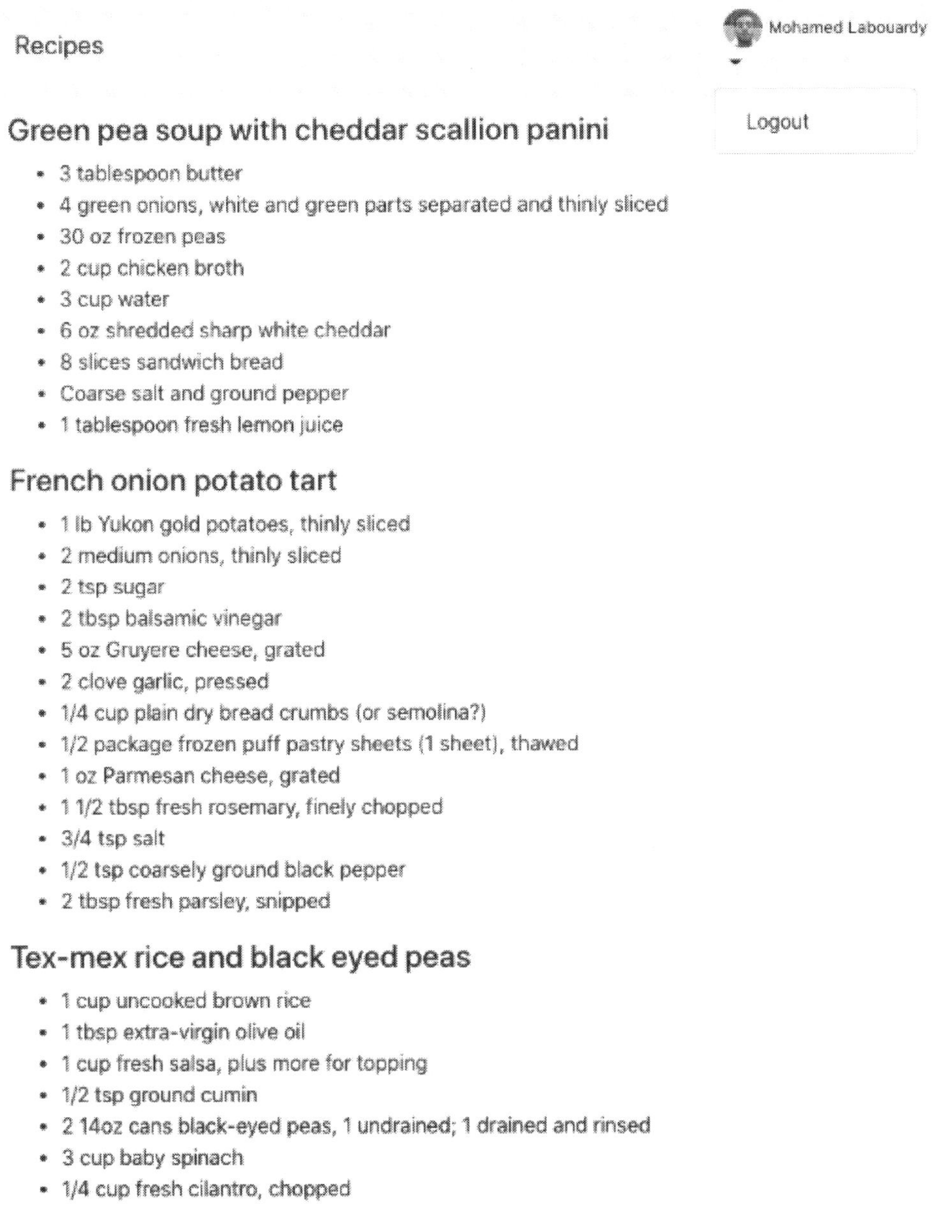

Recipes   Mohamed Labouardy

                                                          Logout

Green pea soup with cheddar scallion panini

- 3 tablespoon butter
- 4 green onions, white and green parts separated and thinly sliced
- 30 oz frozen peas
- 2 cup chicken broth
- 3 cup water
- 6 oz shredded sharp white cheddar
- 8 slices sandwich bread
- Coarse salt and ground pepper
- 1 tablespoon fresh lemon juice

French onion potato tart

- 1 lb Yukon gold potatoes, thinly sliced
- 2 medium onions, thinly sliced
- 2 tsp sugar
- 2 tbsp balsamic vinegar
- 5 oz Gruyere cheese, grated
- 2 clove garlic, pressed
- 1/4 cup plain dry bread crumbs (or semolina?)
- 1/2 package frozen puff pastry sheets (1 sheet), thawed
- 1 oz Parmesan cheese, grated
- 1 1/2 tbsp fresh rosemary, finely chopped
- 3/4 tsp salt
- 1/2 tsp coarsely ground black pepper
- 2 tbsp fresh parsley, snipped

Tex-mex rice and black eyed peas

- 1 cup uncooked brown rice
- 1 tbsp extra-virgin olive oil
- 1 cup fresh salsa, plus more for topping
- 1/2 tsp ground cumin
- 2 14oz cans black-eyed peas, 1 undrained; 1 drained and rinsed
- 3 cup baby spinach
- 1/4 cup fresh cilantro, chopped

Figure 5.27 – Auth0 universal login page

Your authentication has been successful! You'll be redirected to the home page, where you can browse through the list of recipes returned by the `Recipes` API, as illustrated in the following screenshot:

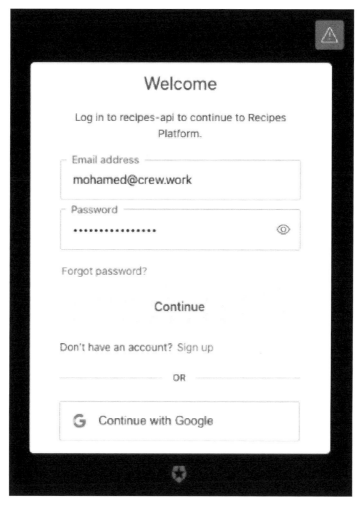

Figure 5.28 – Page listing recipes for a logged-in user

The application also displays the logged-in username and profile picture. The information is available through the `user` property exposed by the `useAuth0()` hook. You have now successfully created a SPA.

Your web application is pretty simple in what it does, but by building it from scratch, we covered almost every little interesting detail React brings to the table. You can take this further and implement a new recipe form for logged-in users to post new recipes.

Summary

In this chapter, we learned how to serve HTML templates with the Gin framework and how to create reusable templates and serve static assets. We covered how to implement a SPA with the React framework to consume a Gin RESTful API and how to resolve CORS issues with Gin.

We have also explored how Auth0 allows you to quickly add authentication to your React application. Finally, we learned how to build a self-contained web application by embedding the application assets during build time.

In the next chapter, we will explore tips and best practices to architect a scalable, distributed web application with Gin.

Questions

1. How would you create reusable templates for the header and footer?
2. How would you create a `NewRecipe` component with React?
3. How would you build a self-contained binary for Windows, Mac, and Linux?

Further reading

- *Full-Stack React Projects - Second Edition*, by Shama Hoque, Packt Publishing
- *Full-Stack React, TypeScript, and Node*, by David Choi, Packt Publishing

6
Scaling a Gin Application

In this chapter, you will learn how to improve the performance and scalability of a distributed web application written with the Gin framework. This chapter will cover how to use caching mechanisms to alleviate performance bottlenecks. Along the way, you will learn how to scale a web app using a message broker solution such as RabbitMQ. Finally, you will learn how to **containerize** the application and scale it out with **Docker Compose**.

In this chapter, we will cover the following topics:

- Scaling workloads with a message broker
- Scaling horizontally with Docker replicas
- Using the Nginx reverse proxy
- Caching assets with HTTP cache headers

By the end of this chapter, you will be able to build a highly available and distributed web application with the Gin framework, Docker, and RabbitMQ.

Technical requirements

To follow the content in this chapter, you will need the following:

- A complete understanding of the previous chapter. This chapter is a follow-up to the previous one as it will use the same source code. Hence, some snippets won't be explained to avoid repetition.

- An understanding of Docker and its architecture. Ideally, some previous experience with a message queue service such as RabbitMQ, ActiveMQ, Kafka, and so on would be beneficial.

The code bundle for this chapter is hosted on GitHub at `https://github.com/PacktPublishing/Building-Distributed-Applications-in-Gin/tree/main/chapter06`.

Scaling workloads with a message broker

When developing a web application, one important aspect of the user experience that is often overlooked is the response time. Nothing can turn away a user more quickly than an application that is slow and sluggish. In the previous chapters, you learned how to reduce database queries with Redis for faster data access. In this chapter, you will take things further and cover how to scale a web application written with the Gin framework.

Before we get into why you need to scale the application workload, let's add another block to the architecture. The new service will parse a Reddit RSS feed and insert feed entries into the MongoDB `recipes` collection. The following diagram illustrates how the new service integrates with the architecture:

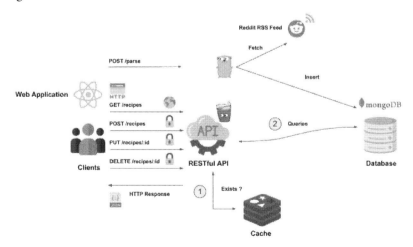

Figure 6.1 – Parsing a Reddit RSS feed

The service will take a subreddit RSS URL as a parameter. We can create an RSS feed by adding `.rss` to the end of an existing subreddit URL:

```
https://www.reddit.com/r/THREAD_NAME/.rss
```

For instance, let's have a look at the recipes subreddit shown in the following screenshot:

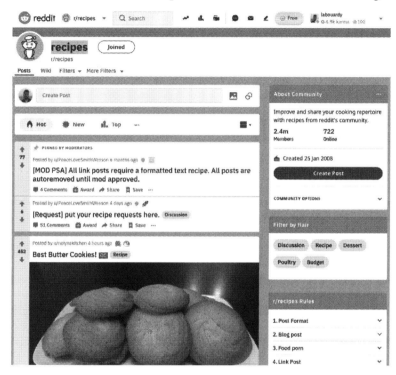

Figure 6.2 – Recipes subreddit

This subreddit will have the following URL for the RSS feed:

```
https://www.reddit.com/r/recipes/.rss
```

If you visit the aforementioned URL, you should receive an XML response. The following is an example of the XML structure that's returned by the recipes subreddit's RSS URL:

```xml
<?xml version="1.0" encoding="UTF-8"?>
<feed
    xmlns="http://www.w3.org/2005/Atom"
    xmlns:media="http://search.yahoo.com/mrss/">
    <title>recipes</title>
    <entry>
```

```
    <author>
        <name>/u/nolynskitchen</name>
        <uri>https://www.reddit.com/user/nolynskitchen
        </uri>
    </author>
    <category term="recipes" label="r/recipes"/>
    <id>t3_m4uvlm</id>
    <media:thumbnail url="https://b.thumbs.
      redditmedia.com
      /vDz3xCmo10TFkokqy9y1chopeIXdOqtGA33joNBtTDA.jpg"
    />
    <link href="https://www.reddit.com/r/recipes
              /comments/m4uvlm/best_butter_cookies/" />
    <updated>2021-03-14T12:57:05+00:00</updated>
    <title>Best Butter Cookies!</title>
  </entry>
</feed>
```

To get started, follow these steps:

1. Create an `rss-parser` project, load it into the VSCode editor, and write a `main.go` file. Within the file, declare a first struct `Entry` and only after that, struct `Feed` which uses Entry:

```
type Feed struct {
    Entries []Entry `xml:"entry"`
}


type Entry struct {
    Link struct {
        Href string `xml:"href,attr"`
    } `xml:"link"`
    Thumbnail struct {
        URL string `xml:"url,attr"`
    } `xml:"thumbnail"`
    Title string `xml:"title"`
}
```

2. Next, write a `GetFeedEntries` method, which takes the RSS URL as a parameter, and return a list of entries:

```go
func GetFeedEntries(url string) ([]Entry, error) {
    client := &http.Client{}
    req, err := http.NewRequest("GET", url, nil)
    if err != nil {
        return nil, err
    }
    req.Header.Add("User-Agent", "Mozilla/5.0 (
        Windows NT 10.0; Win64; x64) AppleWebKit/537.36
        (KHTML, like Gecko) Chrome/70.0.3538.110
        Safari/537.36")

    resp, err := client.Do(req)
    if err != nil {
        return nil, err
    }
    defer resp.Body.Close()

    byteValue, _ := ioutil.ReadAll(resp.Body)
    var feed Feed
    xml.Unmarshal(byteValue, &feed)

    return feed.Entries, nil
}
```

This method uses the HTTP client to issue a GET request into the URL given in the `GetFeedEntries` method parameter. Then, it encodes the response body into a `Feed` struct. Finally, it returns the `Entries` attribute.

Note the usage of the `User-Agent` request header to simulate a request being sent from the browser and avoiding being blocked by the Reddit servers:

```go
req.Header.Add("User-Agent", "Mozilla/5.0 (Windows NT
10.0; Win64; x64) AppleWebKit/537.36 (KHTML, like Gecko)
Chrome/70.0.3538.110 Safari/537.36")
```

> **Note**
> A list of valid User-Agents can be found at the following URL (it's updated regularly): `https://developers.whatismybrowser.com/useragents/explore/`.

3. Next, create a web server with the Gin router and expose a POST request on the `/parse` endpoint. Then, define a route handler called `ParserHandler`:

```
func main() {
    router := gin.Default()
    router.POST("/parse", ParserHandler)
    router.Run(":5000")
}
```

`ParserHandler` is self-explanatory: it marshals the request payload into a `Request` struct. Then, it calls the `GetFeedEntries` method with the URL attribute of the `Request` struct. Finally, based on the method's response, it returns a 500 error code or a 200 status code, along with a list of feed entries:

```
func ParserHandler(c *gin.Context) {
    var request Request
    if err := c.ShouldBindJSON(&request); err != nil {
        c.JSON(http.StatusBadRequest, gin.H{
            "error": err.Error()})
        return
    }

    entries, err := GetFeedEntries(request.URL)
    if err != nil {
        c.JSON(http.StatusInternalServerError,
            gin.H{"error": "error while parsing
                the RSS feed"})
        return
    }

    c.JSON(http.StatusOK, entries)
}
```

The `Request` struct has a `URL` attribute:

```
type Request struct {
    URL string `json:"url"`
}
```

4. To test it out, run the server on a different port (for example, `5000`) to avoid port conflicts with the recipes API (already running on port `8080`):

```
mlabouardy@Mohameds-MBP-001 chapter6 % go run main.go
[GIN-debug] [WARNING] Creating an Engine instance with the Logger and Recovery middleware already attached.

[GIN-debug] [WARNING] Running in "debug" mode. Switch to "release" mode in production.
 - using env:   export GIN_MODE=release
 - using code:  gin.SetMode(gin.ReleaseMode)

[GIN-debug] POST   /parse                     --> main.ParserHandler (3 handlers)
[GIN-debug] Listening and serving HTTP on :5000
```

Figure 6.3 – RSS parser logs

5. On the Postman client, issue a POST request on the `/parse` endpoint with the URL of a subreddit in the request body. The server will parse the RSS feed and return a list of feed entries, as shown in the following screenshot:

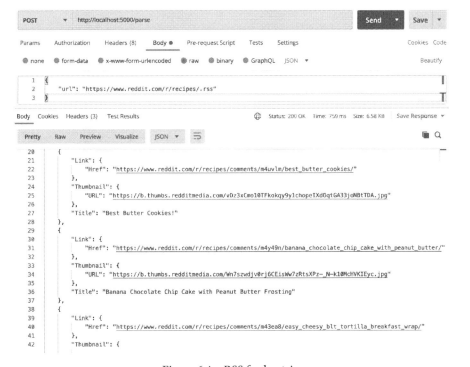

Figure 6.4 – RSS feed entries

6. Now, insert the results into MongoDB by connecting to the MongoDB server deployed in previous chapters. Define the connection instructions on the `init()` method, as follows:

```go
var client *mongo.Client
var ctx context.Context
func init() {
    ctx = context.Background()
    client, _ = mongo.Connect(ctx,
        options.Client().ApplyURI(os.Getenv("MONGO_URI")))
}
```

7. Then, update the HTTP handler to insert entries into the `recipes` collection with the `InsertOne` operation:

```go
func ParserHandler(c *gin.Context) {
    ...
    collection := client.Database(os.Getenv(
        "MONGO_DATABASE")).Collection("recipes")
    for _, entry := range entries[2:] {
        collection.InsertOne(ctx, bson.M{
            "title":     entry.Title,
            "thumbnail": entry.Thumbnail.URL,
            "url":       entry.Link.Href,
        })
    }
    ...
}
```

8. Rerun the application, but this time, provide the MONGO_URI and MONGO_DATABASE environment variables, as follows:

```
MONGO_URI="mongodb://admin:password@localhost:27017/
test?authSource=admin&readPreference=primary&appname=
MongoDB%20Compass&ssl=false" MONGO_DATABASE=demo go run
main.go
```

9. Reissue a POST request with Postman or the `curl` command. Head back to
    MongoDB Compass and refresh the `recipes` collection. The RSS entries should
    have been successfully inserted, as follows:

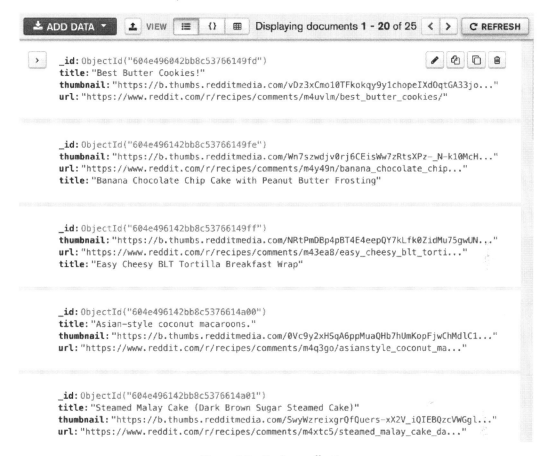

Figure 6.5 – Recipes collection

> **Note**
>
> If you're using the same database and collection that was shown in the previous
> chapters, you might need to drop existing documents before inserting new
> recipes.

The `recipes` collection has now been initialized with a list of recipes.

You can repeat the same steps to parse other subreddit RSS feeds. However, what if you want to parse thousands or millions of subreddits? Handling such a large number of workloads will take a lot of resources (CPU/RAM) and will be time-consuming. That's why we will separate the service logic into multiple loosely coupled services, and then scale them based on the incoming workload.

Those services will need to communicate with each other, and the most effective communication approach is to use message brokers. That's where RabbitMQ comes into the picture.

Deploying RabbitMQ with Docker

RabbitMQ (`https://www.rabbitmq.com/#getstarted`) is a reliable, highly available message broker. The following schema describes how RabbitMQ will be used within the application architecture:

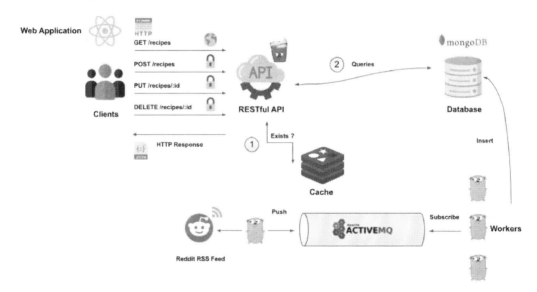

Figure 6.6 – Scaling with RabbitMQ

To deploy RabbitMQ with Docker, use the official RabbitMQ Docker image (`https://hub.docker.com/_/rabbitmq`) and implement the following steps:

1. Issue the following command to run a container from the RabbitMQ image:

```
docker run -d --name rabbitmq -e RABBITMQ_DEFAULT_
USER=user -e RABBITMQ_DEFAULT_PASS=password -p 8080:15672
-p 5672:5672 rabbitmq:3-management
```

The username and password are set through environment variables. The preceding command exposes the RabbitMQ dashboard on port `8080` and the server on port `5672`.

2. Once the container has been deployed, run the following command to display the server logs:

```
docker logs -f CONTAINER_ID
```

Here's how the startup logs will be displayed:

```
2021-03-14 20:20:50.599 [info] <0.44.0> Application mnesia started on node rabbit@93398fbee760
2021-03-14 20:20:50.600 [info] <0.273.0>
 Starting RabbitMQ 3.8.14 on Erlang 23.2.7
 Copyright (c) 2007-2021 VMware, Inc. or its affiliates.
 Licensed under the MPL 2.0. Website: https://rabbitmq.com

  ##  ##      RabbitMQ 3.8.14
  ##  ##
  ##########  Copyright (c) 2007-2021 VMware, Inc. or its affiliates.
  ######  ##
  ##########  Licensed under the MPL 2.0. Website: https://rabbitmq.com

  Doc guides: https://rabbitmq.com/documentation.html
  Support:    https://rabbitmq.com/contact.html
  Tutorials:  https://rabbitmq.com/getstarted.html
  Monitoring: https://rabbitmq.com/monitoring.html

  Logs: <stdout>

  Config file(s): /etc/rabbitmq/rabbitmq.conf

  Starting broker...2021-03-14 20:20:50.602 [info] <0.273.0>
 node            : rabbit@93398fbee760
 home dir        : /var/lib/rabbitmq
 config file(s)  : /etc/rabbitmq/rabbitmq.conf
 cookie hash     : yUZjmlga8ZU/Udux2NXeUw==
 log(s)          : <stdout>
 database dir    : /var/lib/rabbitmq/mnesia/rabbit@93398fbee760
2021-03-14 20:20:52.485 [info] <0.273.0> Feature flags: list of feature flags found:
```

Figure 6.7 – RabbitMQ startup logs

3. Once the server initialization has been completed, navigate to `localhost:8080` via your browser. A RabbitMQ login page will be displayed. Sign in with your user/ password credentials. You will land on the dashboard:

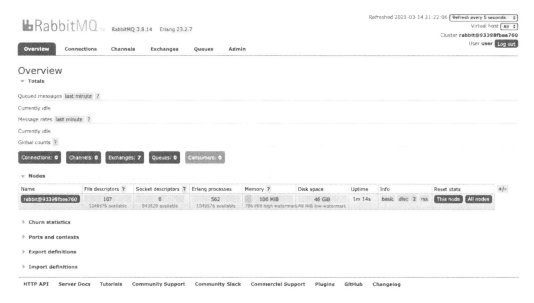

Figure 6.8 – RabbitMQ dashboard

4. Now, create a messaging queue where the RSS URLs will be pushed to by the services. Click on **Queues** from the navigation bar and create a new queue by clicking on **Add a new queue**:

Figure 6.9 – Creating a new RabbitMQ queue

5. Make sure that you set the **Durability** field to **Durable** for the data to be persisted on disk if RabbitMQ ever goes down.

With RabbitMQ up and running, we can move on and implement a producer service to push incoming RSS URLs to RabbitMQ, as well as a consumer service to consume the URLs from the queue.

Exploring the Producer/Consumer pattern

Before we dig deeper into the implementation, we need to explore the Producer/Consumer pattern. The following schema illustrates these two concepts:

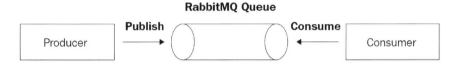

Figure 6.10 – Producer/Consumer pattern

Now that the main concepts are clear, let's get started:

1. Create a new Go project called `producer` and install the RabbitMQ SDK for Golang with the following command:

```
go get github.com/streadway/amqp
```

2. Write a `main.go` file and set up a TCP connection to the RabbitMQ server with the following code snippet:

```
var channelAmqp *amqp.Channel
func init() {
    amqpConnection, err := amqp.Dial(os.Getenv(
        "RABBITMQ_URI"))
    if err != nil {
        log.Fatal(err)
    }

    channelAmqp, _ = amqpConnection.Channel()
}
```

The AMQP connection string will be provided, along with the password, through the `RABBITMQ_URI` environment variable.

3.   Next, define an HTTP handler on the /parse endpoint. The handler will push the URL given in the request body into the RabbitMQ queue using the Publish method:

```
func ParserHandler(c *gin.Context) {
    var request Request
    if err := c.ShouldBindJSON(&request); err != nil {
        c.JSON(http.StatusBadRequest, gin.H{
            "error": err.Error()})
        return
    }

    data, _ := json.Marshal(request)
    err := channelAmqp.Publish(
        "",
        os.Getenv("RABBITMQ_QUEUE"),
        false,
        false,
        amqp.Publishing{
            ContentType: "application/json",
            Body:        []byte(data),
        })
    if err != nil {
        fmt.Println(err)
        c.JSON(http.StatusInternalServerError,
            gin.H{"error": "Error while publishing

            to RabbitMQ"})
        return
    }

    c.JSON(http.StatusOK, map[string]string{
        "message": "success"})
}
func main() {
    router := gin.Default()
    router.POST("/parse", ParserHandler)
```

```
router.Run(":5000")
}
```

4. Finally, run the application with the RABBITMQ_URI and RABBITMQ_QUEUE variables, as follows:

```
RABBITMQ_URI="amqp://user:password@localhost:5672/"
RABBITMQ_QUEUE=rss_urls go run main.go
```

5. Then, execute a POST request on the /parse endpoint. You should receive a 200 **success** message, as shown here:

Figure 6.11 – Publishing data in RabbitMQ

6. Head back to the RabbitMQ dashboard, go to the **Queues** section, and click on the **rss_urls** queue. You should be redirected to the **Queue metrics** page. Here, you will notice a message in the queue:

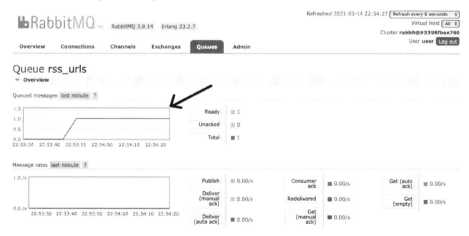

Figure 6.12 – Queue metrics page

With the producer service up and running, you need to build the worker/consumer to consume the messages/URLs available in the RabbitMQ queue:

1. Create a new Go project called `consumer` and create a new file called `main.go`. Write the following code inside the file:

```go
func main() {
    amqpConnection, err := amqp.Dial(os.Getenv(
        "RABBITMQ_URI"))
    if err != nil {
        log.Fatal(err)
    }
    defer amqpConnection.Close()

    channelAmqp, _ := amqpConnection.Channel()
    defer channelAmqp.Close()

    forever := make(chan bool)

    msgs, err := channelAmqp.Consume(
        os.Getenv("RABBITMQ_QUEUE"),
        "",
        true,
        false,
        false,
        false,
        nil,
    )

    go func() {
        for d := range msgs {
            log.Printf("Received a message: %s", d.Body)
        }
    }()

    log.Printf(" [*] Waiting for messages.
            To exit press CTRL+C")
```

```
<-forever
}
```

The code is straightforward: it sets up a connection to the RabbitMQ server and subscribes to the `rss_urls` queue. Then, it creates an infinite loop and fetches a message from the queue, after which it displays the message body to the console and waits for new messages.

2. Run the consumer project by passing the RabbitMQ URI and queue name as environment variables:

```
RABBITMQ_URI="amqp://user:password@localhost:5672/"
RABBITMQ_QUEUE=rss_urls go run main.go
```

Once launched, the consumer will fetch the message that was pushed previously by the producer and display its content on the console. Then, it will delete the message from the queue:

```
mlabouardy@Mohameds-MBP-001 consumer % RABBITMQ_URI="amqp://user:password@localhost:5672/" RABBITMQ_QUEUE=rss_urls go run main.go
2021/03/14 23:03:29   [*] Waiting for messages. To exit press CTRL+C
2021/03/14 23:03:29 Received a message: {"url":"https://www.reddit.com/r/recipes/.rss"}
```

Figure 6.13 – Subscribing and fetching a message from RabbitMQ

3. Verify that the message has been deleted by refreshing the **Queue metrics** page. The **Queued messages** chart should confirm this deletion:

Figure 6.14 – Deleting a message from the queue

With that, your worker/consumer has been built!

So far, you've seen that the consumer displays the message's content. Now, let's take this further and encode the message body in a `Request` struct and get the feed entries by calling the `GetFeedEntries` method, which we mentioned earlier. The entries will then be saved in the `recipes` collection in MongoDB:

```go
go func() {
    for d := range msgs {
        log.Printf("Received a message: %s", d.Body)

        var request Request
        json.Unmarshal(d.Body, &request)

        log.Println("RSS URL:", request.URL)

        entries, _ := GetFeedEntries(request.URL)

        collection := mongoClient.Database(os.Getenv(
            "MONGO_DATABASE")).Collection("recipes")
        for _, entry := range entries[2:] {
            collection.InsertOne(ctx, bson.M{
                "title":     entry.Title,
                "thumbnail": entry.Thumbnail.URL,
                "url":       entry.Link.Href,
            })
        }
    }
}()
```

Rerun the application, but this time, provide the MongoDB connection parameters, in addition to the RabbitMQ parameters:

```
RABBITMQ_URI="amqp://user:password@
localhost:5672/" RABBITMQ_QUEUE=rss_urls MONGO_
URI="mongodb://admin:password@localhost:27017/
test?authSource=admin&readPreference=primary&appname=MongoDB%20
Compass&ssl=false" MONGO_DATABASE=demo go run main.go
```

To test this out, issue a POST request to the producer server with an RSS feed URL in the request body. The producer will publish the URL in the RabbitMQ queue. From there, the consumer will fetch the message and get the XML response of the RSS URL, encode the response in an array of entries, and save the results in MongoDB:

```
2021/03/14 23:09:31  [*] Waiting for messages. To exit press CTRL+C
2021/03/14 23:10:53 Received a message: {"url":"https://www.reddit.com/r/recipes/.rss"}
2021/03/14 23:10:53 RSS URL: https://www.reddit.com/r/recipes/.rss
```

Figure 6.15 – Consumer server logs

You can issue multiple subreddit URLs to the producer server. This time, the consumer will fetch the URLs one by one, as follows:

```
2021/03/14 23:09:31  [*] Waiting for messages. To exit press CTRL+C
2021/03/14 23:10:53 Received a message: {"url":"https://www.reddit.com/r/recipes/.rss"}
2021/03/14 23:10:53 RSS URL: https://www.reddit.com/r/recipes/.rss
2021/03/14 23:11:58 Received a message: {"url":"https://www.reddit.com/r/food/.rss"}
2021/03/14 23:11:58 RSS URL: https://www.reddit.com/r/food/.rss
2021/03/14 23:12:03 Received a message: {"url":"https://www.reddit.com/r/Cooking/.rss"}
2021/03/14 23:12:03 RSS URL: https://www.reddit.com/r/Cooking/.rss
2021/03/14 23:12:07 Received a message: {"url":"https://www.reddit.com/r/vegan/.rss"}
2021/03/14 23:12:07 RSS URL: https://www.reddit.com/r/vegan/.rss
2021/03/14 23:12:12 Received a message: {"url":"https://www.reddit.com/r/Baking/.rss"}
2021/03/14 23:12:12 RSS URL: https://www.reddit.com/r/Baking/.rss
```

Figure 6.16 – Parsing multiple RSS URLs

To view the entries that have been saved in MongoDB, build a simple dashboard to list all the recipes in the `recipes` collection. You can create a new project from scratch or expose an additional route on the web application we built in the previous chapter to serve an HTML representation of the recipes:

```
router.GET("/dashboard", IndexHandler)
```

Then, make sure that you update the `Recipe` struct fields to mirror the MongoDB document field's structure:

```
type Recipe struct {
    Title     string `json:"title" bson:"title"`
    Thumbnail string `json:"thumbnail" bson:"thumbnail"`
    URL       string `json:"url" bson:"url"`
}
```

The route handler will simply call the `Find` operation on the `recipes` collection to return all the recipes. Then, it will encode the results in a `recipes` slice. Finally, it will pass the `recipes` variable into an HTML template to display the results:

```
func IndexHandler(c *gin.Context) {
    cur, err := collection.Find(ctx, bson.M{})
    if err != nil {
        c.JSON(http.StatusInternalServerError,
            gin.H{"error": err.Error()})
        return
    }
    defer cur.Close(ctx)

    recipes := make([]Recipe, 0)
    for cur.Next(ctx) {
        var recipe Recipe
        cur.Decode(&recipe)
        recipes = append(recipes, recipe)
    }

    c.HTML(http.StatusOK, "index.tmpl", gin.H{
        "recipes": recipes,
    })
}
```

The following is the HTML template's content. It uses the Bootstrap framework to build an appealing user interface. It also uses the range keyword to loop through each recipe within the recipes slice and displays its details (title, thumbnail image, and Reddit URL):

```
<section class="container">
        <div class="row">
            <ul class="list-group">
                {{range .recipes}}
                <li class="list-group-item">
                    <div style="width: 100%;">
                        <img src="{{ .Thumbnail }}"
                            class="card-img-top thumbnail">
                        <span class="title">{{ .Title
                        }}</span>
                        <a href="{{ .URL }}" target="_blank"
                            class="btn btn-warning
                            btn-sm see_recipe">See recipe</a>
                    </div>
                </li>
                {{end}}
            </ul>
        </div>
</section>
```

Configure the Gin server to run on port 3000 and execute the server with the go run main.go command with the MONGO_URI and MONGO_DATABASE variables. On your browser, head to Localhost:3000/dashboard Apart from, where a list of recipes should be returned, as shown in the following screenshot:

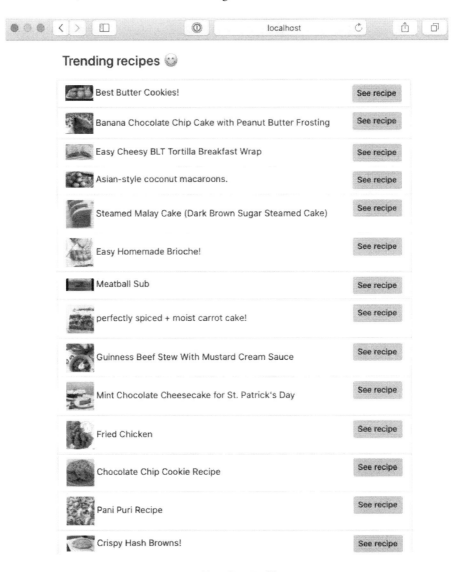

Figure 6.17 – Trending Reddit recipes

> **Note**
>
> The application layout and stylesheet can be found in this book's GitHub repository: `https://github.com/PacktPublishing/Building-Distributed-Applications-in-Gin/blob/main/chapter06/dashboard/templates/index.tmpl`.

Awesome! You are now familiar with how to use a message broker such as RabbitMQ to scale your Gin distributed applications. In the next section, we will demonstrate another technique for scaling a Gin distributed application through Docker.

Scaling horizontally with Docker replicas

So far, you have learned how to build a Producer/Consumer architecture with the Gin framework and RabbitMQ. In this section, we'll cover how to scale the consumer component so that we can split the incoming workload across multiple consumers.

You can achieve this by building a Docker image of the consumer project and building multiple containers based on that image. The Docker image is immutable, which guarantees the same environment each time a container is based on the image that is run.

The following schema illustrates how multiple consumers/workers are used:

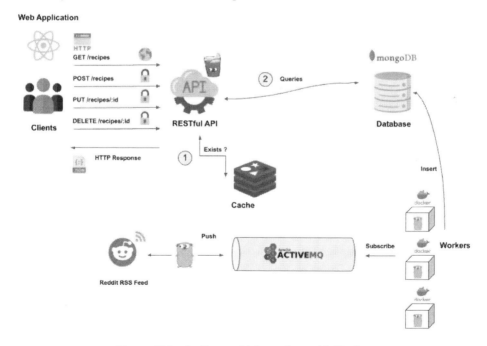

Figure 6.18 – Scaling multiple workers with Docker

To create a Docker image, we need to define a `Dockerfile` – a blueprint that contains all the instructions to run the consumer project. Create a `Dockerfile` in your worker/consumer directory with the following content:

```
FROM golang:1.16
WORKDIR /go/src/github.com/worker
COPY main.go go.mod go.sum ./
RUN go mod download
RUN CGO_ENABLED=0 GOOS=linux go build -a -installsuffix cgo -o
app .
FROM alpine:latest
RUN apk --no-cache add ca-certificates
WORKDIR /root/
COPY --from=0 /go/src/github.com/worker/app .
CMD ["./app"]
```

This `Dockerfile` uses the multi-stage build feature to build a lightweight Docker image. We will see how this works in the next section.

Using Docker multi-stage builds

Multi-stage builds were introduced in Docker Engine 1.17.05. It allows you to use multiple FROM statements in your `Dockerfile` and copy artifacts from one stage to another, leaving behind everything you don't need in the final image.

In the previous example, you used `golang:1.16` as a base image to build a single binary. Then, the second FROM instruction started a new build stage with the Alpine image as its base. From here, you can copy the binary from the previous stage using the COPY –from=0 instruction. As a result, you will end up with a small Docker image.

To build the image, run the following command. The dot at the end is important as it points to the current directory:

```
docker build -t worker .
```

The building process should take a few seconds to be completed. Then, you will find the following Docker build logs:

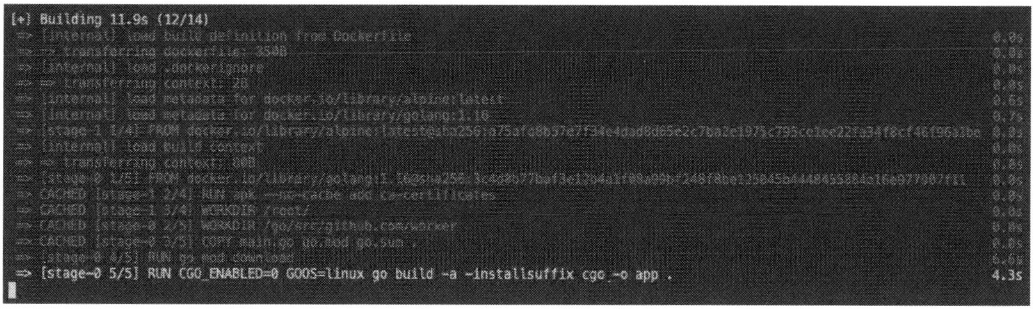

Figure 6.19 – Docker build logs

If you review the preceding output, you will see that Docker logged every instruction of building the worker image according to the steps in our `Dockerfile`. Once the image has been built, run the following command to list the available images in your machine:

```
docker image ls
```

The worker/consumer image should be listed at the top of the list:

Figure 6.20 – Worker Docker image

Run a container based on the image with the `docker run` command. You need to provide the MongoDB and RabbitMQ URIs as environment variables with the `-e` flag. The `-link` flag can be used to interact with MongoDB and RabbitMQ within the container:

```
docker run -d -e MONGO_URI="mongodb://
admin:password@mongodb:27017/
test?authSource=admin&readPreference=primary&appname=MongoDB%20
Compass&ssl=false" -e MONGO_DATABASE=demo2 -e RABBITMQ_
URI="amqp://user:password@rabbitmq:5672/" -e RABBITMQ_
QUEUE=rss_urls --link rabbitmq --link mongodb --name worker
worker
```

The container logs are as follows:

```
mlabouardy@Mohameds-MBP-001 consumer % docker logs -f 4a952c3ce8f4
2021/03/21 15:54:58  [*] Waiting for messages. To exit press CTRL+C
```

Figure 6.21 – Worker's container logs

With that, you have dockerized the worker's service. Next, we will scale it with Docker Compose.

Scaling services with Docker Compose

Docker Compose is a container orchestration tool built on top of Docker Engine. It helps you manage an application stack or multiple containers with a single command line.

Using Docker Compose is as simple as creating a Docker image:

1. Define a `docker-compose.yml` file in the root of your project and type in the following YAML code:

```yaml
version: "3.9"

services:
  worker:
    image: worker
    environment:
      - MONGO_URI="mongodb://admin:password
          @mongodb:27017/test?authSource=admin
          &readPreference=primary&ssl=false"
      - MONGO_DATABASE=demo2
      - RABBITMQ_URI=amqp://user:password@rabbitmq:5672
      - RABBITMQ_QUEUE=rss_urls
    networks:
      - app_network
    external_links:
      - mongodb
      - rabbitmq

networks:
  app_network:
    external: true
```

The configuration specifies the environment variables and network topology that the worker requires.

2. Define an external network where the workers, MongoDB, and RabbitMQ services will be living. Execute the following command:

```
docker network create app_network
```

3. Redeploy the RabbitMQ and MongoDB containers but this time, deploy them within the app_network custom network by passing the –network flag:

```
docker run -d --name rabbitmq -e RABBITMQ_DEFAULT_
USER=user -e RABBITMQ_DEFAULT_PASS=password -p 8080:15672
-p 5672:5672 --network app_network rabbitmq:3-management
```

4. With the containers being configured properly, issue the following command to deploy the worker:

```
docker-compose up -d
```

The -d flag instructs Docker Compose to run the containers in the background (detached mode).

5. Issue the following command to list the running services:

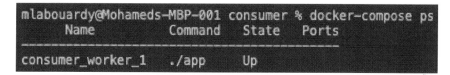

Figure 6.22 – Docker Compose service

6. To scale the worker, rerun the previous command with the –scale flag:

```
docker-compose up -d --scale worker=5
```

The final output will look as follows:

```
Attaching to consumer_worker_2, consumer_worker_3, consumer_worker_4, consumer_worker_5, consumer_worker_1
worker_2 | 2021/03/21 16:30:22  [*] Waiting for messages. To exit press CTRL+C
worker_3 | 2021/03/21 16:30:22  [*] Waiting for messages. To exit press CTRL+C
worker_1 | 2021/03/21 16:28:01  [*] Waiting for messages. To exit press CTRL+C
worker_4 | 2021/03/21 16:30:22  [*] Waiting for messages. To exit press CTRL+C
worker_5 | 2021/03/21 16:30:22  [*] Waiting for messages. To exit press CTRL+C
```

Figure 6.23 – Scaling five workers

7. To test everything out, create a file called `threads` that contains a list of Reddit's best cooking and recipes subreddits. The following list has been cropped for brevity:

```
https://www.reddit.com/r/recipes/.rss
https://www.reddit.com/r/food/.rss
https://www.reddit.com/r/Cooking/.rss
https://www.reddit.com/r/IndianFood/.rss
https://www.reddit.com/r/Baking/.rss
https://www.reddit.com/r/vegan/.rss
https://www.reddit.com/r/fastfood/.rss
https://www.reddit.com/r/vegetarian/.rss
https://www.reddit.com/r/cookingforbeginners/.rss
https://www.reddit.com/r/MealPrepSunday/.rss
https://www.reddit.com/r/EatCheapAndHealthy/.rss
https://www.reddit.com/r/Cheap_Meals/.rss
https://www.reddit.com/r/slowcooking/.rss
https://www.reddit.com/r/AskCulinary/.rss
https://www.reddit.com/r/fromscratch/.rss
```

8. Then, write a `bulk.sh` shell script to read the `threads` file line by line and issue a POST request to the producer service:

```
#!/bin/bash
while IFS= read -r thread
do
    printf "\n$thread\n"
    curl -X POST http://localhost:5000/parse -d
        '{"url":"$thread"}' http://localhost:5000/parse
done < "threads"
```

9. To run the script, add the execution permission and execute the file with the following command:

```
chmod +x bulk.sh
./bulk.sh
```

> **Note**
> Make sure the producer service is running, otherwise the issued HTTP requests with curl command will timeout.

The script will read the threads file line by line and issue a POST request, as follows:

```
mlabouardy@Mohameds-MBP-001 chapter6 % ./bulk.sh

https://www.reddit.com/r/recipes/
{"message":"success"}
https://www.reddit.com/r/food/
{"message":"success"}
https://www.reddit.com/r/Cooking/
{"message":"success"}
https://www.reddit.com/r/IndianFood/
{"message":"success"}
```

Figure 6.24 – Shell script's output

10. Run the docker-compose logs -f command. This time, you should notice multiple workers are being used. Also, Docker Compose assigned colors to instances and each message is being fetched by a different worker:

```
worker_1  | 2021/03/21 17:08:19  [*] Waiting for messages. To exit press CTRL+C
worker_2  | 2021/03/21 17:08:18  [*] Waiting for messages. To exit press CTRL+C
worker_5  | 2021/03/21 17:08:18  [*] Waiting for messages. To exit press CTRL+C
worker_4  | 2021/03/21 17:08:19  [*] Waiting for messages. To exit press CTRL+C
worker_3  | 2021/03/21 17:08:18  [*] Waiting for messages. To exit press CTRL+C
worker_2  | 2021/03/21 17:08:29 Received a message: {"url":"https://www.reddit.com/r/recipes/"}
worker_2  | 2021/03/21 17:08:29 RSS URL: https://www.reddit.com/r/recipes/
worker_3  | 2021/03/21 17:08:29 Received a message: {"url":"https://www.reddit.com/r/food/"}
worker_3  | 2021/03/21 17:08:29 RSS URL: https://www.reddit.com/r/food/
worker_5  | 2021/03/21 17:08:29 Received a message: {"url":"https://www.reddit.com/r/Cooking/"}
worker_5  | 2021/03/21 17:08:29 RSS URL: https://www.reddit.com/r/Cooking/
worker_4  | 2021/03/21 17:08:29 Received a message: {"url":"https://www.reddit.com/r/IndianFood/"}
worker_4  | 2021/03/21 17:08:29 RSS URL: https://www.reddit.com/r/IndianFood/
worker_1  | 2021/03/21 17:08:29 Received a message: {"url":"https://www.reddit.com/r/Baking/"}
```

Figure 6.25 – Splitting the workload across multiple workers

With that, you have successfully split the workload across multiple workers. This approach is called **horizontal scaling**.

> **Note**
>
> In *Chapter 8, Deploying the Application on AWS*, we will cover how to deploy the web application on AWS and how to use a **Simple Queue Service** (**SQS**) instead of RabbitMQ to scale the workers.

Using the NGINX reverse proxy

In the previous section, you learned how to scale the workers responsible for parsing the subreddit URLs. In this section, you will explore how to scale the Recipes API we built in the previous chapters by serving it behind a reverse proxy.

One of the most used reverse proxies is **Nginx**. It faces the client and receives the incoming HTTP(S) requests. It then redirects them to one of the API instances in a round-robin fashion. To deploy multiple instances of the Recipes API, you will be using Docker Compose to orchestrate the containers. The following schema illustrates the difference between a **single instance architecture** and a **load balanced multi-instance architecture** with Nginx:

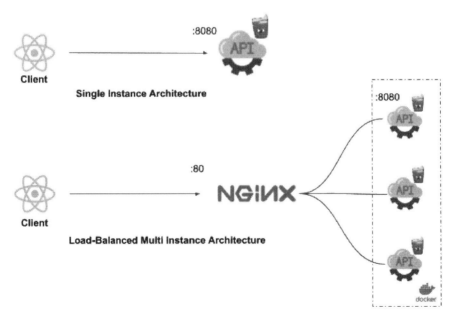

Figure 6.26 – Load balanced multi-instance architecture with Nginx

Another solution for scaling the Recipes API is **vertical scaling**, which consists of increasing the CPU/RAM of the system where the service is running. However, this approach tends to have some limitations in the long run (not cost-effective). That's why, here, you will adopt the horizontal scaling approach and distribute the load across multiple API instances.

> **Note**
>
> An alternative to Nginx is Traefik (`https://doc.traefik.io/traefik/`). It's an open source project built with scalability in mind.

The following is a quick reminder of the Recipes API's output:

```
1   // 20210321185851
2   // http://localhost:3000/recipes
3
4   [
5       {
6           "id": "6057892f5546621cb9d5467e",
7           "name": "Oregano Marinated Chicken",
8           "tags": [
9               "main",
10              "chicken"
11          ],
12          "ingredients": [
13              "4 (6 to 7-ounce) boneless skinless chicken breasts\r",
14              "10 grinds black pepper\r",
15              "1/2 tsp salt\r",
16              "2 tablespoon extra-virgin olive oil\r",
17              "1 teaspoon dried oregano\r",
18              "1 lemon, juiced"
19          ],
20          "instructions": [
21              "To marinate the chicken: In a non-reactive dish, combine the lemon juice, olive oil, oregano, salt, and pepper and mix together",
22              " Add the chicken breasts to the dish and rub both sides in the mixture",
23              " Cover the dish with plastic wrap and let marinate in the refrigerator for at least 30 minutes and up to 4 hours",
24              "\r\n\r\nTo cook the chicken: Heat a nonstick skillet or grill pan over high heat",
25              " Add the chicken breasts and cook, turning once, until well browned, about 4 to 5 minutes on each side or until cooked through",
26              " Let the chicken rest on a cutting board for a few minutes before slicing it into thin strips"
27          ],
28          "publishedAt": "2021-01-17T18:28:52.803062Z"
29      },
```

Figure 6.27 – GET /recipes endpoint response

To deploy multiple instances of the Recipes API, follow these steps:

1. Build a Docker image and write a Dockerfile in the folder with your Recipes API implementation that contains the following content:

```
FROM golang:1.16
WORKDIR /go/src/github.com/api
COPY . .
RUN go mod download
```

```
RUN CGO_ENABLED=0 GOOS=linux go build -a -installsuffix
cgo -o app .

FROM alpine:latest
RUN apk --no-cache add ca-certificates
WORKDIR /root/
COPY --from=0 /go/src/github.com/api/app .
CMD ["./app"]
```

2. This `Dockerfile` uses the multi-stage feature to ship a lightweight image. The `docker build -t recipes-api.` Command's output is as follows:

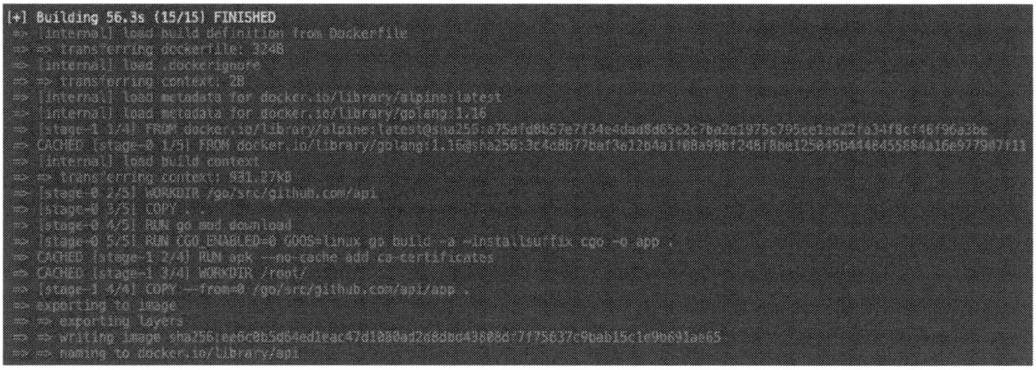

Figure 6.28 – Docker build logs

With the image built, create a `docker-compose.yml` file and define three services:

API: The Recipes API container

Redis: The in-memory caching database

MongoDB: The NoSQL database where the recipes are stored

3. Then, add the following lines to the file:

```
version: "3.9"

services:
  api:
    image: recipes-api
    environment:
      - MONGO_URI=mongodb://admin:password
        @mongodb:27017/test?authSource=admin
```

```
            &readPreference=primary&ssl=false
      - MONGO_DATABASE=demo
      - REDIS_URI=redis:6379
    networks:
      - api_network
    external_links:
      - mongodb
      - redis

  redis:
    image: redis
    networks:
      - api_network

  mongodb:
    image: mongo:4.4.3
    networks:
      - api_network
    environment:
      - MONGO_INITDB_ROOT_USERNAME=admin
      - MONGO_INITDB_ROOT_PASSWORD=password

networks:
  api_network:
```

4. Next, define a Nginx service with the following code block:

```
nginx:
    image: nginx
    ports:
      - 80:80
    volumes:
      - $PWD/nginx.conf:/etc/nginx/nginx.conf
    depends_on:
      - api
    networks:
      - api_network
```

This code maps a local `nginx.conf` file into `/etc/nginx/nginx.conf` inside the container. The file provides instructions to Nginx about how to handle the incoming HTTP requests. The following is a simplified version:

```
events {
    worker_connections 1024;
}


http {
  server_tokens off;
  server {
    listen 80;
    root /var/www;

    location /api/ {
        proxy_set_header X-Forwarded-For $remote_addr;
        proxy_set_header Host            $http_host;
        proxy_pass http://api:8080/;
    }
  }
}
```

5. In `location /api`, set up a reverse proxy to forward the requests to the API running in port `8080` (internally).

6. Deploy the entire stack with the `docker-compose up -d` command. Then, issue the following command to display the running services:

    `docker-compose ps`

    The command's output is as follows:

```
   Name              Command                State            Ports
api_api_1        ./app                       Up      0.0.0.0:3000->8080/tcp
api_mongodb_1    docker-entrypoint.sh mongod Up      27017/tcp
api_nginx_1      /docker-entrypoint.sh ngin… Up      0.0.0.0:80->80/tcp
api_redis_1      docker-entrypoint.sh redis… Up      6379/tcp
```

Figure 6.29 – Application stack

7. The Nginx service is exposed on port `80`. Head to `localhost/api/recipes`; the server will call the Recipes API and forward the recipes list response, as follows:

```
1   // 20210321191537
2   // http://localhost/api/recipes
3
4   [
5     {
6       "id": "60578d20a5b5d7297f47642f",
7       "name": "Oregano Marinated Chicken",
8       "tags": [
9         "main",
10        "chicken"
11      ],
12      "ingredients": [
13        "4 (6 to 7-ounce) boneless skinless chicken breasts\r",
14        "10 grinds black pepper\r",
15        "1/2 tsp salt\r",
16        "2 tablespoon extra-virgin olive oil\r",
17        "1 teaspoon dried oregano\r",
18        "1 lemon, juiced"
19      ],
20      "instructions": [
21        "To marinate the chicken: In a non-reactive dish, combine the lemon juice, olive oil, oregano, salt, and pepper and mix
          together",
22        " Add the chicken breasts to the dish and rub both sides in the mixture",
23        " Cover the dish with plastic wrap and let marinate in the refrigerator for at least 30 minutes and up to 4 hours",
24        "\r\n\r\nTo cook the chicken: Heat a nonstick skillet or grill pan over high heat",
25        " Add the chicken breasts and cook, turning once, until well browned, about 4 to 5 minutes on each side or until cooked
          through",
26        " Let the chicken rest on a cutting board for a few minutes before slicing it into thin strips"
27      ],
28      "publishedAt": "2021-01-17T18:28:52.803062Z"
29    },
```

Figure 6.30 – Forwarding a HTTP response with Nginx

> **Note**
>
> For production usage, it's important that you secure your API endpoints with HTTPS. Luckily, you can use the "Let's Encrypt" add-on for Nginx to generate the TLS certificates automatically.

8. To ensure the response is being forwarded from the Recipes API, check out the Nginx service logs with the following command:

```
docker-compose logs -f nginx
```

9.   You should see something like this:

```
/docker-entrypoint.sh: /docker-entrypoint.d/ is not
empty, will attempt to perform configuration

/docker-entrypoint.sh: Looking for shell scripts in /
docker-entrypoint.d/

/docker-entrypoint.sh: Launching /docker-entrypoint.d/10-
listen-on-ipv6-by-default.sh

10-listen-on-ipv6-by-default.sh: info: Getting the
checksum of /etc/nginx/conf.d/default.conf

10-listen-on-ipv6-by-default.sh: info: Enabled listen on
IPv6 in /etc/nginx/conf.d/default.conf

/docker-entrypoint.sh: Launching /docker-entrypoint.d/20-
envsubst-on-templates.sh

/docker-entrypoint.sh: Launching /docker-entrypoint.d/30-
tune-worker-processes.sh

/docker-entrypoint.sh: Configuration complete; ready for
start up

172.21.0.1 - - [21/Mar/2021:18:11:02 +0000] "GET /api/
recipes HTTP/1.1" 200 2 "-" "Mozilla/5.0 (Macintosh;
Intel Mac OS X 10_15_7) AppleWebKit/537.36 (KHTML, like
Gecko) Chrome/88.0.4324.192 Safari/537.36"
```

10. So far, one instance of the Recipes API container is running. To scale it out, use the
     -scale flag with the docker-compose up command or define the number of
     replicas in the docker-compose.yml file, as follows:

```
api:
    image: recipes-api
    environment:
      - MONGO_URI=mongodb://admin:password
          @mongodb:27017/test?authSource=admin
          &readPreference=primary&ssl=false
      - MONGO_DATABASE=demo
      - REDIS_URI=redis:6379
    networks:
      - api_network
    external_links:
      - mongodb
      - redis
```

```
scale: 5
```

11. Re-execute the docker-compose up command. Four additional services will be created based on the Recipes API Docker image. Following are the service logs:

Figure 6.31 – Scaling the Recipes API

Now, when the client sends a request, it will hit Nginx and then be forwarded to one of the API services in a round-robin fashion. This helps us evenly distribute the load.

> **Note**
>
> In *Chapter 10, Capturing Gin Application Metrics*, we will learn how to set up a monitoring platform to trigger a scale-out event to increase the number of services when the demand increases.

The advantage of using a reverse proxy is that you can set up a single point of entry for your entire distributed web application. Both the backend and the web application will be located at the same URL. That way, you won't need to handle CORS on your API server.

12. Similar to the Recipes API, create a Docker image for the `react-ui` service. The following is the content of our `Dockerfile`:

```
FROM node:14.15.1
COPY package-lock.json .
COPY package.json .
RUN npm install
CMD npm start
```

As you can see, this is dead simple. Here, you are using a pre-built Node.js base image because the `react-ui` service is written in JavaScript.

13. Build the Docker image with `` `docker build -t dashboard` ``. Then, update `docker-compose.yml` so that it runs a Docker service from the image with the following code block:

```
dashboard:
    image: dashboard
    networks:
      - api_network
```

14. Next, update `nginx.conf` so that it forwards incoming requests at the root level of the URL to the dashboard service:

```
events {
    worker_connections 1024;
}

http {
  server_tokens off;
  server {
    listen 80;
      root /var/www;
```

```
location / {
    proxy_set_header X-Forwarded-For $remote_addr;
    proxy_set_header Host            $http_host;
    proxy_pass http://dashboard:3000/;
}

location /api/ {
    proxy_set_header X-Forwarded-For $remote_addr;
    proxy_set_header Host            $http_host;
    proxy_pass http://api:8080/;
    }
  }
}
```

15. Rerun the `docker-compose up -d` command for the changes to take effect:

```
      Name               Command            State              Ports
---------------------------------------------------------------------------------
api_api_1          ./app                    Up
api_api_2          ./app                    Up
api_api_3          ./app                    Up
api_api_4          ./app                    Up
api_api_5          ./app                    Up
api_dashboard_1    docker-entrypoint.sh /bin/ ...  Up
api_mongodb_1      docker-entrypoint.sh mongod     Up      0.0.0.0:27017->27017/tcp
api_nginx_1        /docker-entrypoint.sh ngin ...  Up      0.0.0.0:80->80/tcp
api_redis_1        docker-entrypoint.sh redis ...  Up      6379/tcp
```

Figure 6.32 – Serving the web dashboard from Nginx

16. Head to `localhost/dashboard`; you will be redirected to the web dashboard we wrote in the previous chapter:

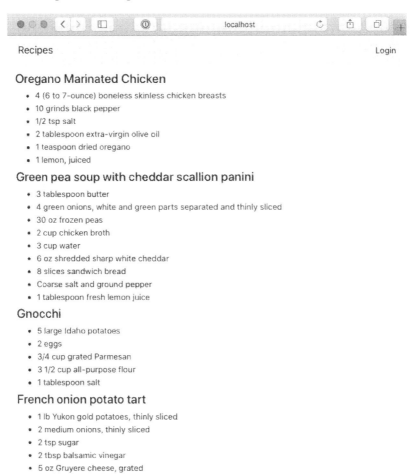

Figure 6.33 – Serving two backends from the same URL

Now, both the RESTful API and dashboard are being served from the same domain name.

To take down your containers, you can use the following command:

```
docker-compose down
```

> **Note**
> If you're using session-based authentication, you'll need to configure cookie stickiness on Nginx to keep a user's session on the server where it was started.

You can also serve the subreddits application (built at the beginning of this chapter) from the Nginx server by replacing the dashboard location with another location section, to the `nginx.conf` file:

```
location /reddit/ {
        proxy_set_header X-Forwarded-For $remote_addr;
        proxy_set_header Host            $http_host;
        proxy_pass http://reddit-trending:3000/;
}
```

Similar to `react-ui`, create a Docker image for the subreddits application. The following is the content of our `Dockerfile`:

```
FROM node:14.15.1
COPY . .
COPY package-lock.json .
COPY package.json .
RUN npm install
CMD npm start
```

Here, you are using a pre-built Node.js base image because the dashboard service is written in JavaScript. Build the Docker image with `"docker build -t dashboard"`.

Also, don't forget to add the application to the `docker-compose.yml` file:

```
  reddit-trending:
    image: web
    networks:
      - api_network
```

Once you have redeployed the stack with `docker-compose`, head to `localhost/reddit`; you will be redirected to the following UI:

Figure 6.34 – Trending recipes application

The application layout is broken because the `app.css` file is being served from the wrong backend. You can confirm this by opening the debug console on Chrome:

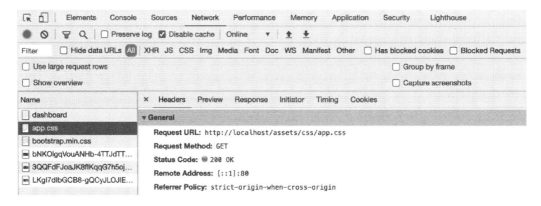

Figure 6.35 – Stylesheet location

You can force Nginx to serve the app.css file from the subreddit application container by adding the following code block to nginx.conf:

```
location /assets/css/app.css {
    proxy_set_header X-Forwarded-For $remote_addr;
    proxy_set_header Host            $http_host;
    proxy_pass http://reddit-trending:3000/assets
      /css/app.css;
}
```

Now, refresh the web page; the application layout will be fixed:

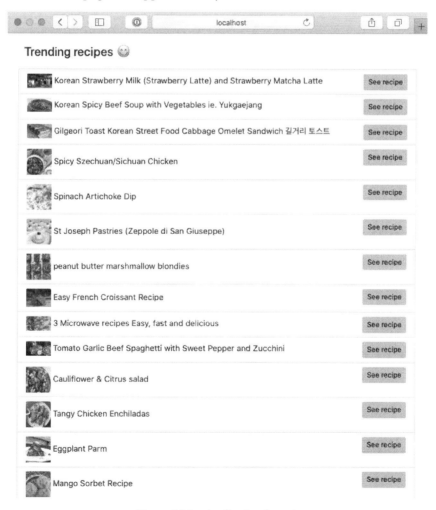

Figure 6.36 – Application layout

As you can see, the dashboard displays the recipes thumbnails. These images are then served from the backend each time you refresh the page. To reduce the stress on the backend, you can configure Nginx to cache the static files. Insert the following code snippet before the `server` section in the Nginx config file:

```
map $sent_http_content_type $expires {
    default                     off;
    text/html                   epoch;
    text/css                    max;
    application/javascript      max;
    ~image/                     max;
}
```

The `~image` keyword will handle all kinds of images (PNG, JPEG, GIF, SVG, and so on). Now, configure expiration with the `expires` instruction in the `server` section:

```
http {
  server {
    listen 80;
    expires $expires;
    ...
  }
}
```

Then, redeploy the stack with the following command:

```
docker-compose up -d
```

The images should now be cached, which reduces the number of requests hitting the backend. In the next section, we will cover how to get the same results in the backend with Gin.

Caching assets with HTTP cache headers

You can also manage caching with the Gin framework. To illustrate this, write a simple web application to serve an image. The code is as follows:

```
func IllustrationHandler(c *gin.Context) {
    c.File("illustration.png")
}


func main() {
    router := gin.Default()
    router.GET("/illustration", IllustrationHandler)
    router.Run(":3000")
}
```

The application should serve an image when the user hits the /illustration resource URL:

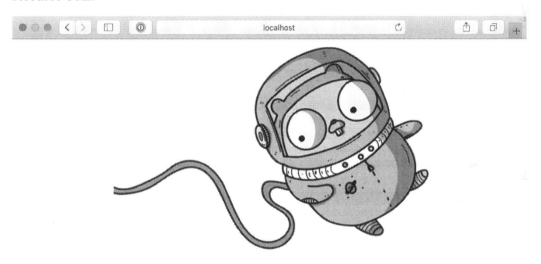

Figure 6.37 – Serving an image with Gin

Because the same image is always delivered, we need to make sure that we're caching the image. That way, we can avoid having unnecessary traffic and have better web performance. Let's see how that is done.

Setting HTTP caching headers

To cache this HTTP request, you can attach an **entity tag** (**ETag**) to the HTTP response header. When a user sends an HTTP request, the server will read the HTTP header and check if the `If-None-Match` field has an `Etag` key value. If there is a match between the `If-None-Match` field and the key that's generated, then a 304 status code will be returned:

```
func IllustrationHandler(c *gin.Context) {
    c.Header("Etag", "illustration")
    c.Header("Cache-Control", "max-age=2592000")

    if match := c.GetHeader("If-None-Match"); match != "" {
        if strings.Contains(match, "illustration") {
            c.Writer.WriteHeader(http.StatusNotModified)
            return
        }
    }

    c.File("illustration.png")
}
```

Once you've updated the HTTP handler with the preceding code, test it out. The first time you ask for the `/illustration` resource, you should get a status of 200 OK. However, for the second request, you should get a 304 StatusNotModified response:

```
[GIN-debug] GET    /illustration              --> main.IllustrationHandler (3 handlers)
[GIN-debug] Listening and serving HTTP on :3000
[GIN] 2021/03/21 - 22:47:35 | 200 |    6.019194ms |        ::1 | GET    "/illustration"
[GIN] 2021/03/21 - 22:47:38 | 304 |      7.909µs |        ::1 | GET    "/illustration"
```

Figure 6.38 – Response caching with Gin

You may also notice that the latency of the second request is shorter than the first one. By keeping the number of queries to a minimum, you can mitigate the API's impact on your application's performance.

Summary

In this chapter, you learned how to build a distributed web application using the Gin framework based on the Microservices architecture.

You also have explored how to set up RabbitMQ as a message broker between the microservices and how to scale out those services with Docker. Along the way, you learned how to maintain the service image's size with Docker's multi-stage build feature, as well as how to improve the API's performance with Nginx and HTTP caching headers.

In the next chapter, you will learn how to write unit and integration tests for a Gin web application.

Further reading

- *RabbitMQ Essentials – Second Edition,* by Lovisa Johansson, Packt Publishing
- *Docker for Developers,* by Richard Bullington-McGuire, Andrew K. Dennis, Michael Schwartz, Packt Publishing.

Section 3: Beyond the Basics

This last part will improve the API built in the previous part and make it production-ready by introducing advanced topics such as testing, troubleshooting, and monitoring. Along the way, you will automate the deployment of the API with a CI/CD pipeline and scale it up for large workloads. This section includes the following chapters:

- *Chapter 7, Testing Gin HTTP Routes*

- *Chapter 8, Deploying the Application on AWS*

- *Chapter 9, Implementing a CI/CD Pipeline*

- *Chapter 10, Capturing Gin Application Metrics*

7

Testing Gin HTTP Routes

In this chapter, you will learn how to test a Gin web-based application, which involves running Go unit and integration tests. Along the way, we will explore how to integrate external tools to identify potential security vulnerabilities within your Gin web application. Finally, we will cover how to test the **API HTTP** methods using the Postman Collection Runner feature.

As such, we will cover the following topics:

- Testing Gin HTTP handlers
- Generating code coverage reports
- Discovering security vulnerabilities
- Running Postman collections

By the end of this chapter, you should be able to write, execute, and automate tests for a Gin web application from scratch.

Technical requirements

To follow the instructions in this chapter, you will need the following:

- A complete understanding of the previous chapter—this chapter is a follow-up of the previous one and it will use the same source code. Hence, some snippets won't be explained, to avoid repetition.

- Previous experience using the Go testing package.

The code bundle for this chapter is hosted on GitHub at `https://github.com/ PacktPublishing/Building-Distributed-Applications-in-Gin/tree/ main/chapter07`.

Testing Gin HTTP handlers

So far, we have learned how to design, build, and scale a distributed web application with Gin framework. In this chapter, we will cover how to integrate different types of tests to eliminate possible errors at release. We will start with **unit testing**.

> **Note**
>
> It's worth mentioning that you need to adopt a **test-driven development (TDD)** approach beforehand to get a head start in writing testable code.

To illustrate how to write a unit test for a Gin web application, you need to dive right into a basic example. Let's take the `hello world` example covered in *Chapter 2, Setting up API Endpoints*. The router declaration and HTTP server setup have been extracted from the `main` function to prepare for the tests, as illustrated in the following code snippet:

```go
package main

import (
    "net/http"

    "github.com/gin-gonic/gin"
)

func IndexHandler(c *gin.Context) {
    c.JSON(http.StatusOK, gin.H{
        "message": "hello world",
    })
}
```

```
    }

func SetupServer() *gin.Engine {
    r := gin.Default()
    r.GET("/", IndexHandler)
    return r
}

func main() {
    SetupServer().Run()
}
```

Run the application, then issue a GET request on localhost:8080. A hello world message will be returned, as follows:

```
curl localhost:8080
{"message":"hello world"}
```

With the refactoring being done, write a unit test in the Go programming language. To do so, apply the following steps:

1. Define a main_test.go file with the following code in the same project directory. The SetupServer() method we previously refactored is injected into a test server:

```
package main
func TestIndexHandler(t *testing.T) {
    mockUserResp := `{"message":"hello world"}`

    ts := httptest.NewServer(SetupServer())
    defer ts.Close()

    resp, err := http.Get(fmt.Sprintf("%s/", ts.URL))
    if err != nil {
        t.Fatalf("Expected no error, got %v", err)
    }
    defer resp.Body.Close()

    if resp.StatusCode != http.StatusOK {
```

```
        t.Fatalf("Expected status code 200, got %v",
            resp.StatusCode)
    }

    responseData, _ := ioutil.ReadAll(resp.Body)

    if string(responseData) != mockUserResp {
        t.Fatalf("Expected hello world message, got %v",
            responseData)
    }
}
```

Each test method must start with a `Test` prefix—so, for example, `TestXYZ` will be a valid test. The previous code sets up a test server using the Gin engine and issues a `GET` request. Then, it checks the status code and response payload. If the actual results don't match the expected results, an error will be thrown. Hence, the test will fail.

2. To run tests in Golang, execute the following command:

```
go test
```

The test will be successful, as seen in the following screenshot:

```
[GIN-debug] [WARNING] Creating an Engine instance with the Logger and Recovery middleware already attached.

[GIN-debug] [WARNING] Running in "debug" mode. Switch to "release" mode in production.
 - using env:   export GIN_MODE=release
 - using code:  gin.SetMode(gin.ReleaseMode)

[GIN-debug] GET    /                         --> _/Users/mlabouardy/github/Building-Distributed-Applications-in-Gin/chap
ter7/basic.IndexHandler (3 handlers)
[GIN] 2021/04/03 - 20:06:35 | 200 |     191.499µs |     127.0.0.1 | GET      "/"
PASS
ok      _/Users/mlabouardy/github/Building-Distributed-Applications-in-Gin/chapter7/basic    0.181s
```

Figure 7.1 – Test execution

While you have the ability to write complete tests with the testing package, you can install a third-party package such as **testify** to use advanced assertions. To do so, follow these steps:

1. Download testify with the following command:

```
Go get github.com/stretchr/testify
```

2. Next, update TestIndexHandler to use the assert property from the testify package to make some assertions about the correctness of the response, as follows:

```
func TestIndexHandler(t *testing.T) {
    mockUserResp := `{"message":"hello world"}`

    ts := httptest.NewServer(SetupServer())
    defer ts.Close()

    resp, err := http.Get(fmt.Sprintf("%s/", ts.URL))
    defer resp.Body.Close()

    assert.Nil(t, err)
    assert.Equal(t, http.StatusOK, resp.StatusCode)

    responseData, _ := ioutil.ReadAll(resp.Body)
    assert.Equal(t, mockUserResp, string(responseData))
}
```

3. Execute the go test command and you will have the same results.

That's how you write a test for a Gin web application.

Let's move forward and write unit tests for the HTTP handlers of the RESTful API covered in previous chapters. As a reminder, the following schema illustrates the operations exposed by the REST API:

Figure 7.2 – API HTTP methods

> **Note**
>
> The API source code is available on the GitHub repository under the
> `chapter07` folder. It's recommended to start this chapter based on the
> source code available in the repository.

The operations in the image are registered in the Gin default router and assigned to different HTTP handlers, as follows:

```go
func main() {
    router := gin.Default()
    router.POST("/recipes", NewRecipeHandler)
    router.GET("/recipes", ListRecipesHandler)
    router.PUT("/recipes/:id", UpdateRecipeHandler)
    router.DELETE("/recipes/:id", DeleteRecipeHandler)
    router.GET("/recipes/:id", GetRecipeHandler)
    router.Run()
}
```

Start with a `main_test.go` file, and define a method to return an instance of the Gin router. Then, write a test method for each HTTP handler. For instance, the `TestListRecipesHandler` handler is shown in the following code snippet:

```go
func SetupRouter() *gin.Engine {
    router := gin.Default()
    return router
}

func TestListRecipesHandler(t *testing.T) {
    r := SetupRouter()
    r.GET("/recipes", ListRecipesHandler)
    req, _ := http.NewRequest("GET", "/recipes", nil)
    w := httptest.NewRecorder()
    r.ServeHTTP(w, req)

    var recipes []Recipe
    json.Unmarshal([]byte(w.Body.String()), &recipes)

    assert.Equal(t, http.StatusOK, w.Code)
```

```
        assert.Equal(t, 492, len(recipes))
}
```

It registers the ListRecipesHandler handler on the GET /recipes resource, then it issues a GET request. The request payload is then encoded into a recipes slice. If the number of recipes is equal to 492 and the status code is a 200-OK response, then the test is considered successful. Otherwise, an error will be thrown, and the test will fail.

Then, issue a go test command, but this time, disable the Gin debug logs and enable verbose mode with a -v flag, as follows:

```
GIN_MODE=release go test -v
```

The command output is shown here:

```
=== RUN   TestListRecipesHandler
[GIN] 2021/04/04 - 13:37:17 | 200 |    3.475079ms |                 | GET     "/recipes"
--- PASS: TestListRecipesHandler (0.01s)
PASS
ok    _/Users/mlabouardy/github/Building-Distributed-Applications-in-Gin/chapter7/api-without-db    0.185s
```

Figure 7.3 – Running tests with verbose output

> **Note**
>
> In *Chapter 10, Capturing Gin Application Metrics*, we will cover how to customize the Gin debug logs and how to ship them into a centralized logging platform.

Similarly, write a test for the NewRecipeHandler handler. It will simply post a new recipe and check if the returned response code is a 200-OK status. The TestNewRecipeHandler method is shown in the following code snippet:

```
func TestNewRecipeHandler(t *testing.T) {
    r := SetupRouter()
    r.POST("/recipes", NewRecipeHandler)

    recipe := Recipe{
        Name: "New York Pizza",
    }
    jsonValue, _ := json.Marshal(recipe)
    req, _ := http.NewRequest("POST", "/recipes",
                                bytes.NewBuffer(jsonValue))
    w := httptest.NewRecorder()
```

```
    r.ServeHTTP(w, req)


    assert.Equal(t, http.StatusOK, w.Code)
}
```

In the preceding test method, you declared a recipe using the `Recipe` structure. The struct is then marshaled into **JSON** format and added as a third parameter of the `NewRequest` function.

Execute the tests, and both `TestListRecipesHandler` and `TestNewRecipeHandler` should be successful, as follows:

```
=== RUN   TestListRecipesHandler
[GIN] 2021/04/04 - 13:39:53 | 200 |    3.525921ms |               | GET    "/recipes"
--- PASS: TestListRecipesHandler (0.01s)
=== RUN   TestNewRecipeHandler
[GIN] 2021/04/04 - 13:39:53 | 200 |    116.241µs |               | POST   "/recipes"
--- PASS: TestNewRecipeHandler (0.00s)
PASS
ok      /Users/mlabouardy/github/Building-Distributed-Applications-in-Gin/chapter7/api-without-db    0.361s
```

Figure 7.4 – Running multiple tests

You are now familiar with writing unit tests for Gin HTTP handlers. Go ahead and write the tests for the rest of the API endpoints.

Generating code coverage reports

In this section, we will cover how to generate **coverage reports** with Go. Test coverage describes how much of a package's code is exercised by running the package's tests.

Run the following command to generate a file that holds statistics about how much code is being covered by the tests you've written in the previous section:

```
GIN_MODE=release go test -v -coverprofile=coverage.out ./...
```

The command will run the tests and display the percentage of statements covered with those tests. In the following example, we're covering 16.9% of statements:

Figure 7.5 – Test coverage

The generated `coverage.out` file contains the number of lines covered by the unit tests. The full code has been cropped for brevity, but you can see an illustration of this here:

```
mode: set
/Users/mlabouardy/github/Building-Distributed-Applications-in-
Gin/chapter7/api-without-db/main.go:51.41,53.2 1 1
/Users/mlabouardy/github/Building-Distributed-Applications-in-
Gin/chapter7/api-without-db/main.go:65.39,67.50 2 1
/Users/mlabouardy/github/Building-Distributed-Applications-in-
Gin/chapter7/api-without-db/main.go:72.2,77.31 4 1
/Users/mlabouardy/github/Building-Distributed-Applications-in-
Gin/chapter7/api-without-db/main.go:67.50,70.3 2 0
/Users/mlabouardy/github/Building-Distributed-Applications-in-
Gin/chapter7/api-without-db/main.go:98.42,101.50 3 0
/Users/mlabouardy/github/Building-Distributed-Applications-in-
Gin/chapter7/api-without-db/main.go:106.2,107.36 2 0
```

You can visualize the code coverage using a **HyperText Markup Language** (**HTML**) presentation, using the `go tool` command, as follows:

```
go tool cover -html=coverage.out
```

The command will open the HTML presentation on your default browser, showing the covered source code in green and the uncovered code in red, as illustrated in the following screenshot:

```
/Users/mlabouardy/github/Building-Distributed-Applications-in-Gin/chapter7/api-without-db/main.go (16.9%) ⌄    not tracked    not covered    covered
//          description: Successful operation
func ListRecipesHandler(c *gin.Context) {
        c.JSON(http.StatusOK, recipes)
}

// swagger:operation POST /recipes recipes newRecipe
// Create a new recipe
// ---
// produces:
// - application/json
// responses:
//     '200':
//          description: Successful operation
//     '400':
//          description: Invalid input
func NewRecipeHandler(c *gin.Context) {
        var recipe Recipe
        if err := c.ShouldBindJSON(&recipe); err != nil {
                c.JSON(http.StatusBadRequest, gin.H{"error": err.Error()})
                return
        }

        recipe.ID = xid.New().String()
        recipe.PublishedAt = time.Now()

        recipes = append(recipes, recipe)

        c.JSON(http.StatusOK, recipe)
}

// swagger:operation PUT /recipes/{id} recipes updateRecipe
// Update an existing recipe
// ---
// parameters:
// - name: id
//   in: path
//   description: ID of the recipe
//   required: true
//   type: string
// produces:
// - application/json
// responses:
//     '200':
//          description: Successful operation
//     '400':
//          description: Invalid input
//     '404':
//          description: Invalid recipe ID
func UpdateRecipeHandler(c *gin.Context) {
        id := c.Param("id")
```

Figure 7.6 – Viewing results

Now that it's easier to spot which methods are covered with your tests, let's write an additional test for the HTTP handler, responsible for updating an existing recipe. To do so, proceed as follows:

1. Add the following code block to the `main_test.go` file:

```go
func TestUpdateRecipeHandler(t *testing.T) {
    r := SetupRouter()
    r.PUT("/recipes/:id", UpdateRecipeHandler)

    recipe := Recipe{
        ID:    "c0283p3d0cvuglq85lpg",
        Name: "Gnocchi",
        Ingredients: []string{
            "5 large Idaho potatoes",
            "2 egges",
            "3/4 cup grated Parmesan",
            "3 1/2 cup all-purpose flour",
        },
    }
    jsonValue, _ := json.Marshal(recipe)
    reqFound, _ := http.NewRequest("PUT",
        "/recipes/"+recipe.ID, bytes.NewBuffer(jsonValue))
    w := httptest.NewRecorder()
    r.ServeHTTP(w, reqFound)

    assert.Equal(t, http.StatusOK, w.Code)

    reqNotFound, _ := http.NewRequest("PUT", "/recipes/1",
        bytes.NewBuffer(jsonValue))
    w = httptest.NewRecorder()
    r.ServeHTTP(w, reqNotFound)

    assert.Equal(t, http.StatusNotFound, w.Code)
}
```

The code issues two HTTP PUT requests.

One of these has a valid recipe ID and checks for the HTTP response code (200-OK).

The other has an invalid recipe ID and checks for the HTTP response code (404-Not found).

2. Re-execute the tests, and the coverage percentage should increase from 16.9% to 39.0%. The following output confirms this:

```
=== RUN   TestListRecipesHandler
[GIN] 2021/04/04 - 14:03:48 | 200 |    3.404191ms |              | GET     "/recipes"
--- PASS: TestListRecipesHandler (0.01s)
=== RUN   TestNewRecipeHandler
[GIN] 2021/04/04 - 14:03:48 | 200 |    118.842µs |               | POST    "/recipes"
--- PASS: TestNewRecipeHandler (0.00s)
=== RUN   TestUpdateRecipeHandler
2021/04/04 14:03:48 c0283p3d0cvuglq85lpg
[GIN] 2021/04/04 - 14:03:48 | 200 |    55.682µs |               | PUT     "/recipes/c0283p3d0cvuglq85lpg"
2021/04/04 14:03:48 1
[GIN] 2021/04/04 - 14:03:48 | 404 |    41.665µs |               | PUT     "/recipes/1"
--- PASS: TestUpdateRecipeHandler (0.00s)
PASS
coverage: 39.0% of statements
ok      /Users/mlabouardy/github/Building-Distributed-Applications-in-Gin/chapter7/api-without-db  0.361s  coverage: 39.0% of statements
```

Figure 7.7 – More code coverage

Awesome! You are now able to run unit tests and get code coverage reports. So, go forth, test, and cover.

While unit tests are an important part of software development, it is equally important that the code you write is not just tested in isolation. Integration and end-to-end tests give you that extra confidence by testing parts of your application together. These parts may work just fine on their own, but in a large system, units of code rarely work separately. That's why, in the next section, we will cover how to write and run integration tests.

Performing integration tests with Docker

The purpose of **integration tests** is to verify that separated developed components work together properly. Unlike unit tests, integration tests can depend on databases and external services.

The distributed web application written so far interacts with the external services MongoDB and Reddit, as illustrated in the following screenshot:

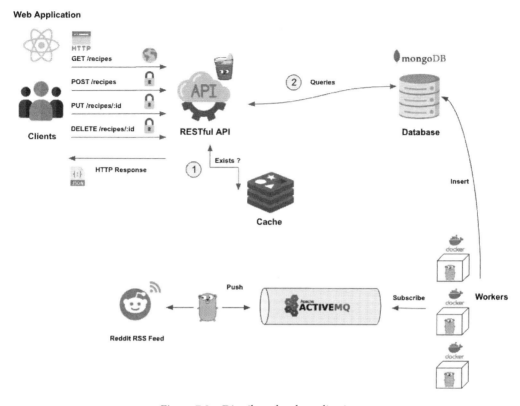

Figure 7.8 – Distributed web application

To get started with integration tests, proceed as follows:

1. Run the needed services for our integration tests with Docker Compose. The following `docker-compose.yml` file will start a MongoDB and Redis container:

```
version: "3.9"
services:
  redis:
    image: redis
    ports:
      - 6379:6379

  mongodb:
    image: mongo:4.4.3
```

```
ports:
  - 27017:27017
environment:
  - MONGO_INITDB_ROOT_USERNAME=admin
  - MONGO_INITDB_ROOT_PASSWORD=password
```

2. Now, test each endpoint exposed by the RESTful API. For example, to test out the endpoint responsible for listing all recipes, we can use the following code block:

```
func TestListRecipesHandler(t *testing.T) {
    ts := httptest.NewServer(SetupRouter())
    defer ts.Close()

    resp, err := http.Get(fmt.Sprintf("%s/recipes",
                                      ts.URL))
    defer resp.Body.Close()
    assert.Nil(t, err)
    assert.Equal(t, http.StatusOK, resp.StatusCode)
    data, _ := ioutil.ReadAll(resp.Body)

    var recipes []models.Recipe
    json.Unmarshal(data, &recipes)
    assert.Equal(t, len(recipes), 10)
}
```

3. To run tests, provide the MongoDB **Uniform Resource Identifier** (**URI**) and database before the `go test` command, as follows:

```
MONGO_URI="mongodb://admin:password@localhost:27017/
test?authSource=admin&readPreference=primary&ssl=false"
MONGO_DATABASE=demo REDIS_URI=localhost:6379 go test
```

Great! The test will pass successfully, as illustrated here:

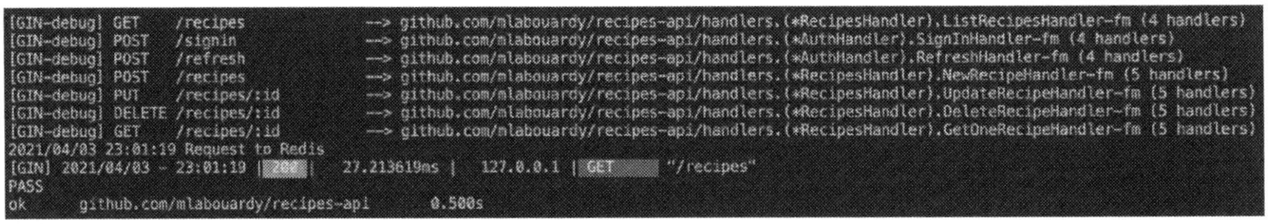

Figure 7.9 – Running integration tests

The test issues a GET request on the /recipes endpoint and verifies if the number of recipes returned by the endpoint is equal to 10.

Another important but neglected test is the **security test**. It's mandatory to ensure your application is free from major security vulnerabilities, otherwise risks of data breaches and data leaks are high.

Discovering security vulnerabilities

There are many tools that help in identifying major security vulnerabilities in your Gin web application. In this section, we will cover two tools, out of a few, that you can adopt while building a Gin application: **Snyk** and **Golang Security Checker** (**Gosec**).

In the upcoming sections, we will demonstrate how to use these tools to inspect security vulnerabilities in a Gin application.

Gosec

Gosec is a tool written in Golang that inspects the source code for security problems by scanning the Go **abstract syntax tree** (**AST**). Before we inspect the Gin application code, we need to install the Gosec binary.

The binary can be downloaded with the following cURL command. Here, version 2.7.0 is being used:

```
curl -sfL https://raw.githubusercontent.com/securego/gosec/
master/install.sh | sh -s -- -b $(go env GOPATH)/bin v2.7.0
```

Once the command is installed, run the following command on your project folder. The ./... argument is set to recursively scan all the Go packages:

```
gosec ./...
```

The command will identify three major issues related to unhandled errors (**Common Weakness Enumeration (CWE)** *703* (`https://cwe.mitre.org/data/definitions/703.html`), as illustrated in the following screenshot:

```
[gosec] 2021/04/04 17:21:38 Including rules: default
[gosec] 2021/04/04 17:21:38 Excluding rules: default
[gosec] 2021/04/04 17:21:38 Import directory: /Users/mlabouardy/github/Building-Distributed-Applications-in-Gin/chapter7/api-with-db/handlers
[gosec] 2021/04/04 17:21:39 Checking package: handlers
[gosec] 2021/04/04 17:21:39 Checking file: /Users/mlabouardy/github/Building-Distributed-Applications-in-Gin/chapter7/api-with-db/handlers/auth.go
[gosec] 2021/04/04 17:21:39 Checking file: /Users/mlabouardy/github/Building-Distributed-Applications-in-Gin/chapter7/api-with-db/handlers/recipes.go
[gosec] 2021/04/04 17:21:39 Import directory: /Users/mlabouardy/github/Building-Distributed-Applications-in-Gin/chapter7/api-with-db
[gosec] 2021/04/04 17:21:40 Checking package: main
[gosec] 2021/04/04 17:21:40 Checking file: /Users/mlabouardy/github/Building-Distributed-Applications-in-Gin/chapter7/api-with-db/main.go
[gosec] 2021/04/04 17:21:40 Import directory: /Users/mlabouardy/github/Building-Distributed-Applications-in-Gin/chapter7/api-with-db/models
[gosec] 2021/04/04 17:21:40 Checking package: models
[gosec] 2021/04/04 17:21:40 Checking file: /Users/mlabouardy/github/Building-Distributed-Applications-in-Gin/chapter7/api-with-db/models/recipe.go
[gosec] 2021/04/04 17:21:40 Checking file: /Users/mlabouardy/github/Building-Distributed-Applications-in-Gin/chapter7/api-with-db/models/user.go
Results:

[/Users/mlabouardy/github/Building-Distributed-Applications-in-Gin/chapter7/api-with-db/main.go:81] - G104 (CWE-703): Errors unhandled. (Confidence: HI
GH, Severity: LOW)
    80: func main() {
  > 81:     SetupServer().Run()
    82: }


[/Users/mlabouardy/github/Building-Distributed-Applications-in-Gin/chapter7/api-with-db/handlers/recipes.go:67] - G104 (CWE-703): Errors unhandled. (Co
nfidence: HIGH, Severity: LOW)
    66:        recipes := make([]models.Recipe, 0)
  > 67:        json.Unmarshal([]byte(val), &recipes)
    68:        c.JSON(http.StatusOK, recipes[:10])


[/Users/mlabouardy/github/Building-Distributed-Applications-in-Gin/chapter7/api-with-db/handlers/recipes.go:54] - G104 (CWE-703): Errors unhandled. (Co
nfidence: HIGH, Severity: LOW)
    53:            var recipe models.Recipe
  > 54:            cur.Decode(&recipe)
    55:            recipes = append(recipes, recipe)


Summary:
   Files: 5
   Lines: 473
   Nosec: 0
  Issues: 3
```

Figure 7.10 – Unhandled errors

By default, Gosec will scan your project and validate it against the rules. However, it's possible to exclude some rules. For instance, to exclude the rule responsible for the Errors unhandled issue, issue the following command:

```
gosec -exclude=G104 ./...
```

> **Note**
> A complete list of available rules can be found here:
>
> `https://github.com/securego/gosec#available-rules`

The command output is shown here:

```
[gosec] 2021/04/04 17:24:23 Including rules: default
[gosec] 2021/04/04 17:24:23 Excluding rules: G104
[gosec] 2021/04/04 17:24:23 Import directory: /Users/mlabouardy/github/Building-Distributed-Applications-in-Gin/chapter7/api-with-db/handlers
[gosec] 2021/04/04 17:24:23 Checking package: handlers
[gosec] 2021/04/04 17:24:23 Checking file: /Users/mlabouardy/github/Building-Distributed-Applications-in-Gin/chapter7/api-with-db/handlers/auth.go
[gosec] 2021/04/04 17:24:23 Checking file: /Users/mlabouardy/github/Building-Distributed-Applications-in-Gin/chapter7/api-with-db/handlers/recipes.go
[gosec] 2021/04/04 17:24:23 Import directory: /Users/mlabouardy/github/Building-Distributed-Applications-in-Gin/chapter7/api-with-db
[gosec] 2021/04/04 17:24:24 Checking package: main
[gosec] 2021/04/04 17:24:24 Checking file: /Users/mlabouardy/github/Building-Distributed-Applications-in-Gin/chapter7/api-with-db/main.go
[gosec] 2021/04/04 17:24:24 Import directory: /Users/mlabouardy/github/Building-Distributed-Applications-in-Gin/chapter7/api-with-db/models
[gosec] 2021/04/04 17:24:24 Checking package: models
[gosec] 2021/04/04 17:24:24 Checking file: /Users/mlabouardy/github/Building-Distributed-Applications-in-Gin/chapter7/api-with-db/models/recipe.go
[gosec] 2021/04/04 17:24:24 Checking file: /Users/mlabouardy/github/Building-Distributed-Applications-in-Gin/chapter7/api-with-db/models/user.go
Results:

Summary:
   Files: 5
   Lines: 473
   Nosec: 0
   Issues: 0
```

Figure 7.11 – Excluding Gosec rules

You should now be able to scan your application source code for potential security vulnerabilities or sources of errors.

Securing Go modules with Snyk

Another way to detect potential security vulnerabilities is by scanning the Go modules. The go.mod file holds all the dependencies used by the Gin web application. **Snyk** (https://snyk.io) is a **software-as-a-service (SaaS)** solution used to identify and fix security vulnerabilities in your Go application.

> **Note**
> Snyk supports all main programming languages including Java, Python, Node.js, Ruby, Scala, and so on.

The solution is pretty simple. To get started, proceed as follows:

1. Create a free account by signing in with your GitHub account.

2. Then, install the Snyk official **command-line interface (CLI)** using **Node Package Manager (npm)**, as follows:

   ```
   npm install -g snyk
   ```

3. Next, associate your Snyk account with the CLI by running the following command:

   ```
   snyk auth
   ```

   The preceding command will open a browser tab and redirect you to authenticate the CLI with your Snyk account.

4. Now, you should be ready to scan the project vulnerabilities with the following command:

```
snyk test
```

The preceding command will list all identified vulnerabilities (major or minor), including their path and remediation guidance, as illustrated in the following screenshot:

```
Testing /Users/mlabouardy/github/Building-Distributed-Applications-in-Gin/chapter7/api-with-db...

× High severity vulnerability found in github.com/gin-gonic/gin
  Description: HTTP Response Splitting
  Info: https://snyk.io/vuln/SNYK-GOLANG-GITHUBCOMGINGONICGIN-1041736
  Introduced through: github.com/gin-gonic/gin@1.6.3, github.com/gin-contrib/cors@1.3.1
  From: github.com/gin-gonic/gin@1.6.3
  From: github.com/gin-contrib/cors@1.3.1 > github.com/gin-gonic/gin@1.6.3

× High severity vulnerability found in github.com/dgrijalva/jwt-go
  Description: Access Restriction Bypass
  Info: https://snyk.io/vuln/SNYK-GOLANG-GITHUBCOMDGRIJALVAJWTGO-596515
  Introduced through: github.com/dgrijalva/jwt-go@3.2.0
  From: github.com/dgrijalva/jwt-go@3.2.0
  Fixed in: 4.0.0-preview1

Organization:     mlabouardy
Package manager:  gomodules
Target file:      go.mod
Project name:     github.com/mlabouardy/recipes-api
Open source:      no
Project path:     /Users/mlabouardy/github/Building-Distributed-Applications-in-Gin/chapter7/api-with-db
Licenses:         enabled

Tested 118 dependencies for known issues, found 2 issues, 3 vulnerable paths.
```

Figure 7.12 – Snyk vulnerability findings

5. According to the output, Snyk identified two major issues. One of them is with the current version of the Gin framework. Click on the Info URL—you will be redirected to a dedicated page where you can learn more about the vulnerability, as illustrated in the following screenshot:

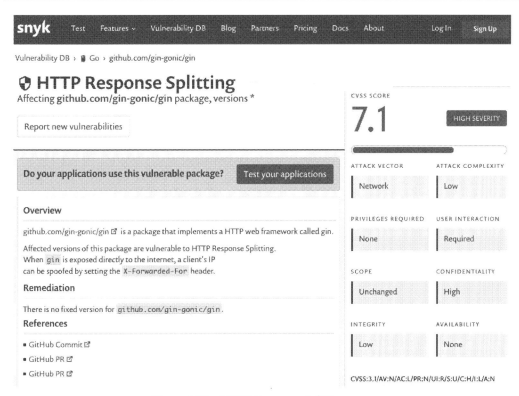

Figure 7.13 – HTTP Response Splitting page

6. Most security vulnerabilities can be fixed by upgrading the packages to the latest stable version. Run the following command to upgrade your project dependencies:

```
go get -u
```

All dependencies listed in your go.mod file will be upgraded to the latest available version, as illustrated in the following screenshot:

```
go: github.com/leodido/go-urn upgrade => v1.2.1
go: github.com/golang/snappy upgrade => v0.0.3
go: github.com/go-playground/validator/v10 upgrade => v10.4.1
go: golang.org/x/sync upgrade => v0.0.0-20210220032951-036812b2e83c
go: github.com/golang/protobuf upgrade => v1.5.2
go: github.com/modern-go/concurrent upgrade => v0.0.0-20180306012644-bacd9c7ef1dd
go: gopkg.in/yaml.v2 upgrade => v2.4.0
go: github.com/ugorji/go/codec upgrade => v1.2.5
go: golang.org/x/text upgrade => v0.3.6
go: github.com/gin-gonic/gin upgrade => v1.6.3
go: github.com/pkg/errors upgrade => v0.9.1
go: github.com/xdg/scram upgrade => v1.0.2
go: github.com/aws/aws-sdk-go upgrade => v1.38.12
go: golang.org/x/sys upgrade => v0.0.0-20210403161142-5e06dd20ab57
go: golang.org/x/net upgrade => v0.0.0-20210331212208-0fccb6fa2b5c
go: github.com/mattn/go-isatty upgrade => v0.0.12
go: github.com/json-iterator/go upgrade => v1.1.10
go: github.com/go-playground/locales upgrade => v0.13.0
go: golang.org/x/crypto upgrade => v0.0.0-20210322153248-0c34fe9e7dc2
go: google.golang.org/protobuf upgrade => v1.26.0
go: go.mongodb.org/mongo-driver upgrade => v1.5.1
go: github.com/modern-go/reflect2 upgrade => v1.0.1
go: github.com/xdg/stringprep upgrade => v1.0.2
go: github.com/go-playground/universal-translator upgrade => v0.17.0
go: github.com/klauspost/compress upgrade => v1.11.13
go get: github.com/xdg/scram@v0.0.0-20180814205039-7eeb5667e42c updating to
        github.com/xdg/scram@v1.0.2: parsing go.mod:
        module declares its path as: github.com/xdg-go/scram
                but was required as: github.com/xdg/scram
```

Figure 7.14 – Upgrading Go packages

For the spotted vulnerabilities, there's an open pull request on GitHub that is merged and available in the Gin 1.7 version, as illustrated in the following screenshot:

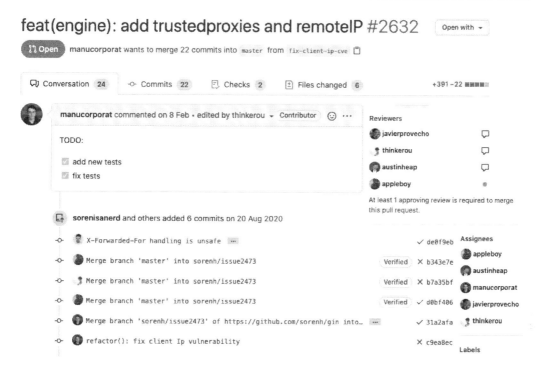

Figure 7.15 – Vulnerability fix

That's it—you now know how to scan your Go modules with Snyk as well!

> **Note**
>
> We'll cover how to embed Snyk in the **continuous integration/continuous deployment (CI/CD)** pipeline in *Chapter 9, Implementing a CI/CD pipeline*, to continuously inspect the application's source code for security vulnerabilities.

Running Postman collections

Throughout the book, you have learned how to use the **Postman** REST client to test out the API endpoints. In addition to sending API requests, Postman can be used to build test suites by defining a group of API requests within a collection.

To set this up, proceed as follows:

1. Open the Postman client and click on the **New** button from the header bar, then select **Collection**, as illustrated in the following screenshot:

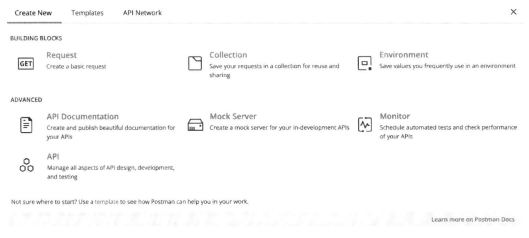

Figure 7.16 – New Postman collection

2. A new window will pop up— name your collection `Recipes API` and click on the **Create** button to save the collection. Then, click on **Add request** to create a new API request and call it `List Recipes`, as illustrated in the following screenshot:

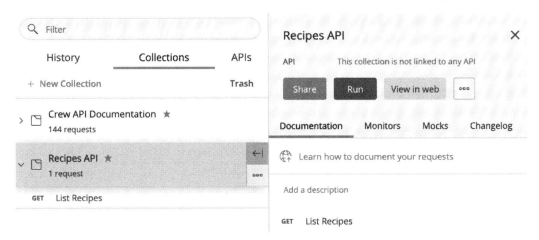

Figure 7.17 – New request

3. Click on the **Save** button—a new tab will open with your given request name. Enter `http://localhost:8080/recipes` in the address bar and select a `GET` method.

All right—now, once that is done, you will write some JavaScript code in the **Tests** section.

In Postman, you can write JavaScript code that will be executed before sending a request (pre-request script) or after receiving a response. Let's explore how to achieve that in the next section.

Scripting in Postman

Test scripts can be used to test whether your API is working accordingly or not or to check that new features have not affected any functionality of existing requests.

To write a script, proceed as follows:

1. Click on the **Tests** section and paste the following code:

```
pm.test("More than 10 recipes", function () {
    var jsonData = pm.response.json();
    pm.expect(jsonData.length).to.least(10)
});
```

The script will check if the number of recipes returned by the API requests is equal to 10 recipes, as illustrated in the following screenshot:

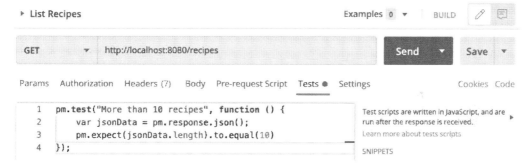

Figure 7.18 – Scripting in Postman

2. Press the **Send** button and check the Postman console, which is shown in the following screenshot:

Figure 7.19 – Running a test script

You can see in *Figure 7.19* that the test script has passed.

You may have noticed that the API URL is hardcoded in the address bar. While this is working fine, if you're maintaining multiple environments (sandbox, staging, and production), you'll need some way to test your API endpoints without duplicating your collection requests. Luckily, you can create environment variables in Postman.

To use the URL parameter, proceed as follows:

1. Click the *eye* icon available in the top-right corner and click on **Edit**. In the **VARIABLE** column, set the name and the URL, which is http://localhost:8080, as illustrated in the following screenshot. Click on **Save**:

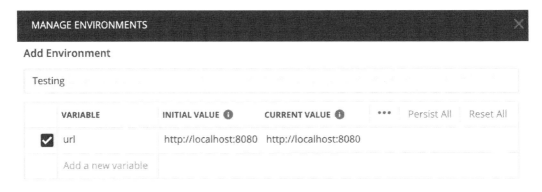

Figure 7.20 – Environment variables

2. Go back to your GET request and use the following URL variable. Make sure to select the **Testing** environment from the drop-down menu in the top-right corner, as illustrated in the following screenshot:

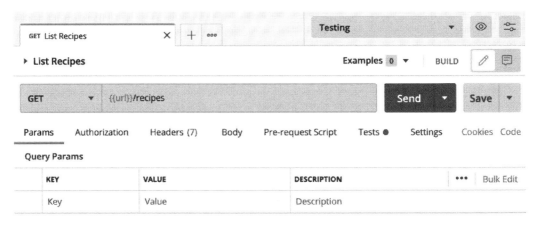

Figure 7.21 – Parameterizing request

3. Now, go ahead and add another test script for the API request. The following script will look for a particular recipe in the response payload:

```
pm.test("Gnocchi recipe", function () {
    var jsonData = pm.response.json();
    var found = false;
    jsonData.forEach(recipe => {
        if (recipe.name == 'Gnocchi') {
            found = true;
        }
    })
    pm.expect(found).to.true
});
```

4. Press the **Send** button, and both test scripts should be successful, as depicted here:

Figure 7.22 – Running multiple test scripts

You can now define multiple test case scenarios for your API endpoints.

Let's take this further and create another API request, this time for the endpoint responsible for adding a new recipe, as illustrated in the following screenshot:

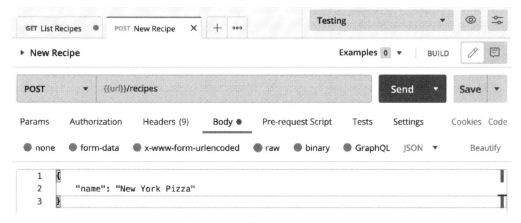

Figure 7.23 – New recipe request

To do so, proceed as follows:

1. Define a test script to check if the HTTP status code returned upon successful insert operation is a `200-OK` code, as follows:

    ```
    pm.test("Status code is 200", function () {
        pm.response.to.have.status(200);
    });
    ```

2. Define another one to check if the ID of inserted is a string of 24 characters, as follows:

    ```
    pm.test("Recipe ID is not null", function(){
        var id = pm.response.json().id;
        pm.expect(id).to.be.a("string");
        pm.expect(id.length).to.eq(24);
    })
    ```

3. Click the **Send** button. The test script will fail because the actual status code is `401 - Unauthorized`, which is normal because the endpoint expects an authorization header in the HTTP request. You can see the output in the following screenshot:

Figure 7.24 – 401 Unauthorized response

> **Note**
> To learn more about API authentication, head back to *Chapter 4, Building API Authentication*, for a step-by-step guide.

4. Add an `Authorization` header with a valid **JSON Web Token** (**JWT**). This time, the test scripts pass successfully!

5. You now have two different API requests in a collection. Run the collection by clicking on the **Run** button. A new window will pop up, as illustrated in the following screenshot:

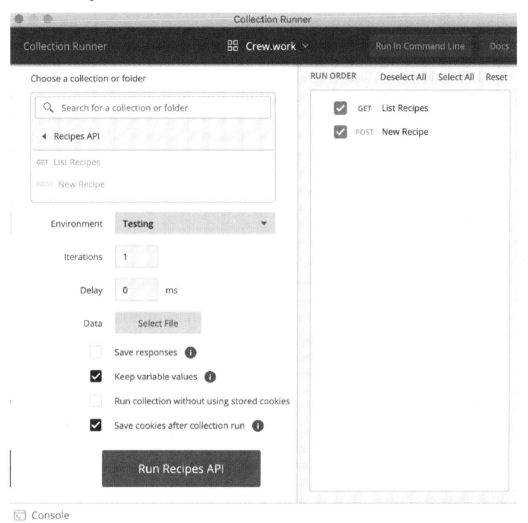

Figure 7.25 – Collection Runner

6. Click on the **Run Recipes API** button, and both API requests will be executed sequentially, as illustrated in the following screenshot:

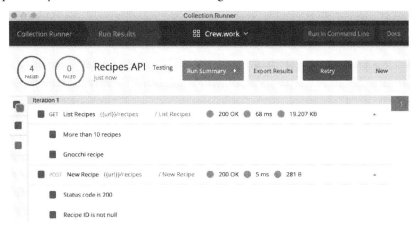

Figure 7.26 – Run Results screen

7. You can export the collection and all API requests by clicking the **Export** button. A JSON file should be created with the following structure:

```
{
    "info": {},
    "item": [
        {
            "name": "New Recipe",
            "event": [
                {
                    "listen": "test",
                    "script": {
                        "exec": [
                            "pm.test(\"Recipe ID is not
                                null\", function(){",
                            "var id = pm.response
                                .json().id;",
                            "pm.expect(id).
                                to.be.a(\"string\");",
                            "pm.expect(id.length)
                                .to.eq(24);",
                            "})"
```

```
                        ],
                        "type": "text/javascript"
                    }
                }
            ],
            "request": {
                "method": "POST",
                "header": [],
                "body": {
                    "mode": "raw",
                    "raw": "{\n    \"name\": \"New York
                        Pizza\"\n}",
                    "options": {
                        "raw": {
                            "language": "json"
                        }
                    }
                },
                "url": {
                    "raw": "{{url}}/recipes",
                    "host": [
                        "{{url}}"
                    ],
                    "path": [
                        "recipes"
                    ]
                }
            },
            "response": []
        }
    ],
    "auth": {}
}
```

With the Postman collection exported, you can run it from the terminal using **Newman**
(`https://github.com/postmanlabs/newman`).

In the next section, we will run the previous Postman collection with the Newman CLI.

Running collections with Newman

With all tests being defined, let's execute them using the Newman command line. It's worth mentioning that you can take this further and run those tests within your CI/CD workflow as post-integration tests to ensure the new API changes and that the features are not generating any regression.

To get started, proceed as follows:

1. Install **Newman** with npm. Here, we are using version 5.2.2:

    ```
    npm install -g newman
    ```

2. Once installed, run Newman with the exported collection file as an argument, as follows:

    ```
    newman run postman.json
    ```

    The API requests should fail because the URL parameter isn't being defined, as illustrated in the following screenshot:

    ```
    mlabouardy@Mohameds-MBP-001 chapter7 % newman run postman.json
    newman

    Recipes API

    → List Recipes
      GET {{url}}/recipes [errored]
        getaddrinfo ENOTFOUND {{url}} {{url}}:80
      2. More than 10 recipes
      3. Gnocchi recipe

    → New Recipe
      POST {{url}}/recipes [errored]
        getaddrinfo ENOTFOUND {{url}} {{url}}:80
      5. Status code is 200
      6. Recipe ID is not null
    ```

    Figure 7.27 – Collection with failing tests

3. You can set its value using a --env-var flag, as follows:

    ```
    newman run postman.json --env-var "url=http://
    localhost:8080"
    ```

    This should be the output if all calls are passed:

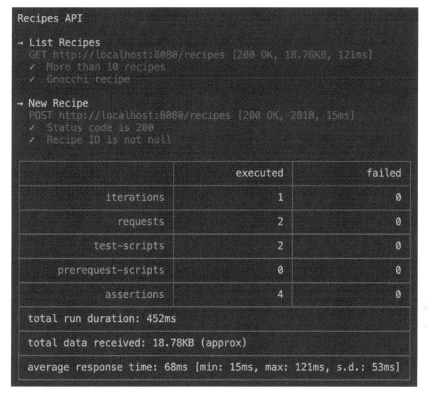

Figure 7.28 – Collection with successful tests

You should now be able to automate your API endpoints testing with Postman.

> **Note**
>
> In *Chapter 10, Capturing Gin Application Metrics*, we will cover how to trigger `newman run` commands within a CI/CD pipeline upon a successful application release.

Summary

In this chapter, you have learned how to run different automated tests for a Gin web application. You have also explored how to integrate external tools such as Gosec and Snyk to inspect code quality, detect bugs, and find potential security vulnerabilities.

In the next chapter, we will cover our distributed web application on the cloud, mainly on **Amazon Web Services (AWS)** using Docker and Kubernetes. You should now be able to ship an almost bug-free applications and spot potential security vulnerabilities ahead of releasing new features to production.

Questions

1. Write a unit test for the `UpdateRecipeHandler` HTTP handler.

2. Write a unit test for the `DeleteRecipeHandler` HTTP handler.

3. Write a unit test for the `FindRecipeHandler` HTTP handler.

Further reading

Go Design Patterns by Mario Castro Contreras, Packt Publishing

8
Deploying the Application on AWS

This chapter will teach you how to deploy the **API** on **Amazon Web Services** (**AWS**). It also goes on to explain how to serve the application through **HTTPS** using a custom domain name, and scale the Gin-based API on Kubernetes and **Amazon Elastic Container Service** (**Amazon ECS**).

As such, we will focus on the following topics:

- Deploying a Gin web application on an **Amazon Elastic Compute Cloud** (**Amazon EC2**) instance

- Deploying on Amazon **ECS** (**Elastic Container Service**)

- Deploying on Kubernetes with **Amazon Elastic Kubernetes Service** (**Amazon EKS**)

Technical requirements

To follow the instructions in this chapter, you will need the following:

- A complete understanding of the previous chapter—this chapter is a follow-up to the previous one and it will use the same source code. Hence, some snippets won't be explained, to avoid repetition.

- Previous experience of using AWS is mandatory.

- A basic understanding of Kubernetes is required.

The code bundle for this chapter is hosted on GitHub at `https://github.com/ PacktPublishing/Building-Distributed-Applications-in-Gin/tree/ main/chapter08`.

Deploying on EC2 instance

Throughout the course of the book, you have learned how to build a distributed web application using the Gin framework and how to scale the API for loading and testing it locally. In this section, we will cover how to deploy the following architecture on the cloud and serve it to external users.

An overview of the application architecture can be seen here:

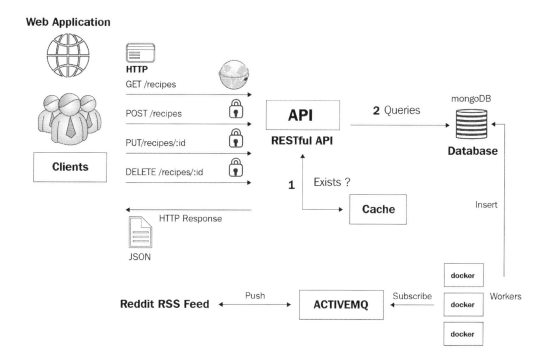

Figure 8.1 – Application architecture

AWS is the leader when it comes to cloud providers—it offers a huge range of infrastructure services such as load balancers, servers, databases, and network services.

To get started, create an AWS account (`https://aws.amazon.com`). Most AWS services offer an abundance of Free Tier resources, so deploying your application will cost you little or nothing.

Launching an EC2 instance

With the AWS account created, you are now ready to launch an EC2 instance. To do so, proceed as follows:

1. Sign in to the **AWS Management Console** (`https://console.aws.amazon.com`) and search for **EC2**. In the **EC2** dashboard, click on the **Launch Instance** button to provision a new EC2 instance.

2. Choose **Amazon Linux 2 AMI** as an **Amazon Machine Image** (**AMI**). This is the **operating system** (**OS**) that will run the EC2 instance. The following screenshot provides an overview of this:

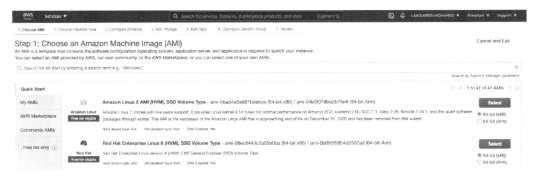

Figure 8.2 – AMI

3. Next, select an instance type. You can start with a t2.micro instance and upgrade later if needed. Then, click on **Configure Instance Details** and leave the settings at their defaults, as illustrated in the following screenshot:

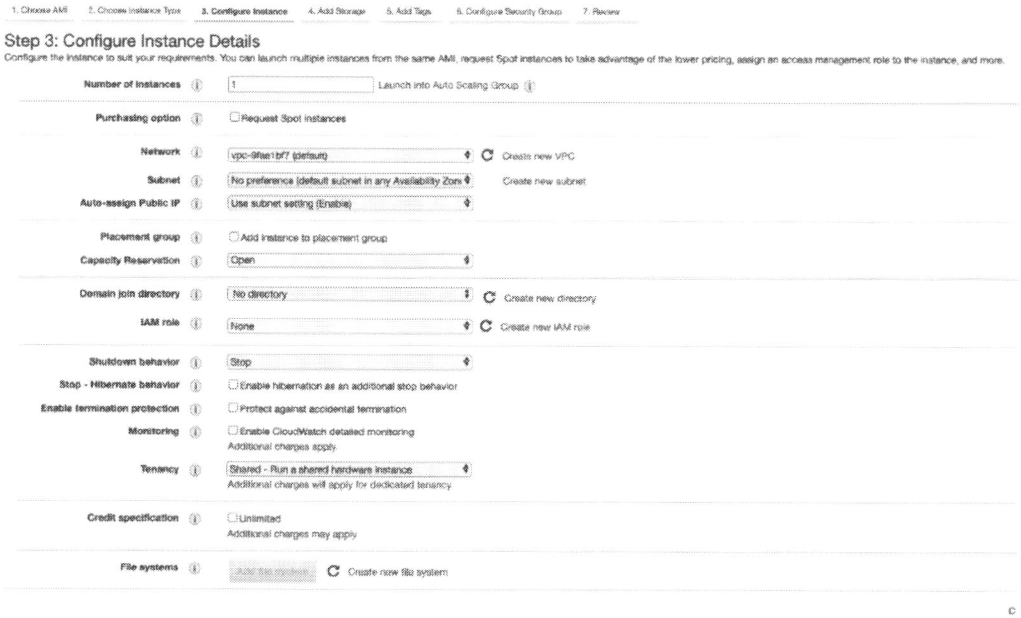

Figure 8.3 – Instance configuration

4. Now, click on the **Add Storage** button and leave the **Elastic Block Store** (**EBS**) volume size as 8 **gigabytes** (**GB**). For **Volume type**, you might change it from GP2 to GP3 or provisioned IOPS.

> **Note**
>
> MongoDB requires fast storage. Therefore, if you're planning to host a MongoDB container on EC2, an EBS-optimized type can improve the **input/output** (**I/O**) operations.

5. Then, click on **Add Tags** and create a new one called `Name=application-sg`, as illustrated in the following screenshot. Leave the security group at its default setting (allow inbound traffic on port 22 for SSH). Then, click on **Review and launch**:

Figure 8.4 – Security group

> **Note**
>
> As a best practice, you should always restrict **Secure Shell** (**SSH**) solely to known static **Internet Protocol** (**IP**) addresses or networks.

6. Click on **Launch** and assign a key pair or create a new SSH key pair. Then, click on **Create instance**.

7. Head back to the **Instances** dashboard by clicking on the **View instances** button—it will take a few seconds for the instance to be up and running but you should then see it on the screen, as per the following screenshot:

Figure 8.5 – EC2 dashboard

8. Once the instance is ready, open your terminal session and SSH to the instance using the public **IP version 4** (**IPv4**) address. Replace `key.pem` with your SSH key pair, as illustrated here:

```
ssh ec2-user@IP -I key.pem
```

9. A confirmation message will appear—enter `Yes`. Then, issue the following commands to install Git, **Docker Community Edition (Docker CE)**, and Docker Compose:

```
sudo su
yum update -y
yum install -y docker git
usermod -a -G docker ec2-user
service docker restart
curl -L "https://github.com/docker/compose/releases/
download/1.29.0/docker-compose-$(uname -s)-$(uname -m)"
-o /usr/bin/docker-compose
chmod +x /usr/bin/docker-compose
```

> **Note**
>
> The `sudo su` command is used to provide the privileges at the root level.

Here, we are using the Docker `19.03.13-ce` and Docker Compose `1.29.0` versions:

```
[ec2-user@ip-172-31-14-226 ~]$ docker --version
Docker version 19.03.13-ce, build 4484c46
[ec2-user@ip-172-31-14-226 ~]$ docker-compose --version
docker-compose version 1.29.0, build 07737305
[ec2-user@ip-172-31-14-226 ~]$
```

Figure 8.6 – Docker version

You have successfully provisioned and launched an EC2 instance.

With the EC2 instance up and running, you can deploy your **Docker Compose** stack covered in *Chapter 6, Scaling a Gin Application*. To do so, perform the following steps:

1. Clone the following GitHub repository, which includes the components and files for the distributed Gin web application:

```
git clone https://github.com/PacktPublishing/Building-
Distributed-Applications-in-Gin.git
cd Building-Distributed-Applications-in-Gin/chapter06
```

Here is the content of the `chapter06/docker-compose.yml` file:

```yaml
version: "3.9"


services:
 api:
    image: api
    environment:
      - MONGO_URI=mongodb://admin:password
            @mongodb:27017/test?authSource=admin
            &readPreference=primary&ssl=false
      - MONGO_DATABASE=demo
      - REDIS_URI=redis:6379
    external_links:
      - mongodb
      - redis
    scale: 5

 dashboard:
    image: dashboard

 redis:
    image: redis

 mongodb:
    image: mongo:4.4.3
    environment:
      - MONGO_INITDB_ROOT_USERNAME=admin
      - MONGO_INITDB_ROOT_PASSWORD=password

 nginx:
    image: nginx
    ports:
      - 80:80
    volumes:
      - $PWD/nginx.conf:/etc/nginx/nginx.conf
```

```
depends_on:
    - api
    - dashboard
```

The stack consists of the following services:

a. RESTful API written with Go and the Gin framework

b. A dashboard written with JavaScript and the React framework

c. MongoDB for data storage

d. Redis for in-memory storage and API caching

e. Nginx as a reverse proxy

2. Before deploying the stack, build the Docker images for the RESTful API and the web dashboard. Head to the corresponding folder of each service and run the docker build command. For instance, the following commands are used to build the Docker image for the RESTful API:

```
cd api
docker build -t api .
```

The command output is shown here:

```
[ec2-user@ip-172-31-14-226 api]$ docker build -t api .
Sending build context to Docker daemon  941.6kB
Step 1/10 : FROM golang:1.16
1.16: Pulling from library/golang
bd8f6a7501cc: Pull complete
44718e6d535d: Pull complete
efe9738af0cb: Pull complete
f37aabde37b8: Pull complete
c4c446e03742: Pull complete
03fadb054608: Pull complete
46075c0b6765: Pull complete
Digest: sha256:d62be43251761e201a023716ea8100c4e4ec4a5f6eecfa6911746510dfef9e7d
Status: Downloaded newer image for golang:1.16
 ---> cbf5edf38f6b
Step 2/10 : WORKDIR /go/src/github.com/api
 ---> Running in 80e6b66a7285
Removing intermediate container 80e6b66a7285
 ---> 97643050c43d
Step 3/10 : COPY . .
 ---> 550ddf1d37ae
Step 4/10 : RUN go mod download
 ---> Running in 0528d3eec44b
```

Figure 8.7 – Docker build logs

3. After building the images, issue the following command:

```
cd ..
docker-compose up -d
```

The services will be deployed, and five instances of the API will be created, as illustrated in the following screenshot:

```
Creating chapter6_api_1         ... done
Creating chapter6_api_2         ... done
Creating chapter6_api_3         ... done
Creating chapter6_api_4         ... done
Creating chapter6_api_5         ... done
Creating chapter6_dashboard_1 ... done
Creating chapter6_mongodb_1     ... done
Creating chapter6_redis_1       ... done
Creating chapter6_nginx_1       ... done
```

Figure 8.8 – Docker application

With the application up and running, go to the web browser and paste the IP address that is used to connect to your EC2 instance. You should then see the following error message:

Figure 8.9 – Request timeout

To fix that, you need to allow inbound traffic on port 80, which is the port the nginx proxy is exposed to. Head to **Security Groups** from the EC2 dashboard and search for the security group assigned to the EC2 instance in which the application is running. Once found, add an inbound rule, as follows:

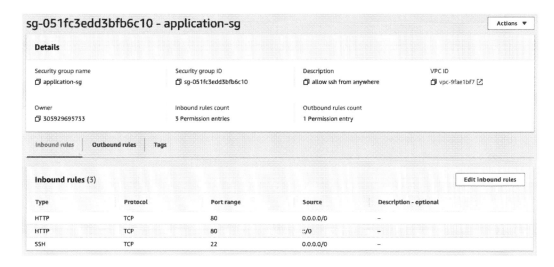

Figure 8.10 – Inbound rule on port 80

Head back to your web browser and issue an HTTP request to the instance IP. This time, the nginx proxy will be hit and a response will be returned. If you issue a request to the /api/recipes endpoint, an empty array should be returned, as illustrated in the following screenshot:

[]

Figure 8.11 – RESTful API response

The MongoDB recipes collection is empty. So, create a new recipe by issuing a POST request on the /api/recipes endpoint with the following JSON payload:

Figure 8.12 – A POST request to create a new recipe

Make sure to include an `Authorization` header in the `POST` request. Refresh the web browser page and a recipe should then be returned on the web dashboard, as illustrated in the following screenshot:

Not Secure — 52.28.238.126
Recipes
Login
Margherita Pizza
pizza dough
shredded cheese
fresh basil leaves
tomato sauce

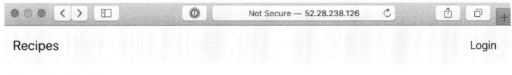

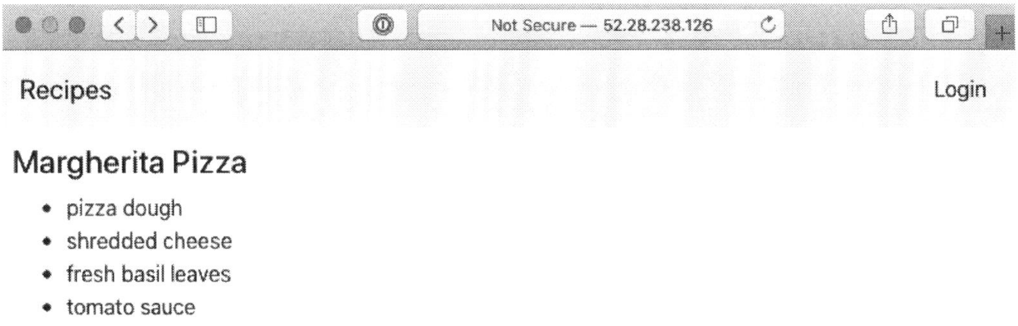

Figure 8.13 – New recipe

Now, click on the **Login** button, and you should have an unsecure origin error, as follows:

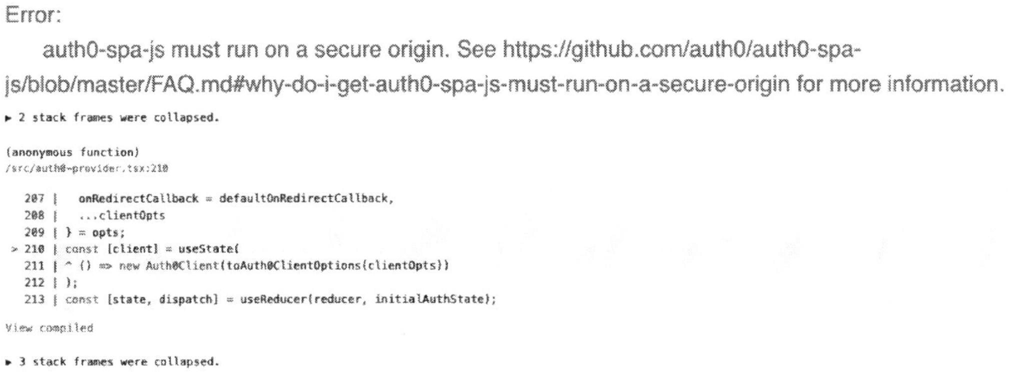

Error:
auth0-spa-js must run on a secure origin. See https://github.com/auth0/auth0-spa-js/blob/master/FAQ.md#why-do-i-get-auth0-spa-js-must-run-on-a-secure-origin for more information.
▸ 2 stack frames were collapsed.
(anonymous function)
/src/auth0-provider.tsx:210
207 | onRedirectCallback = defaultOnRedirectCallback,
208 | ...clientOpts
209 | } = opts;
> 210 | const [client] = useState(
211 | ^ () => new Auth0Client(toAuth0ClientOptions(clientOpts))
212 |);
213 | const [state, dispatch] = useReducer(reducer, initialAuthState);
View compiled
▸ 3 stack frames were collapsed.

Figure 8.14 – Auth0 requires the client to be run though HTTPS

The error is due to Auth0 needing to be run on a web application served through the HTTPS protocol. You can serve the application through HTTPS by setting up a **load balancer** on top of the EC2 instance.

SSL offloading with an application load balancer

To run the API through HTTPS, we need a **Secure Sockets Layer** (**SSL**) certificate. You can easily get an SSL certificate with **AWS Certificate Manager** (**ACM**). This service makes it easy to provision, manage, and deploy SSL/**Transport Layer Security** (**TLS**) certificates on AWS-managed resources. To generate an SSL certificate, proceed as follows:

1. Head to the ACM dashboard and request a free SSL certificate for your domain name by clicking on the **Request a certificate** button and choosing **Request a public certificate**.

2. On the **Add domain names** page, enter a **fully qualified domain name (FQDN)**, such as domain.com.

> **Note**
> The domain.com domain name can have multiple subdomains, such as sandbox.domain.com, production.domain.com, and api.domain.com.

3. On the **Select validation method** page, choose **DNS validation** and add a **Canonical Name** (**CNAME**) record provided by ACM to your **Domain Name System** (**DNS**) configuration. Issuing public certificates might take a few minutes, but once the domain name is validated, the certificate will be issued and will appear in the ACM dashboard with the status set to **Issued**, as illustrated in the following screenshot:

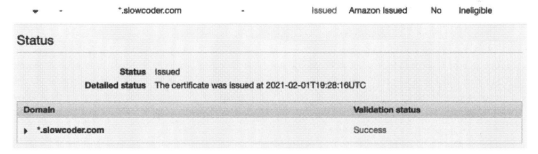

Figure 8.15 – Requesting a public certificate with ACM

4. Next, create an application load balancer from the **Load Balancers** section within the EC2 dashboard, as illustrated in the following screenshot:

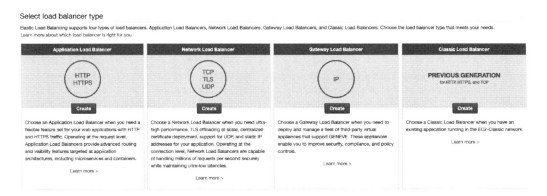

Figure 8.16 – Application load balancer

5. On the subsequent page, enter a name for the load balancer and specify the scheme as **Internet facing** from the drop-down list. In the **Availability Zones** section, select a subnet from each **availability zone (AZ)** for resiliency. Then, under the **Listeners** section, add an HTTPS listener and an HTTP listener on ports 443 and 80, respectively, as illustrated in the following screenshot:

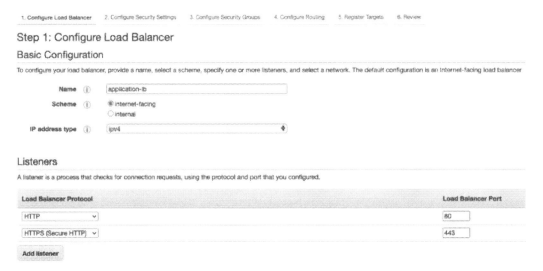

Figure 8.17 – HTTP and HTTPS listeners

6. Click on the **Configure Security Settings** button to proceed and select the certificate created in ACM from the drop-down list, as illustrated in the following screenshot:

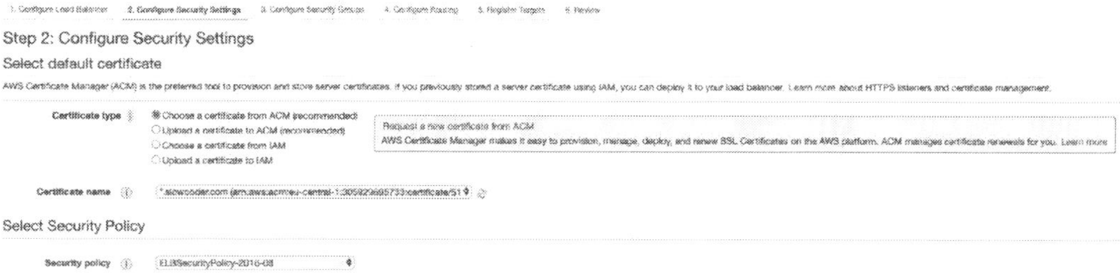

Figure 8.18 – Certificate configuration

7. Now, click on **Configure Routing** and create a new target group called **application**. Ensure the protocol is set to HTTP and the port to 80 because the nginx proxy is listening on port 80. With this configuration, traffic between the load balancer and the instance will be transmitted using HTTP, even for HTTPS requests made by the client to the load balancer. You can see the configuration in the following screenshot:

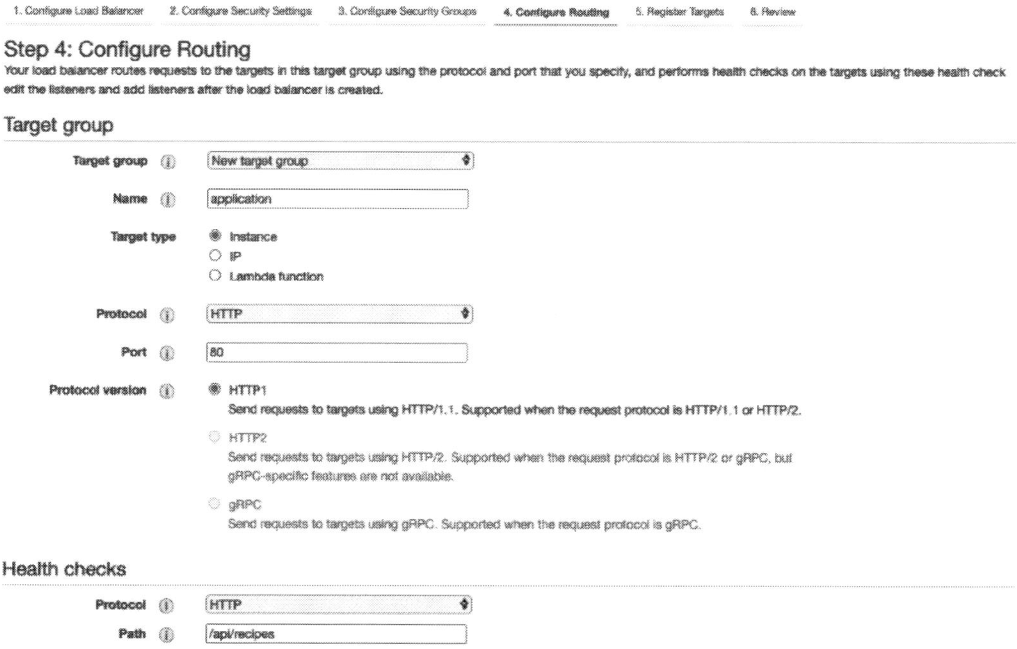

Figure 8.19 – Configuring a target group

8. In the **Health checks** section, define the protocol as HTTP and the path as /api/ recipes.

9. Click on **Register Targets**, select the EC2 instance on which the application is running, and click on **Add to registered**, as follows:

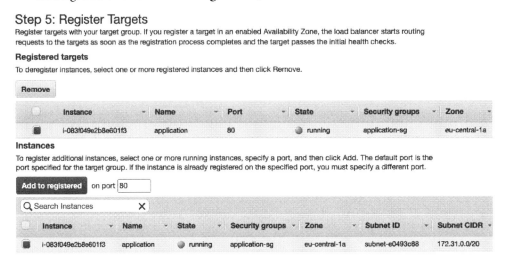

Figure 8.20 – Registering an EC2 instance

10. When you have finished selecting instances, choose **Next: Review**. Review the settings that you selected and click on the **Create** button. The provisioning process should take a few minutes, but you should then see a screen like this:

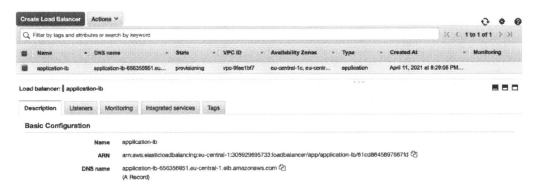

Figure 8.21 – Load balancer DNS name

11. Once the state is **active**, copy the load balancer DNS name and create an A record that points to the public DNS name of the load balancer in Route 53 (https:// aws.amazon.com/route53/) or in your DNS registrar, as illustrated in the following screenshot:

Figure 8.22 – Route 53 new A record

Once you make the necessary changes, it can take up to 48 hours for the change to propagate across other DNS servers.

Verify that the changes to your domain name record have propagated by browsing to HTTPS://recipes.domain.com. This should result in the load balancer displaying the secure web dashboard of the application. Click on the *padlock* icon in the browser address bar and it should display the details of the domain and the SSL certificate, as illustrated in the following screenshot:

Figure 8.23 – Serving through HTTPS

Your application load balancer has now been configured with an SSL certificate for your Gin application running on AWS. You can use the Auth0 service to sign in and add new recipes from the web dashboard.

Deploying on Amazon ECS

In the previous section, we learned how to deploy an EC2 instance and configure it to run our Gin application on it. In this section, we will learn how to get the same results without managing an EC2 instance. AWS proposes two container orchestration services: **ECS** and **EKS**.

In this section, you will learn about ECS, which is a fully managed container orchestration service. Before deploying our application to ECS, we need to store the application Docker images in a remote repository. That's where an **Elastic Container Registry** (**ECR**) repository comes into play.

Storing images in a private repository

ECR is a widely used private Docker registry. To store images in a private repository, you need to create a repository in ECR first. To achieve that, follow these steps:

1. Jump to the ECR dashboard from the **AWS Management Console**, click on the **Create repository** button, and choose `mlabouardy/recipes-api` as a name for your Gin RESTful API repository, as illustrated in the following screenshot:

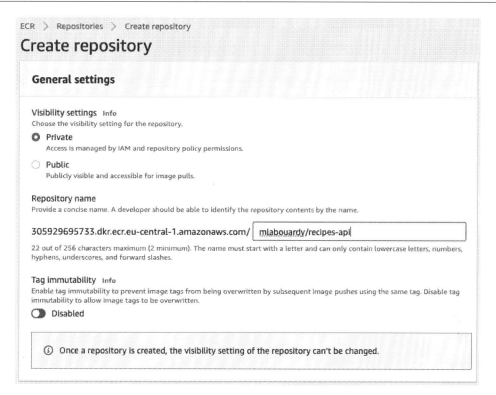

Figure 8.24 – New ECR repository

> **Note**
>
> You can host your Docker images in Docker Hub. If you go with this approach, you can skip this part.

2.   Click on the **Create repository** button, and then select the repository and click on **View push commands**. Copy the commands to authenticate and push the API image to the repository, as illustrated in the following screenshot:

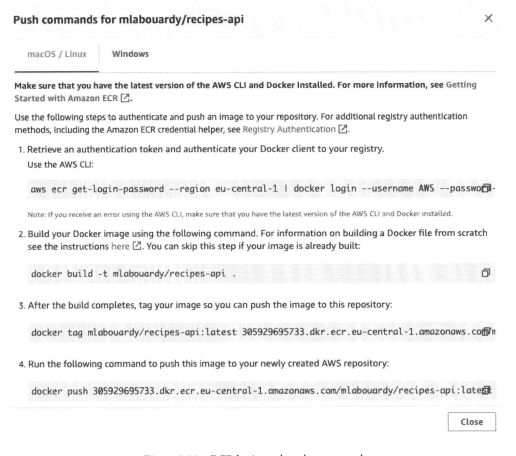

Push commands for mlabouardy/recipes-api   ✕

macOS / Linux   **Windows**

Make sure that you have the latest version of the AWS CLI and Docker installed. For more information, see Getting Started with Amazon ECR [↗].

Use the following steps to authenticate and push an image to your repository. For additional registry authentication methods, including the Amazon ECR credential helper, see Registry Authentication [↗].

1. Retrieve an authentication token and authenticate your Docker client to your registry.
   Use the AWS CLI:

   ```
   aws ecr get-login-password --region eu-central-1 | docker login --username AWS --password-
   ```

   Note: If you receive an error using the AWS CLI, make sure that you have the latest version of the AWS CLI and Docker installed.

2. Build your Docker image using the following command. For information on building a Docker file from scratch see the instructions here [↗]. You can skip this step if your image is already built:

   ```
   docker build -t mlabouardy/recipes-api .
   ```

3. After the build completes, tag your image so you can push the image to this repository:

   ```
   docker tag mlabouardy/recipes-api:latest 305929695733.dkr.ecr.eu-central-1.amazonaws.com/m
   ```

4. Run the following command to push this image to your newly created AWS repository:

   ```
   docker push 305929695733.dkr.ecr.eu-central-1.amazonaws.com/mlabouardy/recipes-api:latest
   ```

                                                                        [Close]

Figure 8.25 – ECR login and push commands

> **Note**
>
> For a step-by-step guide on how to install the AWS **command-line interface (CLI)**, refer to the official documentation at `https://docs.aws.amazon.com/cli/latest/userguide/cli-configure-files.html`.

3. Follow the commands shown in *Figure 8.25* to authenticate with ECR. Tag the image and push it to the remote repository, as follows (substitute the ID, REGION, and USER variables with your own values):

```
aws ecr get-login-password --region REGION | docker login
--username AWS --password-stdin ID.dkr.ecr.REGION.amazonaws.com
```

```
docker tag api ID.dkr.ecr.REGION.amazonaws.com/USER/recipes-
api:latest
```

```
docker push ID.dkr.ecr.REGION.amazonaws.com/USER/recipes-
api:latest
```

The command logs are shown here:

```
mlabouardy@Mohameds-MBP-001 chapter8 % docker push 305929695733.dkr.ecr.eu-central-1.amazonaws.com/mlabouardy/recipes-api:latest
The push refers to repository [305929695733.dkr.ecr.eu-central-1.amazonaws.com/mlabouardy/recipes-api]
97303b99f8d9: Pushed
5f70bf18a086: Pushed
e717bd539fbe: Pushed
cb381a32b229: Pushed
latest: digest: sha256:e64ed4d6c2923049623d0fbbfc58e75c10286cbddd8ae2ca2f58387f51b6fe23 size: 1155
```

Figure 8.26 – Pushing an image to ECR

The image will now be available on ECR, as illustrated in the following screenshot:

Figure 8.27 – Image stored on ECR

With the Docker image stored in ECR, you can go ahead and deploy the application in ECS.

Now, update the docker-compose.yml file to reference the ECR repository URI in the image section, as follows:

```
version: "3.9"


services:
  api:
    image: ACCOUNT_ID.dkr.ecr.eu-central-1.amazonaws.com/
      mlabouardy/recipes-api:latest
```

```
    environment:
        - MONGO_URI=mongodb://admin:password@mongodb:27017/
            test?authSource=admin&readPreference=
            primary&ssl=false
        - MONGO_DATABASE=demo
        - REDIS_URI=redis:6379
    external_links:
        - mongodb
        - redis
    scale: 5

dashboard:
    image: ACCOUNT_ID.dkr.ecr.eu-central-1.amazonaws.com/
        mlabouardy/dashboard:latest
```

Creating an ECS cluster

Our `docker-compose.yml` file now references the images stored in ECR. We're ready to spin up the ECS cluster and deploy the application on it.

You can deploy an ECS cluster either manually from the **AWS Management Console** or through the AWS ECS CLI. Follow the official instructions to install the Amazon ECS CLI based on your OS from `https://docs.aws.amazon.com/AmazonECS/latest/developerguide/ECS_CLI_installation.htm`.

Once installed, configure the Amazon ECS CLI by providing the AWS credentials and the AWS region in which to create the cluster, as follows:

```
ecs-cli configure profile --profile-name default --access-key
KEY --secret-key SECRET
```

Before provisioning an ECS cluster, define a task execution `IAM` role to allow the Amazon ECS container agent to make AWS API calls on our behalf. Create a file named `task-execution-assule-role.json` with the following content:

```
{
    "Version": "2012-10-17",
    "Statement": [
        {
            "Sid": "",
```

```
            "Effect": "Allow",
            "Principal": {
                "Service": "ecs-tasks.amazonaws.com"
            },
            "Action": "sts:AssumeRole"
        }
    ]
}
```

Create a task execution role using the JSON file, and attach the
`AmazonECSTaskExecutionRolePolicy` task execution role policy to it, as follows:

```
aws iam --region REGION create-role --role-name
ecsTaskExecutionRole --assume-role-policy-document file://task-
execution-assume-role.json
```

```
aws iam --region REGION attach-role-policy --role-name
ecsTaskExecutionRole --policy-arn arn:aws:iam::aws:policy/
service-role/AmazonECSTaskExecutionRolePolicy
```

Complete the configuration with the following command, the default cluster name, and
launch type. Then, create an Amazon ECS cluster with the `ecs-cli` up command:

```
ecs-cli configure --cluster sandbox --default-launch-type
FARGATE --config-name sandbox --region REGION
```

```
ecs-cli up --cluster-config sandbox --aws-profile default
```

This command may take a few minutes to complete as your resources (EC2 instances, load
balancers, security groups, and so on) are created. The output of this command is shown
here:

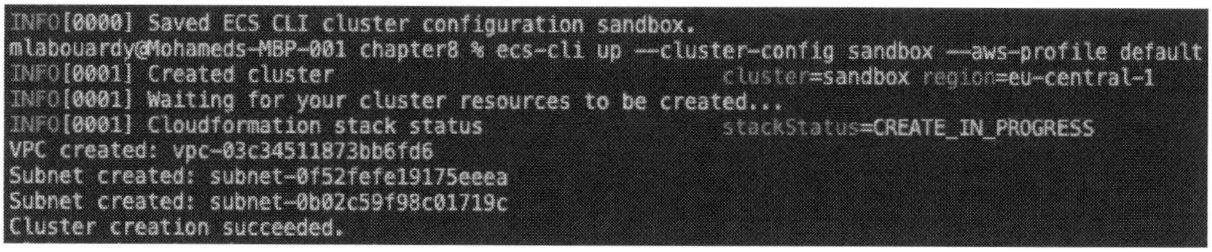

Figure 8.28 – Creating an ECS cluster

Jump to the ECS dashboard—the sandbox cluster should be up and running, as it is in the following screenshot:

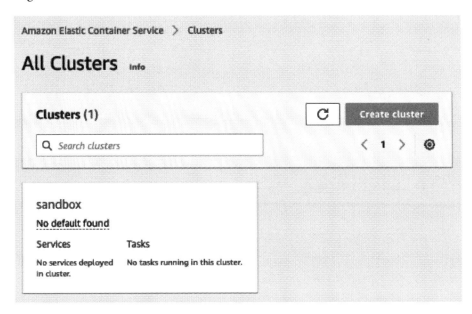

Figure 8.29 – Sandbox cluster

To deploy the application, you can use the docker-compose file provided in the previous section. In addition to that, there are certain parameters specific to Amazon ECS that you need to provide in the config file, such as the following:

- **Subnets**: To be replaced with a list of public subnets where the EC2 instances should be deployed

- **Security group and resource usage**: **Central processing unit (CPU)** and memory

Create an `ecs-params.yml` file with the following content:

```
version: 1
task_definition:
  task_execution_role: ecsTaskExecutionRole
  ecs_network_mode: awsvpc
  task_size:
    mem_limit: 2GB
    cpu_limit: 256
run_params:
  network_configuration:
    awsvpc_configuration:
      subnets:
        - "subnet-e0493c88"
        - "subnet-7472493e"
      security_groups:
        - "sg-d84cb3b3"
      assign_public_ip: ENABLED
```

Next, deploy the `docker compose` file to the cluster with the following command. The `--create-log-groups` option creates the CloudWatch log groups for the container logs:

```
ecs-cli compose --project-name application -f
docker-compose.ecs.yml up --cluster sandbox
--create-log-groups
```

The deployment logs are shown here:

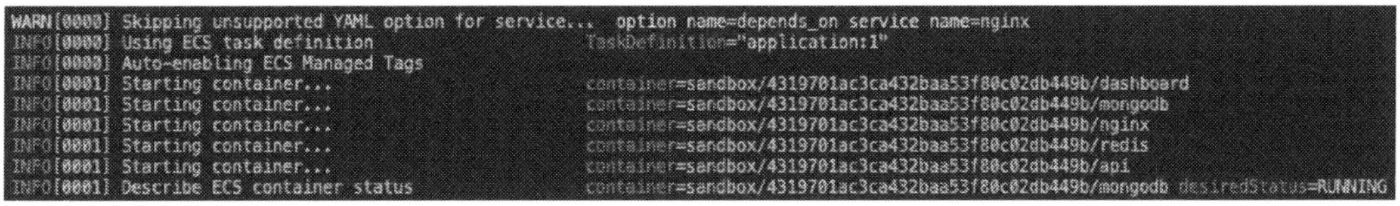

Figure 8.30 – Task deployment

An `application` task will be created. A **task** is a set of metadata (memory, CPU, port mapping, environment variables) that describes how a container should be deployed. You can see an overview of this here:

Figure 8.31 – Task definition

Using the AWS CLI, add a security group rule to allow inbound traffic on port 80, as follows:

```
aws ec2 authorize-security-group-ingress --group-id SG_ID
--protocol tcp --port 80 --cidr 0.0.0.0/0 --region REGION
```

Issue the following command to view the containers that are running in ECS:

```
ecs-cli compose --project-name application service ps -cluster-
-config sandbox --ecs-profile default
```

The command will list the containers running and also the IP address and port of the nginx service. If you point your web browser at that address, you should see the web dashboard.

Great! You now have a running ECS cluster with the Dockerized Gin application.

Deploying on Kubernetes with Amazon EKS

ECS might be a good solution for beginners and small workloads. However, for large deployment and at a certain scale, you might want to consider shifting to Kubernetes (also known as **K8s**). For those of you who are AWS power users, Amazon EKS is a natural fit.

AWS offers a managed Kubernetes solution under the EKS service.

To get started, we need to deploy an EKS cluster, as follows:

1. Jump to the EKS dashboard and create a new cluster with the following parameters:

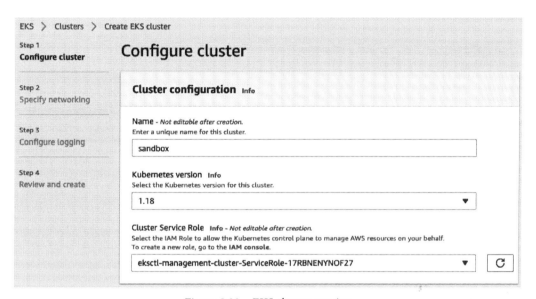

Figure 8.32 – EKS cluster creation

The cluster `IAM` role should include the following **Identity and Access Management (IAM)** policies: `AmazonEKSWorkerNodePolicy`, `AmazonEKS_ CNI_Policy`, and `AmazonEC2ContainerRegistryReadOnly`.

2. On the **Specify networking** page, select an existing **virtual private cloud (VPC)** to use for the cluster and subnets, as illustrated in the following screenshot. Leave the rest at their default settings:

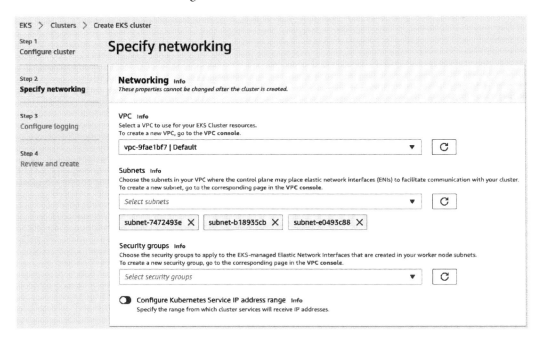

Figure 8.33 – EKS network configuration

3. For cluster endpoint access, enable public access for simplicity. For a production usage, restrict access to your network **Classless Inter-Domain Routing (CIDR)** or enable only private access to the cluster API.

4. Then, on the **Configure Logging** page, enable all log types to be able to troubleshoot or debug network issues from the CloudWatch console easily.

5. Review the information and click on **Create**. The status file will show **Creating** while the cluster provisioning process is running. Once completed, the status will become **Active**, as illustrated in the following screenshot:

Figure 8.34 – New EKS cluster

Optionally, create an EKS cluster with the EKS CLI through a single command, as follows:

```
eksctl create cluster --name sandbox --version 1.19 --with-oidc
--region REGION
```

> **Note**
>
> For a step-by-step guide on how to provision EKS with `eksctl`, head over to the official guide at `https://docs.aws.amazon.com/eks/latest/userguide/create-cluster.html`.

6. Once the cluster is in an **Active** state, create a managed Node Group on which the containers will be running.

7. Click on the cluster name and select the **Configuration** tab. On the **Compute** tab, click on **Add Node Group**. Set the group name to `workers` and create a Node IAM role, as illustrated in the following screenshot:

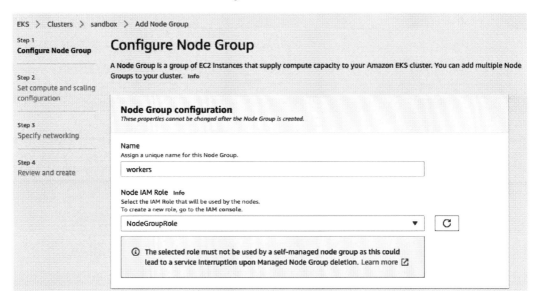

Figure 8.35 – EKS Node Group

Note

For more information on how to configure a Node Group, refer to the official documentation at `https://docs.aws.amazon.com/eks/latest/userguide/create-node-role.html#create-worker-node-role`.

---

8. On the subsequent page, choose Amazon Linux 2 as an AMI and select t3.medium On-Demand instances, as illustrated in the following screenshot:

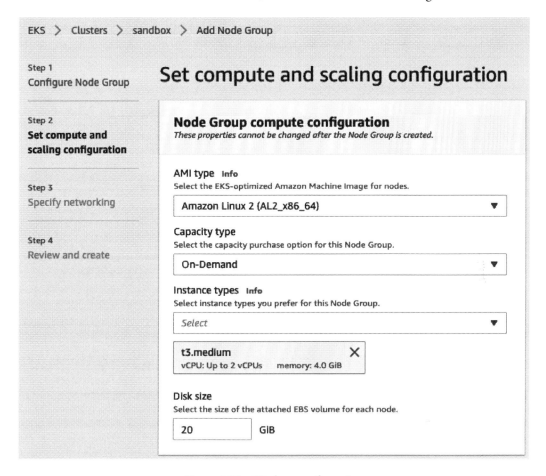

Figure 8.36 – Workers configuration

> **Note**
>
> For a production usage, you might use `Spot-Instances` instead of `On-Demand`. `Spot-Instances` usually comes with a good discount in price because of possibile spontaneous interruptions. Those interruptions can be gracefully handled by Kubernetes, leaving you with extra money.

The following figure shows how configuration is scaled:

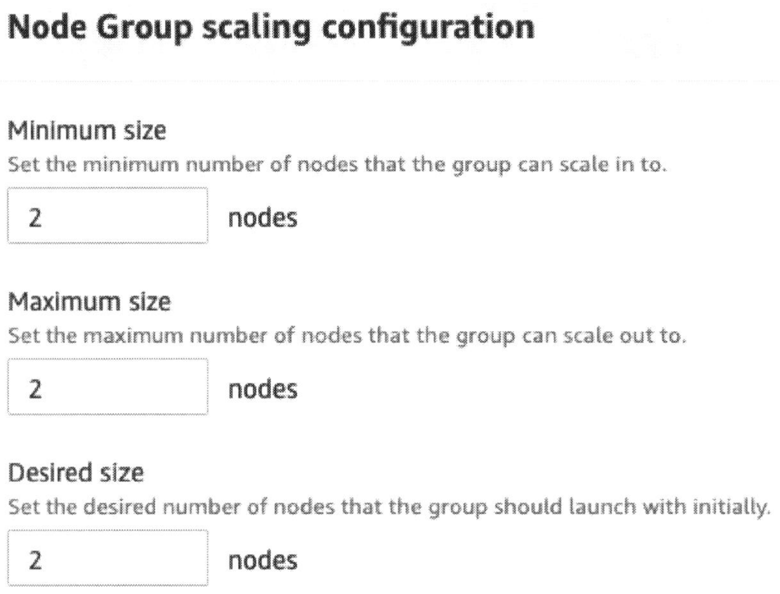

Node Group scaling configuration

Minimum size
Set the minimum number of nodes that the group can scale in to.

| 2 | nodes |

Maximum size
Set the maximum number of nodes that the group can scale out to.

| 2 | nodes |

Desired size
Set the desired number of nodes that the group should launch with initially.

| 2 | nodes |

Figure 8.37 – Scaling configuration

9. Finally, specify the subnets where the two nodes will be deployed. On the **Review and create** page, review your managed Node Group configuration and click on **Create**.

Now that you've provisioned your EKS cluster, you need to configure `kubectl`.

Configuring kubectl

`kubectl` is a command-line utility for communicating with the cluster API server. To install the utility, execute the following commands:

```
curl -LO "https://dl.k8s.io/release/$(curl -L -s https://
dl.k8s.io/release/stable.txt)/bin/darwin/amd64/kubectl
chmod +x ./kubectl
mv kubectl /usr/local/bin/
```

In this book, we are using the latest version of `kubectl`, which is 1.21.0, as you can see here:

```
Client Version: version.Info{Major:"1",
Minor:"21", GitVersion:"v1.21.0",
GitCommit:"cb303e613a121a29364f75cc67d3d580833a7479",
GitTreeState:"clean", BuildDate:"2021-04-08T16:31:21Z",
GoVersion:"go1.16.1", Compiler:"gc", Platform:"darwin/amd64"}
```

Next, generate a `kubeconfig` file with the needed credentials for `kubectl` to interact with the EKS cluster, as follows:

```
aws eks update-kubeconfig --name sandbox --region eu-central-1
```

You can now test the credentials by listing the nodes of the cluster with the following command:

```
kubectl get nodes
```

The command will list two nodes as expected, as we can see here:

```
mlabouardy@Mohameds-MBP-001 chapter8 % kubectl get nodes
NAME                                          STATUS   ROLES    AGE    VERSION
ip-192-168-52-8.eu-central-1.compute.internal    Ready    <none>   7m54s  v1.19.6-eks-49a6c0
ip-192-168-8-121.eu-central-1.compute.internal   Ready    <none>   7m52s  v1.19.6-eks-49a6c0
```

Figure 8.38 – EKS nodes

Awesome! You have successfully configured `kubectl`.

Now that you've set up your EKS cluster, to run services on Kubernetes, you will need to translate your `compose service` definition to Kubernetes objects. **Kompose** is an open source tool that can speed up the translation process.

> **Note**
>
> Instead of writing multiple Kubernetes **YAML Ain't Markup Language (YAML)** files, you can package your whole application in a Helm chart (`https://docs.helm.sh/`) and store it in a remote registry for distribution.

Migrating a Docker Compose workflow to Kubernetes

Kompose is an open source tool that converts `docker-compose.yml` files into Kubernetes deployment files. To get started with Kompose, proceed as follows:

1. Navigate to the project's GitHub release page (`https://github.com/kubernetes/kompose/releases`) and download the binary based on your OS. Here, version 1.22.0 is used:

   ```
   curl -L https://github.com/kubernetes/kompose/releases/
   download/v1.22.0/kompose-darwin-amd64 -o kompose
   chmod +x kompose
   sudo mv ./kompose /usr/local/bin/kompose
   ```

2. With Kompose installed, convert your service definitions with the following command:

   ```
   kompose convert -o deploy
   ```

3. After running this command, Kompose will output information about the files it has created, as follows:

```
INFO Network api_network is detected at Source, shall be converted to equivalent NetworkPolicy at Destination
INFO Network api_network is detected at Source, shall be converted to equivalent NetworkPolicy at Destination
INFO Network api_network is detected at Source, shall be converted to equivalent NetworkPolicy at Destination
INFO Network api_network is detected at Source, shall be converted to equivalent NetworkPolicy at Destination
INFO Network api_network is detected at Source, shall be converted to equivalent NetworkPolicy at Destination
INFO Kubernetes file "mongodb-service.yaml" created
INFO Kubernetes file "nginx-service.yaml" created
INFO Kubernetes file "redis-service.yaml" created
INFO Kubernetes file "api-deployment.yaml" created
INFO Kubernetes file "api_network-networkpolicy.yaml" created
INFO Kubernetes file "dashboard-deployment.yaml" created
INFO Kubernetes file "mongodb-deployment.yaml" created
INFO Kubernetes file "nginx-deployment.yaml" created
INFO Kubernetes file "redis-deployment.yaml" created
```

Figure 8.39 – Translating Docker Compose to Kubernetes resources with Kompose

Here is an example of a generated `Deployment` file:

```yaml
apiVersion: apps/v1
kind: Deployment
metadata:
  annotations:
    kompose.cmd: kompose convert
    kompose.version: 1.22.0 (955b78124)
  creationTimestamp: null
  labels:
    io.kompose.service: api
  name: api
spec:
  replicas: 1
  selector:
    matchLabels:
      io.kompose.service: api
  strategy: {}
  template:
    metadata:
      annotations:
        kompose.cmd: kompose convert
        kompose.version: 1.22.0 (955b78124)
      creationTimestamp: null
      labels:
        io.kompose.network/api_network: "true"
        io.kompose.service: api
    spec:
      containers:
        - env:
            - name: MONGO_DATABASE
              value: demo
            - name: MONGO_URI
              value: mongodb://admin:password
                @mongodb:27017/test?authSource=admin
                &readPreference=primary&ssl=false
            - name: REDIS_URI
```

```
            value: redis:6379
          image: ID.dkr.ecr.REGION.amazonaws.com/USER
            /recipes-api:latest
        name: api
        resources: {}
    restartPolicy: Always
  status: {}
```

4. Now, create Kubernetes objects and test whether your application is working as expected by issuing the following command:

```
kubectl apply -f .
```

You will see the following output, indicating that the objects have been created:

```
deployment.apps/api configured
deployment.apps/dashboard configured
deployment.apps/mongodb configured
service/mongodb configured
deployment.apps/nginx configured
service/nginx configured
deployment.apps/redis configured
service/redis configured
```

Figure 8.40 – Deployments and services

5. To check that your Pods are running, deploy the Kubernetes dashboard with the following command:

```
kubectl apply -f https://raw.githubusercontent.com/
kubernetes/dashboard/v2.0.5/aio/deploy/recommended.yaml
```

6. Next, create an eks-admin service account and cluster role binding that you can use to securely connect to the dashboard with admin-level permissions, as follows:

```
apiVersion: v1
kind: ServiceAccount
metadata:
  name: eks-admin
  namespace: kube-system
---
apiVersion: rbac.authorization.k8s.io/v1beta1
kind: ClusterRoleBinding
metadata:
```

```
  name: eks-admin
roleRef:
  apiGroup: rbac.authorization.k8s.io
  kind: ClusterRole
  name: cluster-admin
subjects:
- kind: ServiceAccount
  name: eks-admin
  namespace: kube-system
```

7. Save the content in an `eks-admin-service-account.yml` file and apply the service account to your cluster with the following command:

```
kubectl apply -f eks-admin-service-account.yml
```

8. Before connecting to the dashboard, retrieve an authentication token with the following command:

```
kubectl -n kube-system describe secret $(kubectl -n kube-system get secret | grep eks-admin | awk '{print $1}')
```

Here's how the Kubernetes dashboard token looks like:

Figure 8.41 – Kubernetes dashboard token

9. Run the proxy locally with the following command:

```
kubectl proxy
```

10. Go to `http://localhost:8001/api/v1/namespaces/kubernetes-dashboard/services/https:kubernetes-dashboard:/proxy/#!/login` and paste the authentication token.

You should be redirected to the dashboard where you can view the distributed application containers, as well as their metrics and status, as illustrated in the following screenshot:

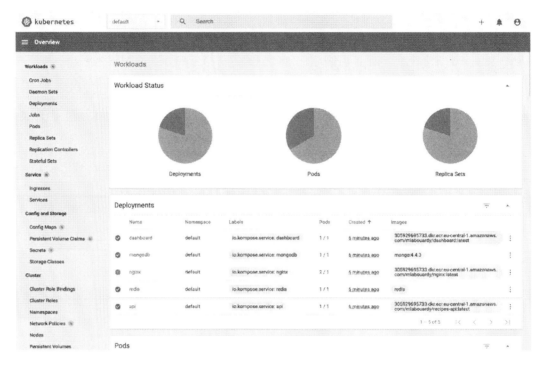

Figure 8.42 – Kubernetes dashboard

You can monitor your application running in EKS easily and scale the API Pods if needed.

> **Note**
>
> When you're done experimenting with EKS, it's a good idea to remove all the resources you created so that AWS doesn't charge you for them.

Summary

In this chapter, you learned how to run a Gin web application on AWS using the Amazon EC2 service and how to serve it though HTTPS with an application load balancer and ACM.

You have also explored how to deploy the application to a managed cluster with ECS without managing the underlying EC2 nodes. Along the way, you covered how to store the Docker images in a remote registry with ECR, and how to deploy the application for scale with Amazon EKS.

In the next chapter, you will see how to automate the deployment of your Gin application on AWS with a **continuous integration/continuous deployment** (**CI/CD**) pipeline.

Questions

1. How will you configure a persistent volume for MongoDB container data?
2. Deploy RabbitMQ on AWS EC2.
3. Create MongoDB credentials with Kubernetes Secrets.
4. Scale the API pods with `kubectl` to five instances.

Further reading

- *Docker for Developers,* by Richard Bullington-McGuire, Andrew K. Dennis, and Michael Schwartz. Packt Publishing
- *Mastering Kubernetes – Third Edition,* by Gigi Sayfan. Packt Publishing
- *Docker on Amazon Web Services,* by Justin Menga. Packt Publishing

9
Implementing a CI/CD Pipeline

This chapter will show you how to build a CI/CD workflow to automate the deployment of a Gin service. We will also discuss the importance of embracing a GitFlow approach while building a Gin-based API.

In this chapter, we will cover the following topics:

- Exploring CI/CD practices
- Building a continuous integration workflow
- Maintaining multiple runtime environments
- Implementing continuous delivery

By the end of this chapter, you will be able to automate the test, build, and deploy process of a Gin web application.

Technical requirements

To follow the content in this chapter, you will need the following:

- A complete understanding of the previous chapter. This chapter is a follow-up of the previous one as it will be using the same source code. Hence, some snippets won't be explained to avoid repetition.

- Previous experience with CI/CD practices is highly recommended so that you can follow this chapter with ease.

The code bundle for this chapter is hosted on GitHub at `https://github.com/ PacktPublishing/Building-Distributed-Applications-in-Gin/tree/ main/chapter09`.

Exploring CI/CD practices

In the previous chapters, you learned how to design, build, and deploy a Gin web application on AWS. Currently, deploying new changes can be a time-consuming process. When deploying to an EC2 instance, Kubernetes, or **Platform as a Service** (**PaaS**), there are manual steps involved that help the new changes be pushed out of the door.

Luckily, many of these deployment steps can be automated, thus saving development time, removing possibilities for human errors, and reducing release cycle times. That's why in this section, you will learn how to embrace **continuous integration** (**CI**), **continuous deployment** (**CD**) and **continuous delivery** to accelerate the **time to market** (**TTM**) of your application, as well as to ensure high-quality features shipment through each iteration. But first, what do these practices mean?

Continuous integration

Continuous integration (**CI**) is the process of having a centralized code repository (for example, GitHub, Bitbucket, GitLab, and so on) and making all the changes and features go through a pipeline before integrating them into the remote repository. A classic pipeline triggers a build whenever a code commit (or push event) occurs, runs pre-integrations tests, builds the artifact (for example, Docker image, JAR, an npm package, and so on), and pushes the results into a private registry for versioning:

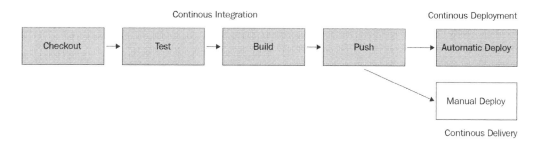

Figure 9.1 – CI/CD practices

As shown in the preceding diagram, the CI workflow consists of the following stages: **Checkout**, **Test**, **Build**, and **Push**.

Continuous deployment

Continuous deployment (CD), on the other hand, is an extension of the CI workflow. Every change that passes through all the stages of the CI pipeline is released automatically placed onto a staging or preprod environment, where the QA team can run validation and acceptance tests.

Continuous delivery

Continuous delivery is similar to CD but requires human intervention or business validation before you can deploy the new release to a production environment. This human involvement could include manual deployment, which is typically performed by a QA engineer, or something as simple as clicking a button. This differs from CD, where every successful build is released to the staging environment.

Embracing these three practices can help in improving the code's quality and testability, and also helps reduce the risk of shipping broken releases to production.

Now that you understand what these three components are, by the end of this chapter, you will be able to build an end-to-end deployment process for our Gin web application, similar to the one shown in the following diagram:

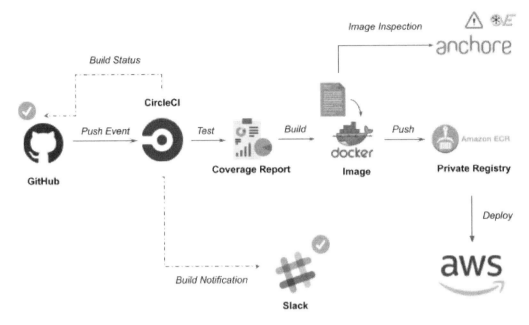

Figure 9.2 – CI/CD pipeline

The preceding pipeline is divided into the following stages:

- **Checkout**: Pulls the latest changes from the project's GitHub repository.

- **Test**: Runs unit and quality tests within a Docker container.

- **Build**: Compiles and builds a Docker image from a Dockerfile.

- **Push**: Tags the image and stores it in a private registry.

- **Deploy**: Deploys and promotes the changes to an AWS environment (EC2, EKS, or ECS).

> **Note**
> We're using CircleCI as a CI server, but the same workflow can be implemented with other CI solutions such as Jenkins, Travis CI, GitHub Actions, and so on.

Building a CI workflow

The application we built for this book is versioned in a GitHub repository. This repository uses the GitFlow model as a branching strategy, where three main branches are used. Each branch represents a runtime environment for the application:

- **Master branch**: This branch corresponds to the code running in the production environment.

- **Preprod branch**: The staging environment – a mirror of the production environment.

- **Develop branch**: The sandbox or development environment.

To promote the application from one environment to another, you can create **feature branches**. You can also create **hotfix branches** for major bugs or issues.

> **Note**
>
> To learn more about GitFlow workflows and best practices, check out the official documentation: `https://www.atlassian.com/git/tutorials/comparing-workflows/gitflow-workflow`.

The following figure shows what your Project's GitHub repository would look like:

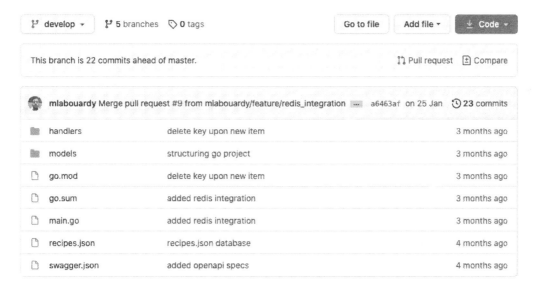

Figure 9.3 – Project's GitHub repository

You will be using **CircleCI** to automate the CI/CD workflow. If you don't have a CircleCI account already, sign up for free using your GitHub account at `https://circleci.com`. The principles of CI/CD remain the same, regardless of the CI server:

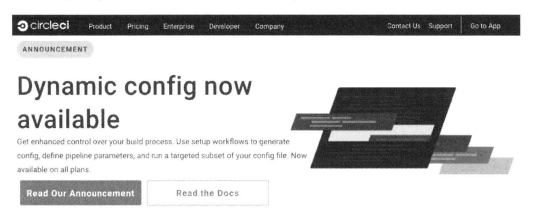

Figure 9.4 – CircleCI landing page

Once you've signed up, you need to configure CircleCI to run the application tests and build the Docker image. To do so, you need to describe all the steps in a template file and save it within the code's GitHub repository. This approach is called **Pipeline as Code**.

Pipeline as Code

When a CircleCI build is triggered, it looks for a `.circleci/config.yml` file. This file contains the instructions to be executed on the CI server.

Start by creating a `.circleci` folder and a `.config.yml` file with the following content:

```yaml
version: 2.1

executors:
  environment:
    docker:
      - image: golang:1.15.6
    working_directory:
jobs:
  test:
    executor: environment
    steps:
```

```
      - checkout

workflows:
  ci_cd:
    jobs:
      - test
```

The preceding code snippet will run the workflow inside an environment powered by a Golang v1.15.6 Docker image. Most of the CI/CD steps will be performed with Docker, which makes running builds locally a breeze and keeps our options open if we want to migrate to a different CI server in the future (versus vendor lock-in). The first job to be run is the test stage, which consists of the following steps:

```
jobs:
  test:
    executor: environment
    steps:
      - checkout
      - restore_cache:
          keys:
            - go-mod-v4-{{ checksum "go.sum" }}
      - run:
          name: Install Dependencies
          command: go mod download
      - save_cache:
          key: go-mod-v4-{{ checksum "go.sum" }}
          paths:
            - "/go/pkg/mod"
      - run:
          name: Code linting
          command: >
            go get -u golang.org/x/lint/golint
            golint ./...
      - run:
          name: Unit tests
          command: go test -v ./...
```

The `test` job will fetch the latest changes from this project's GitHub repository using the `checkout` instruction. Then, it will download the project dependencies and cache them for future usage (to reduce the workflow duration), after which, it will run a series of tests:

- **Code linting**: This checks if the code respects standard coding conventions.

- **Unit tests**: This executes the unit tests we wrote in previous chapters.

With the CircleCI config ready, let's create a project on CircleCI for the Gin application. To do so, follow these steps:

1. Jump to the CircleCI console and click on **Set up Project**, next to the project's repository:

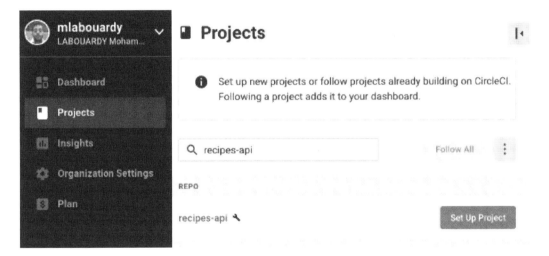

Figure 9.5 – Setting up a CircleCI project

2. Click on the **Use Existing Config** button, since we already have a CircleCI configuration, and click on **Start Building**:

Figure 9.6 – CircleCI configuration

3. A new pipeline will start; however, it will fail due to no `config.yml` file existing in the code repository. This error is shown in the following screenshot:

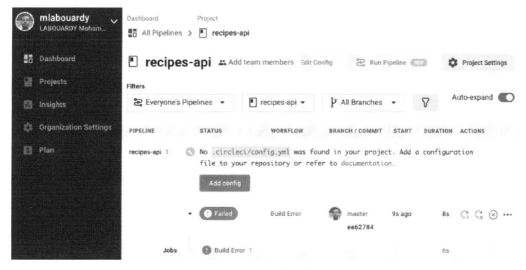

Figure 9.7 – Pipeline failed

4. Push the CircleCI configuration to the GitHub repository on the develop branch by running the following commands:

```
git add .
git commit -m "added test stage"
git push origin develop
```

A new pipeline will be triggered automatically. The output will be something similar to the following:

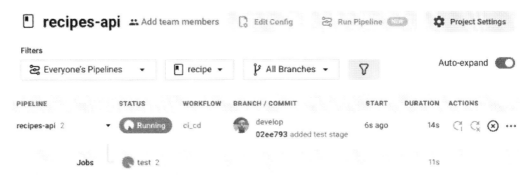

Figure 9.8 – Pipeline has been triggered automatically

5. Click on the **test** job.

    You should see the steps described in the `config.yml` file. All the tests will pass, and you will be able to build your Docker image:

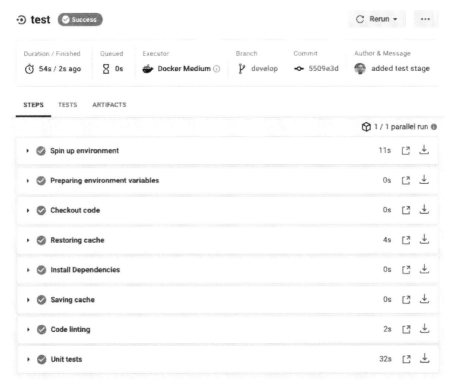

Figure 9.9 – Running automated tests

It's worth mentioning that the pipeline was triggered automatically because upon setting up the CircleCI project, a webhook was created automatically in the project's GitHub repository. This way, for each push event, a notification is sent to CircleCI servers to trigger the corresponding CircleCI pipeline:

Figure 9.10 – GitHub Webhook

Let's move on to the next step of integrating the application by building a Docker image.

6. Add a `build` job to the CI/CD workflow:

```
workflows:
  ci_cd:
    jobs:
      - test
      - build
```

7. The `build` job is responsible for building a Docker image based on our `Dockerfile`, which is stored within the code repository. Then, it tags the built image and stores it in a remote Docker registry for versioning:

```
build:
    executor: environment
  steps:
    - checkout
    - setup_remote_docker:
        version: 19.03.13
    - run:
        name: Build image
        command: >
```

```
         TAG=0.1.$CIRCLE_BUILD_NUM
         docker build -t USER/recipes-api:$TAG .
 - run:
     name: Push image
     command: >
       docker tag USER/recipes-api:$TAG
           ID.dkr.ecr.REGION.amazonaws.com/USER/
       recipes-api:$TAG
       docker tag USER/recipes-api:$TAG
           ID.dkr.ecr.REGION.amazonaws.com/USER/
       recipes-api:develop
       docker push ID.dkr.ecr.REGION.amazonaws.com/
           USER/recipes-api:$TAG
       docker push ID.dkr.ecr.REGION.amazonaws.com/
           USER/recipes-api:develop
```

> **Note**
>
> If you're interested in the Dockerfile, you can find it in this book's GitHub repository at `https://github.com/PacktPublishing/Building-Distributed-Applications-in-Gin/blob/main/chapter10/Dockerfile`.

To tag the image, we will be using semantic versioning (`https://semver.org`). The version's format is three digits, separated by a dot:

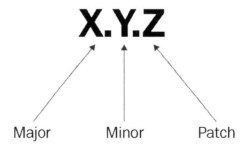

Figure 9.11 – Semantic versioning

The major version is increased when new changes break the API (backward-incompatible changes). The minor version is incremented when new features are released, while the patch version is incremented with bug fixes.

In the CircleCI configuration, you're using the $CIRCLE_BUILD_NUM environment variable to create a unique version for each Docker image that's built via the development cycle of our Gin application. Another alternative is using the CIRCLE_SHA1 variable, which is the SHA1 hash of the Git commit that triggered the CI build.

8. Once the image has been tagged, store it in a private registry. In the previous example, you were using an **Elastic Container Registry (ECR)** as a private repository, but another solution such as DockerHub can be used as well.

9. Push the changes to the develop branch with the following command:

```
git add .
git commit -m "added build stage"
git push origin develop
```

A new pipeline will be triggered. Once the test job has completed, the build job will be executed, as shown in the following screenshot:

Figure 9.12 – Running a "build" job

The following are the `build` job's steps. The test should fail at the **Push image** step because CircleCI wasn't able to push the image to ECR due to a lack of AWS permissions:

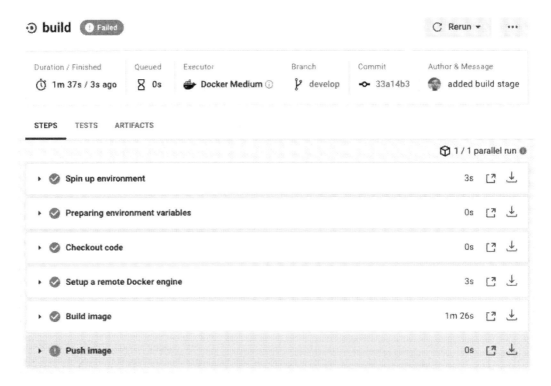

Figure 9.13 – Push image step

Let us now see how you can configure your CI and CD workflows:

1. To allow CircleCI to interact with your ECR repository, create a dedicated IAM user with proper IAM policies.

2. Jump to the AWS Management Console (`https://console.aws.amazon.com/`) and navigate to the **Identity and Access Management** (**IAM**) console. Then, create a new IAM user for CircleCI. Check the **Programmatic access** box, as shown in the following screenshot:

Add user

Set user details

You can add multiple users at once with the same access type and permissions. Learn more

User name*   circleci

⊕ **Add another user**

Select AWS access type

Select how these users will access AWS. Access keys and autogenerated passwords are provided in the last step. Learn more

Access type* ✔ **Programmatic access**
Enables an **access key ID** and **secret access key** for the AWS API, CLI, SDK, and other development tools.

☐ **AWS Management Console access**
Enables a **password** that allows users to sign-in to the AWS Management Console.

Figure 9.14 – CircleCI IAM user

3. Attach the following IAM policy to the IAM user. This statement allows CircleCI to push a Docker image to the ECR repository. Make sure that you substitute ID as needed:

```
{
    "Version": "2008-10-17",
    "Statement": [
        {
            "Sid": "AllowPush",
            "Effect": "Allow",
            "Principal": {
                "AWS": [
                    "arn:aws:iam::ID:circleci/
                                    push-pull-user-1"
                ]
            },
            "Action": [
                "ecr:PutImage",
                "ecr:InitiateLayerUpload",
                "ecr:UploadLayerPart",
                "ecr:CompleteLayerUpload"
```

```
            ]
        }
    ]
}
```

4. Once the IAM user has been created, create an access key from the **Security credentials** tab. Then, head back to the CircleCI dashboard and jump to **Project Settings**:

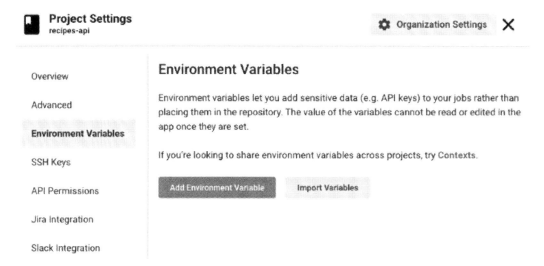

Figure 9.15 – CircleCI environment variables

5. Under the **Environment Variables** section, click on the **Add Environment Variable** button and add the following variables:

    AWS_ACCESS_KEY_ID: Specifies an AWS access key associated with the CircleCI IAM user.

    AWS_SECRET_ACCESS_KEY: Specifies an AWS secret access key associated with the CircleCI IAM user.

    AWS_DEFAULT_REGION: Specifies the AWS region where the ECR repository is located:

Name	Value	Add Environment Variable	Import Variables
AWS_ACCESS_KEY_ID	xxxx4TKE		✕
AWS_DEFAULT_REGION	xxxxal-1		✕
AWS_SECRET_ACCESS_KEY	xxxxUolq		✕

Figure 9.16 – AWS credentials as environment variables

6. Once the environment variables have been set up, update the CircleCI configuration by adding an instruction to authenticate with ECR, before executing the `docker push` commands. The new changes will look as follows:

```
-run:
    name: Push image
    command: |
        TAG=0.1.$CIRCLE_BUILD_NUM
      docker tag USER/recipes-api:$TAG
          ID.dkr.ecr.REGION.amazonaws.com/USER/
          recipes-api:$TAG
      docker tag USER/recipes-api:$TAG ID.dkr.ecr.
          REGION.amazonaws.com/USER/
          recipes-api:develop
      aws ecr get-login-password --region REGION |
          docker login --username AWS --password-
          stdin ID.dkr.ecr.REGION.amazonaws.com
      docker push ID.dkr.ecr.REGION.amazonaws.com
          /USER/recipes-api:$TAG
    docker push ID.dkr.ecr.REGION.amazonaws.com
          /USER/recipes-api:develop
```

7. Substitute the USER, ID, and REGION variables appropriately with your own values and, once again, push the changes to the remote repository, under the develop branch:

```
git add .
git commit -m "authenticate with ecr"
git push origin develop
```

> **Note**
>
> Instead of hardcoding the USER, ID, and REGION values in the configuration file, you can pass their values as environment variables from the CircleCI project settings.

A new pipeline will be triggered. This time, the build job should be successful, and you should see something similar to the following:

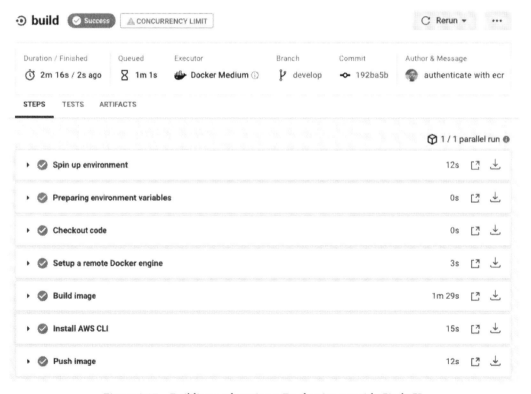

Figure 9.17 – Building and storing a Docker image with CircleCI

Now, click on the **Push image** step. You should see logs that confirm that the image has been stored in ECR:

Figure 9.18 – Docker tag and push logs

For each image of the application built with CI, there will also be a corresponding tag in the ECR repository:

ECR > Repositories > mlabouardy/recipes-api

mlabouardy/recipes-api

Image tag	Pushed at	Size (MB)	Image URI	Digest	Scan status	Vulnerabilities
develop, 0.1.28	10 May 2021 00:29:41	12.96	Copy URI	sha256:26f4de326845effe0afe7c2dea3af40...	-	-

Figure 9.19 – Docker image in ECR

Note

In addition to the dynamically built version, we're storing a `develop` tag that points to the latest built image in the develop branch.

With the test and build stages being automated, you can go even further and automate the deployment process as well.

8. Similar to the previous jobs, add a `deploy` job to the current workflow:

```
workflows:
  ci_cd:
    jobs:
      - test
      - build
      - deploy
```

The `deploy` job will simply use the `docker-compose.yml` file we covered in the previous chapter to deploy the application stack on an EC2 instance. The file will look as follows (the full YAML file has been cropped for brevity):

```
version: "3"

services:
  api:
    image: ID.dkr.ecr.REGION.amazonaws.com/USER/
           recipes-api:develop
    environment:
      - MONGO_URI=mongodb://admin:password@mongodb
          :27017/test?authSource=admin
          &readPreference=primary&ssl=false
      - MONGO_DATABASE=demo
      - REDIS_URI=redis:6379
    external_links:
      - mongodb
      - redis

  redis:
    image: redis

  mongodb:
    image: mongo:4.4.3
    environment:
```

```
            - MONGO_INITDB_ROOT_USERNAME=admin
            - MONGO_INITDB_ROOT_PASSWORD=password
```

9. To deploy the new changes to the EC2 instance where the containers are running, you will have to SSH to the remote server and issue two `docker-compose` commands – `pull` and `up`:

```
deploy:
    executor: environment
    steps:
      - checkout
      - run:
          name: Deploy with Docker Compose
          command: |
              ssh -oStrictHostKeyChecking=no ec2-user@IP
                  docker-compose pull && docker-compose up
 -d
```

10. Make sure that you substitute the `IP` variable with the IP or the DNS name of the EC2 instance where the sandbox environment is running.

11. To SSH to the EC2 instance, add the SSH key pair you used to deploy the EC2 instance in AWS to your CircleCI project settings. Under **SSH Keys**, click on **Add SSH Key** and paste the content of the SSH key pair:

Additional SSH Keys

Add keys to the build VMs that you need to deploy to your machines. If the hostname field is blank, the key will be used for all hosts.

Hostname	Fingerprint	Add SSH Key
3.66.175.83	72:6a:2f:bb:61:d3:08:3f:7e:d0:81:ac:64:ea:85:5b	✕

Figure 9.20 – Adding an SSH key pair

12. Commit and push the new CircleCI config to GitHub with the following commands:

```
git add .
git commit -m "added deploy stage"
git push origin develop
```

A new pipeline will be triggered, and the test, build, and deploy jobs will be executed sequentially. At the end of the **deploy** job, the newly built image will be deployed to the sandbox environment:

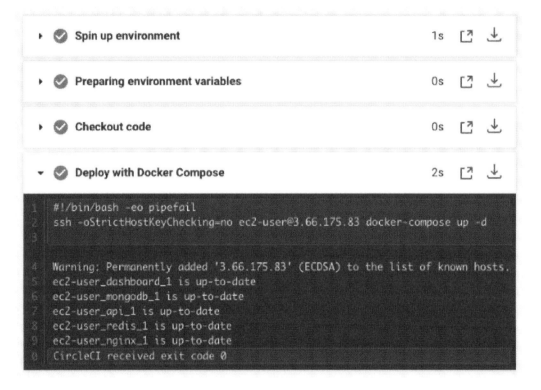

Figure 9.21 – Continuous deployment

If you're running **Elastic Container Service** (**ECS**), you can force ECS to pull the new image with the following CircleCI config:

```
version: 2.1

orbs:
  aws-ecs: circleci/aws-ecs@0.0.11
```

```
workflows:
ci_cd:
  jobs:
    - test
    - build
    - aws-ecs/deploy-service-update:
        aws-region: AWS_DEFAULT_REGION
        family: 'demo'
        cluster-name: 'sandbox'
        container-image-name-updates:
            'container=api,tag=0.1.${CIRCLE_BUILD_NUM}'
```

> **Note**
>
> Make sure that you assign ECS permissions to the CircleCI IAM user to perform the task update successfully.

The major change is that we're using CircleCI orbs instead of Docker images as a runtime environment. By using orbs, we can use pre-built commands, which reduces the lines of code in our config file. The deploy job will deploy the updated image to a sandbox ECS cluster.

If you're running Kubernetes, you can use the following CircleCI specification file to update the image:

```
version: 2.1
orbs:
  aws-eks: circleci/aws-eks@0.2.0
  kubernetes: circleci/kubernetes@0.3.0

jobs:
  deploy:
    executor: aws-eks/python3
    steps:
      - checkout
      - aws-eks/update-kubeconfig-with-authenticator:
          cluster-name: sandbox
          install-kubectl: true
          aws-region: AWS_REGION
```

```
        - kubernetes/create-or-update-resource:
            resource-file-path: "deployment/
            api.deployment.yaml"
            get-rollout-status: true
            resource-name: deployment/api
        - kubernetes/create-or-update-resource:
            resource-file-path: "deployment/api.service.
  yaml"


workflows:
  ci_cd:
    jobs:
      - test
      - build
      - deploy
```

With your CI and CD workflows configured, you can test them out by building a new feature for the Gin RESTful API. You can do so by implementing the following steps:

1. Update the `main.go` file and expose a new endpoint on the `/version` resource using the Gin router. The endpoint will display the running API version:

```
router.GET("/version", VersionHandler)
```

The HTTP handler is self-explanatory; it returns the value of the `API_VERSION` environment variable:

```
func VersionHandler(c *gin.Context) {
    c.JSON(http.StatusOK, gin.H{"version": os.Getenv(
        "API_VERSION")})
}
```

2. To inject the environment variable dynamically, you can use the Docker arguments feature, which allows you to pass values at build time. Update our `Dockerfile` and declare `API_VERSION` as a build argument and environment variable:

```
FROM golang:1.16
WORKDIR /go/src/github.com/api
COPY . .
RUN go mod download
RUN CGO_ENABLED=0 GOOS=linux go build -a -installsuffix
cgo -o app .

FROM alpine:latest
ARG API_VERSION
ENV API_VERSION=$API_VERSION
RUN apk --no-cache add ca-certificates
WORKDIR /root/
COPY --from=0 /go/src/github.com/api/app .
CMD ["./app"]
```

3. Next, update the `Build image` step by injecting the `$TAG` variable as a value for the `API_VERSION` build argument:

```
run:
    name: Build image
    command: |
        TAG=0.1.$CIRCLE_BUILD_NUM
        docker build -t mlabouardy/
            recipes-api:$TAG --build-arg API_VERSION=${TAG}
        .
```

4. Push the new changes to the develop branch with the following code:

```
git add .
git commit -m "inject api version"
git push origin develop
```

A build will start to run as soon as we push. Once the CI pipeline has finished and produced a success message, the `deploy` job will run and deploy the application on EC2:

```bash
#!/bin/bash -eo pipefail
ssh -oStrictHostKeyChecking=no ec2-user@3.66.175.83 "docker-compose pull && docker-compose up -d"

Warning: Permanently added '3.66.175.83' (ECDSA) to the list of known hosts.
Pulling api          ...
Pulling dashboard ...
Pulling redis        ...
Pulling mongodb   ...
Pulling nginx        ...
Pulling nginx        ... pulling from mlabouardy/nginx
Pulling nginx        ... digest: sha256:b800f73c1f2163829c...
Pulling nginx        ... status: image is up to date for 3...
Pulling dashboard ... pulling from mlabouardy/dashboard
Pulling nginx        ... done
Pulling dashboard ... digest: sha256:b19fc80f86185eba6c...
Pulling dashboard ... status: image is up to date for 3...
Pulling dashboard ... done
Pulling api          ... pulling from mlabouardy/recipes-api
Pulling api          ... already exists
Pulling api          ... pulling fs layer
Pulling api          ... pulling fs layer
Pulling api          ... downloading (3.0%)
Pulling api          ... download complete
Pulling api          ... extracting (11.7%)
Pulling api          ... downloading (1.0%)
Pulling api          ... extracting (100.0%)
Pulling api          ... extracting (100.0%)
Pulling api          ... pull complete
Pulling api          ... downloading (51.9%)
Pulling api          ... verifying checksum
Pulling api          ... download complete
```

Figure 9.22 – Deploying Docker Stack

5. To test out the new changes, navigate to the instance IP address and point your browser to the `/api/version` resource path:

```
←  →  C    ⚠ Not Secure | 3.66.175.83/api/version

⠿ Apps   📁 Personal   📁 Crew   📁 DevOps Bulletin

{"version":"0.1.38"}
```

Figure 9.23 – API running version

This will return the version of the running Docker image of the Gin RESTful API.

It's worth mentioning that the current CirlceCI config doesn't guarantee the jobs will always run in the same order (test -> build -> deploy). To maintain the CI/CD order, use the `requires` keyword, as follows:

```
workflows:
  ci_cd:
    jobs:
      - test
      - build:
        requires:
          - test
      - deploy:
        requires:
          - test
          - build
```

This way, you can ensure the deploy job is only executed if both the test and build jobs are successful:

Figure 9.24 – CI/CD workflow

Awesome! Now, we have a complete CI/CD pipeline for our Gin application.

Maintaining multiple runtime environments

In a real-world scenario, you'll need multiple environments to avoid pushing broken features or major bugs to a sandbox or staging environment (or worse, a production environment) before validating them.

You can create an EC2 instance to host the staging environment by running a new EC2 instance based on the sandbox environment we created in previous chapters:

1. Select the **sandbox** instance and click on **Actions** from the action bar. Then, click on **Launch more like this** from the **Image and template** drop-down list:

Figure 9.25 – Replicating the sandbox environment

This option will automatically populate the Amazon EC2 launch wizard with configuration details from the selected instance.

2. Update the Name tag value to staging and click on **Launch** to provision the instance:

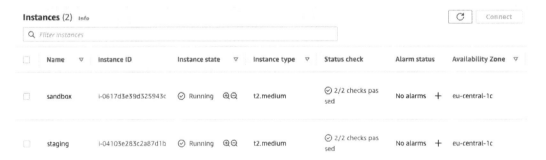

Figure 9.26 – Staging environment running in an EC2 instance

3. Once the instance is up and running, update CircleCI so that it tags the Docker image based on the branch name where the pipeline is running. In addition to the `dynamic` tag we created via the `CIRCLE_BUILD_NUM` environment variable, push a `fixed` tag (develop, preprod, or master) if the current branch is either develop, preprod, or master:

```
run:
    name: Push image
    command: |
        TAG=0.1.$CIRCLE_BUILD_NUM
        aws ecr get-login-password --region REGION | docker
            login --username AWS --password-stdin
            ID.dkr.ecr.REGION.amazonaws.com
        docker tag USER/recipes-api:$TAG
            ID.dkr.ecr.REGION.amazonaws.com/USER/recipes-
api:$TAG
        docker push ID.dkr.ecr.REGION.amazonaws.com/
            USER/recipes-api:$TAG
        if [ "${CIRCLE_BRANCH}" == "master" ] || [
            "${CIRCLE_BRANCH}" == "preprod" ] || [
            "${CIRCLE_BRANCH}" == "develop" ];
    then
            docker tag USER/recipes-api:$TAG
                ID.dkr.ecr.REGION.amazonaws.com/USER/
                recipes-api:${CIRCLE_BRANCH}
                docker push ID.dkr.ecr.REGION.amazonaws.com/
                    USER/recipes-api:${CIRCLE_BRANCH}
        fi
```

4. Next, update the `deploy` job so that you can SSH it to the right EC2 instance IP address based on the current Git branch name:

```
run:
    name: Deploy with Docker Compose
    command: |
        if [ "${CIRCLE_BRANCH}" == "master" ]
        then
            ssh -oStrictHostKeyChecking=no ec2-user@IP_PROD
```

```
            "docker-compose pull && docker-compose up -d"
    elif [ "${CIRCLE_BRANCH}" == "preprod" ]
    then
        ssh -oStrictHostKeyChecking=no
            ec2-user@IP_STAGING
            "docker-compose pull && docker-compose up -d"
    else
        ssh -oStrictHostKeyChecking=no
            ec2-user@IP_SANDBOX
            "docker-compose pull && docker-compose up -d"
    fi
```

> **Note**
>
> The IP addresses (IP_PROD, IP_STAGING, and IP_SANDBOX) should be
> defined as environment variables in the CircleCI project's settings.

5. Finally, update the workflow so that it deploys the changes, but only if the current
    Git branch is a develop, preprod, or master branch:

```
workflows:
  ci_cd:
    jobs:
      - test
      - build:
          requires:
            - test
      - deploy:
          requires:
            - test
            - build
          filters:
            branches:
              only:
                - develop
                - preprod
                - master
```

6. Commit and store the changes in GitHub using the following commands:

```
git add .
git commit -m "continuous deployment"
git push origin develop
```

A new pipeline will be triggered automatically on the develop branch, where the changes will be deployed to a sandbox environment:

Figure 9.27 – Deploying to a sandbox environment

Once the new changes have been validated in the sandbox environment, you should be ready to promote the code to the staging environment.

To deploy to the staging environment, follow these steps:

1. Create a **pull request** (**PR**) to merge the develop branch into the preprod branch, as follows:

Figure 9.28 – Creating a pull request

Notice that the PR is ready to be merged because all the checks have passed:

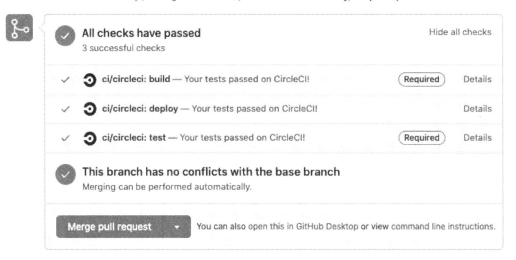

Figure 9.29 – Successful Git checks

2. Click on the **Merge pull request** button. A new pipeline will be triggered on the preprod branch and three jobs – **test**, **build**, and **deploy** – will be executed one by one:

Figure 9.30 – Deploying to a staging environment

3. At the end of the **build** stage, a new image from the preprod branch, as well as its CircleCI build number, will be stored in the ECR repository, as follows:

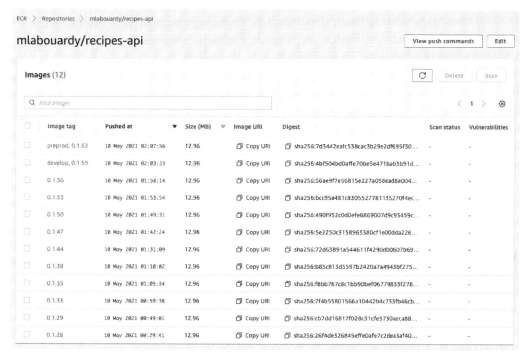

Figure 9.31 – Preprod Docker image

4. Now, deploy the image to the staging environment using the `docker-compose up` command. Hit the IP address of the staging environment; you should see the version of the running Docker image:

```
{"version":"0.1.62"}
```

Figure 9.32 – Docker image version.

Great! You now have a staging environment where you can validate your API functionalities before promoting them to production.

So far, you have learned how to achieve continuous deployment via a push event. However, in a production environment, you might want to add extra validation before shipping a new release to production. That's where **continuous delivery practices** come into play.

Implementing continuous delivery

To deploy the Gin application to production, you need to spin up a dedicated EC2 instance or EKS cluster. You must ask for manual validation before deploying to production.

With CircleCI, you can use the pause_workflow job to interact with the user and ask for approval before resuming the pipeline. To do so, follow these steps:

1. Add the pause_workflow job before the deploy job and define a release job, as follows:

```
workflows:
  ci_cd:
    jobs:
      - test
      - build:
          requires:
            - test
      - deploy:
          requires:
            - test
            - build
          filters:
            branches:
              only:
                - develop
                - preprod
      - pause_workflow:
          requires:
            - test
            - build
```

```
            type: approval
            filters:
              branches:
                only:
                  - master
        - release:
            requires:
              - pause_workflow
            filters:
              branches:
                only:
                  - master
```

2. Push the changes to the develop branch. A new pipeline will be triggered and the changes will be deployed to your sandbox environment. Next, create a pull request and merge the develop and preprod branches. Now, raise a pull request to merge the preprod branch and the master branch:

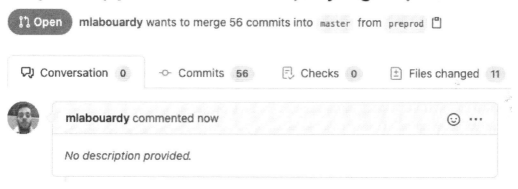

Figure 9.33 – Pull request to merge into the master branch

3. Once the PR has been merged, a new pipeline will be triggered on the master branch and both the test and build jobs will be executed:

Figure 9.34 – Running a CI/CD workflow on the master branch

4. When the `pause_workflow` job is reached, the pipeline will be paused, as follows:

Figure 9.35 – Asking the user for approval

5. If you click on the **pause_workflow** box, a confirmation dialog will pop up, where you can allow the workflow to continue running:

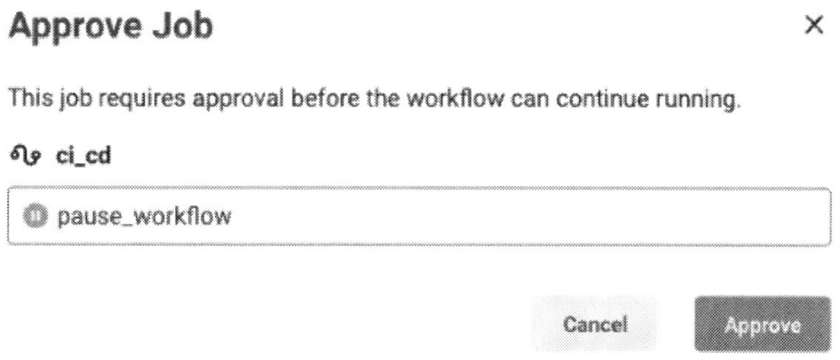

Approve Job   ✕

This job requires approval before the workflow can continue running.

ᐁ ci_cd

> pause_workflow

Cancel   Approve

Figure 9.36 – Approving the deployment

6. Once approved, the pipeline will resume, and the deploy stage will be executed. At the end of the CI/CD pipeline, the application will be deployed into a production environment:

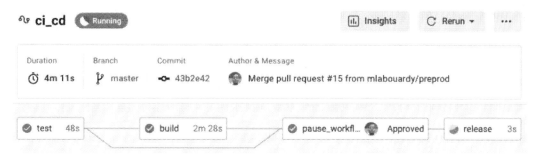

Figure 9.37 – Deploying an application to production

Awesome! With that, you have achieved continuous delivery!

Before wrapping up, you can improve the workflow by adding a **Slack** notification to raise awareness within the development team when a new build is being triggered on CircleCI.

Improving the feedback loop with Slack

You can use the **Slack RESTful API** to post a notification on a Slack channel or use the CircleCI Slack orb with pre-built Slack commands to improve the feedback loop.

To do so, follow these steps:

1. Add the following code block to the `test` job:

```
- slack/notify:
        channel: "#ci"
        event: always
        custom: |
          {
            "blocks": [
              {
                "type": "section",
                "text": {
                  "type": "mrkdwn",
                  "text": "*Build has started*!
                            :crossed_fingers:"
                }
              },
              {
                "type": "divider"
              },
              {
                "type": "section",
                "fields": [
                  {
                    "type": "mrkdwn",
                    "text": "*Project*:\
                      n$CIRCLE_PROJECT_REPONAME"
                  },
                  {
                    "type": "mrkdwn",
                    "text": "*When*:\n$(date +'%m/%d/%Y
                            %T')"
                  },
```

```
                    {
                        "type": "mrkdwn",
                        "text": "*Branch*:\n$CIRCLE_BRANCH"
                    },
                    {
                        "type": "mrkdwn",
                        "text": "*Author*:
                                \n$CIRCLE_USERNAME"
                    }
                ],
                "accessory": {
                    "type": "image",
                    "image_url": "https://media.giphy.com/
                    media/3orieTfp1MeFLiBQR2/giphy.gif",
                    "alt_text": "CircleCI logo"
                }
            },
            {
                "type": "actions",
                "elements": [
                    {
                        "type": "button",
                        "text": {
                            "type": "plain_text",
                            "text": "View Workflow"
                        },
                        "url": "https://circleci.com/
                        workflow-run/${
                                CIRCLE_WORKFLOW_ID}"
                    }
                ]
            }
        ]
    }
```

2. Then, create a new Slack application on your Slack workspace by navigating to `https://api.slack.com/apps` and clicking on **Build app** from the page's header:

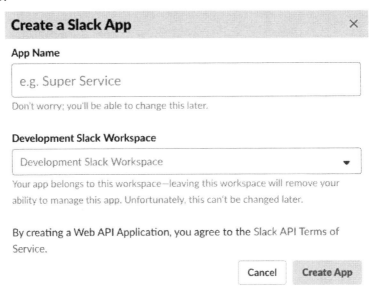

Figure 9.38 – New Slack application

3. Give the application a meaningful name and click on the **Create App** button. On the **OAuth & Permissions** page, add the following permissions under **Bot Token Scopes**:

Scopes

A Slack app's capabilities and permissions are governed by the scopes it requests.

Bot Token Scopes
Scopes that govern what your app can access.

OAuth Scope	Description	
chat:write	Send messages as @circleci	🗑
chat:write.public	Send messages to channels @circleci isn't a member of	🗑
files:write	Upload, edit, and delete files as CircleCI	🗑

Add an OAuth Scope

Figure 9.39 – Slack bot permissions

4. From the left navigation menu, click on **OAuth & Permissions** and copy the OAuth token:

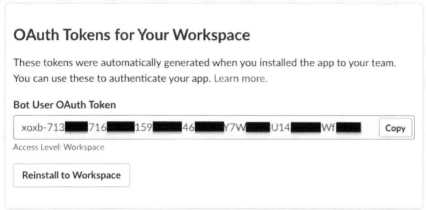

Figure 9.40 – Bot user OAuth token

5. Go back to the CircleCI project settings and add the following environment variables:

SLACK_ACCESS_TOKEN: The OAuth Token we generated previously.

SLACK_DEFAULT_CHANNEL: The Slack channel where you want to post CircleCI build notifications.

You should see the following:

Name	Value		
AWS_ACCESS_KEY_ID	xxxx4TKE		×
AWS_DEFAULT_REGION	xxxxal-1		×
AWS_SECRET_ACCESS_KEY	xxxxUolq		×
SLACK_ACCESS_TOKEN	xxxxA26X		×
SLACK_DEFAULT_CHANNEL	xxxxi		×

Figure 9.41 – Slack environment variables

6. Push the new CircleCI config updates to GitHub. At this point, a new pipeline will be executed:

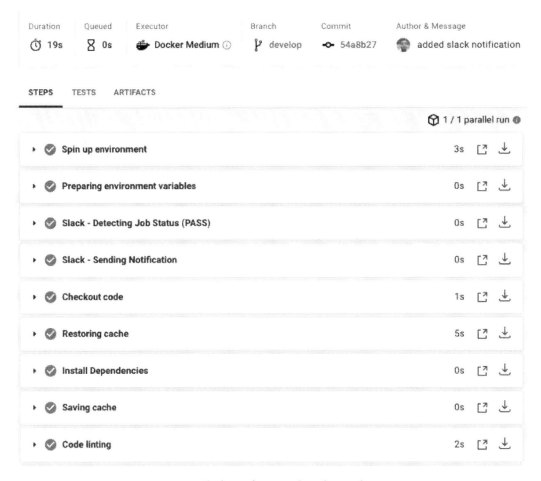

Figure 9.42 – Slack notification when the pipeline starts

A Slack notification will be sent on the configured Slack channel containing the name of the project and the name of the Git branch:

Mohamed 2:37 AM
joined ci along with CircleCI.

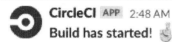 **CircleCI** APP 2:48 AM
Build has started! 🤞

Project:	**When:**	
recipes-api	05/10/2021 00:48:01	
Branch:	**Author:**	
develop	mlabouardy	

 View Workflow

Figure 9.43 – Sending a Slack notification

You can take this even further and send a notification based on the pipeline's status. For instance, add the following code if you want to be alerted when the pipeline fails (the full JSON has been cropped for brevity):

```
- slack/notify:
    channel: "#ci"
    event: fail
    custom: |
      {
        "blocks": [
          {
            "type": "section",
            "text": {
              "type": "mrkdwn",
              "text": "*Tests failed, run for your
                    life*! :fearful:"
            }
          }
        ]
      }
```

You can simulate a pipeline failure by throwing an error with a code error different than `0`:

```
- run:
    name: Unit tests
    command: |
      go test -v ./...
      exit 1
```

Now, push the changes to the develop branch. When the pipeline reaches the `Unit tests` step, an error will be thrown, and the pipeline will fail:

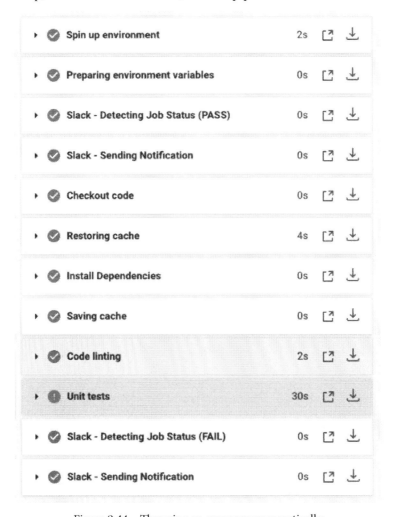

Figure 9.44 – Throwing an error programmatically

On the Slack channel, you should receive a notification similar to the one shown in the following screenshot:

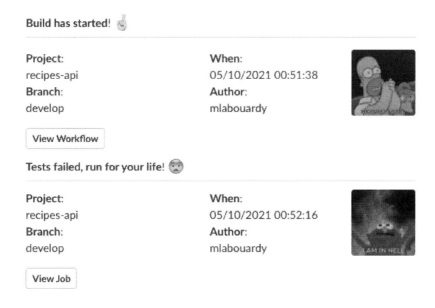

Figure 9.45 – Sending a notification when the pipeline fails

That's pretty much it. This chapter has merely scratched the surface of what can be done with the CI/CD pipeline. However, it should provide enough of a foundation for you to start experimenting and building your own end-to-end workflows for your Gin applications.

Summary

In this chapter, you learned how to set up a CI/CD pipeline from scratch to automate the deployment process of a Gin application with CircleCI. Additionally, using CircleCI orbs improves productivity by simplifying how we write our Pipeline as Code configuration.

You also explored how to run automated tests with Docker and how to achieve continuous deployment with GitFlow and multiple AWS environments. Along the way, you set up Slack notifications so that you're alerted about a build failure or success.

The final chapter in this book will cover how to troubleshoot and debug Gin applications running in production.

Questions

1. Build a CI/CD pipeline to automate the deployment process for the React web application we built in Chapter 5, *Serving Static HTML in Gin*.

2. Add a Slack notification for when a successful production deployment is made.

Further reading

-   *Hands-On Serverless Applications with Go* by Mohamed Labouardy, Packt publishing

-   *Implementing DevOps with AWS* by Salle Ingle, Packt publishing

10
Capturing Gin Application Metrics

In this final chapter, you will learn how to debug, troubleshoot, and monitor the RESTful API in near-real time. You will also learn how to collect Gin application metrics to measure the of the Gin application and to profile for abnormal behavior. Besides that, you will also explore how to stream Gin debug logs to a centralized logging platform using the ELK stack.

As such, we will cover the following topics:

- Exposing Gin application metrics with Prometheus

- Monitoring server-side metrics

- Streaming Gin logs to the ELK platform

By the end of this chapter, you will be able to instrument and monitor a Dockerized Gin web application running in production and debug its logs with ease.

Technical requirements

To follow the content in this chapter, you will need the following:

- A complete understanding of the previous chapter. This chapter is a follow-up to the previous one as it will use the same source code. Hence, some snippets won't be explained to avoid repetition.

- It is assumed that you already have knowledge of Docker and containerization.

The code bundle for this chapter is hosted on GitHub at `https://github.com/PacktPublishing/Building-Distributed-Applications-in-Gin/tree/main/chapter10`.

Exposing Gin metrics with Prometheus

In the previous chapter, you learned how to automate the deployment process for a Gin application. However, no app is immune from downtime or external attacks (**DDoS**). That's why you need to set up the right tools to constantly monitor the performance of your application. **Prometheus** (`https://prometheus.io`) is a common open source tool for monitoring applications.

You can install the Go client by running the following command from your terminal session:

```
go get github.com/prometheus/client_golang
```

Next, update the `main.go` file so that it exposes an HTTP route on the `/prometheus` path. The route handler will call the Prometheus HTTP handler, which will return a list of runtime and application metrics:

```
router.GET("/prometheus", gin.WrapH(promhttp.Handler()))
```

Then, import the following package to use the `promhttp` struct:

```
"github.com/prometheus/client_golang/prometheus/promhttp"
```

Next, redeploy the application. If you navigate to `http://localhost:8080/prometheus`, you should see the following metrics:

```
# HELP go_gc_duration_seconds A summary of the pause duration of garbage collection cycles.
# TYPE go_gc_duration_seconds summary
go_gc_duration_seconds{quantile="0"} 4.0122e-05
go_gc_duration_seconds{quantile="0.25"} 4.0122e-05
go_gc_duration_seconds{quantile="0.5"} 4.0122e-05
go_gc_duration_seconds{quantile="0.75"} 4.0122e-05
go_gc_duration_seconds{quantile="1"} 4.0122e-05
go_gc_duration_seconds_sum 4.0122e-05
go_gc_duration_seconds_count 1
# HELP go_goroutines Number of goroutines that currently exist.
# TYPE go_goroutines gauge
go_goroutines 11
# HELP go_info Information about the Go environment.
# TYPE go_info gauge
go_info{version="go1.15.6"} 1
# HELP go_memstats_alloc_bytes Number of bytes allocated and still in use.
# TYPE go_memstats_alloc_bytes gauge
go_memstats_alloc_bytes 2.981544e+06
# HELP go_memstats_alloc_bytes_total Total number of bytes allocated, even if freed.
# TYPE go_memstats_alloc_bytes_total counter
go_memstats_alloc_bytes_total 4.00576e+06
# HELP go_memstats_buck_hash_sys_bytes Number of bytes used by the profiling bucket hash table.
# TYPE go_memstats_buck_hash_sys_bytes gauge
go_memstats_buck_hash_sys_bytes 1.446447e+06
# HELP go_memstats_frees_total Total number of frees.
# TYPE go_memstats_frees_total counter
go_memstats_frees_total 10373
# HELP go_memstats_gc_cpu_fraction The fraction of this program's available CPU time used by the GC since the program started.
# TYPE go_memstats_gc_cpu_fraction gauge
go_memstats_gc_cpu_fraction 0.0169374283894136
# HELP go_memstats_gc_sys_bytes Number of bytes used for garbage collection system metadata.
# TYPE go_memstats_gc_sys_bytes gauge
go_memstats_gc_sys_bytes 4.366912e+06
# HELP go_memstats_heap_alloc_bytes Number of heap bytes allocated and still in use.
# TYPE go_memstats_heap_alloc_bytes gauge
go_memstats_heap_alloc_bytes 2.981544e+06
# HELP go_memstats_heap_idle_bytes Number of heap bytes waiting to be used.
# TYPE go_memstats_heap_idle_bytes gauge
go_memstats_heap_idle_bytes 6.1415424e+07
# HELP go_memstats_heap_inuse_bytes Number of heap bytes that are in use.
# TYPE go_memstats_heap_inuse_bytes gauge
go_memstats_heap_inuse_bytes 5.005312e+06
# HELP go_memstats_heap_objects Number of allocated objects.
# TYPE go_memstats_heap_objects gauge
go_memstats_heap_objects 13451
# HELP go_memstats_heap_released_bytes Number of heap bytes released to OS.
# TYPE go_memstats_heap_released_bytes gauge
go_memstats_heap_released_bytes 6.1366272e+07
# HELP go_memstats_heap_sys_bytes Number of heap bytes obtained from system.
# TYPE go_memstats_heap_sys_bytes gauge
go_memstats_heap_sys_bytes 6.6420736e+07
# HELP go_memstats_last_gc_time_seconds Number of seconds since 1970 of last garbage collection.
# TYPE go_memstats_last_gc_time_seconds gauge
go_memstats_last_gc_time_seconds 1.620860934984183e+09
# HELP go_memstats_lookups_total Total number of pointer lookups.
# TYPE go_memstats_lookups_total counter
go_memstats_lookups_total 0
# HELP go_memstats_mallocs_total Total number of mallocs.
```

Figure 10.1 – Prometheus default metrics

This application only exposes the default metrics. You can also expose your own custom metrics by instrumenting the Gin application code. Let's learn how to do that.

Instrumenting a Gin application

Instrumentation is the ability to monitor and measure performance, detect errors, and get trace information that represents the application's state. Prometheus allows us to inject code to monitor a Gin application up close.

To add a custom metric, such as counting the number of incoming requests, follow these steps:

1. First, we need to create a piece of middleware to intercept incoming HTTP requests and increment the counter:

```
var totalRequests = prometheus.NewCounterVec(
    prometheus.CounterOpts{
        Name: "http_requests_total",
        Help: "Number of incoming requests",
    },
    []string{"path"},
)
```

2. Then, we must define a piece of Gin middleware with the following code block:

```
func PrometheusMiddleware() gin.HandlerFunc {
    return func(c *gin.Context) {
        totalRequests.WithLabelValues(
            c.Request.URL.Path).Inc()
        c.Next()
    }
}
```

3. Next, register the totalRequests counter within the init() method's body:

```
prometheus.Register(totalRequests)
```

4. Then, pass the PrometheusMiddleware middleware to the Gin router:

```
router.Use(PrometheusMiddleware())
```

5. Restart the application and then refresh the /prometheus URL.

In the response, you'll see the number of requests per path:

```
# HELP http_requests_total Number of incoming requests
# TYPE http_requests_total counter
http_requests_total{path="/"} 1
http_requests_total{path="/css/main.css"} 1
http_requests_total{path="/favicon.ico"} 2
http_requests_total{path="/img/rabbitmqlogo.svg"} 1
http_requests_total{path="/js/base64.js"} 1
http_requests_total{path="/js/charts.js"} 1
http_requests_total{path="/js/ejs-1.0.min.js"} 1
http_requests_total{path="/js/formatters.js"} 1
http_requests_total{path="/js/global.js"} 1
http_requests_total{path="/js/jquery-3.5.1.min.js"} 1
http_requests_total{path="/js/jquery.flot-0.8.1.min.js"} 1
http_requests_total{path="/js/jquery.flot-0.8.1.time.min.js"} 1
http_requests_total{path="/js/json2-2016.10.28.js"} 1
http_requests_total{path="/js/main.js"} 1
http_requests_total{path="/js/prefs.js"} 1
http_requests_total{path="/js/sammy-0.7.6.min.js"} 1
http_requests_total{path="/js/singular/singular.js"} 1
http_requests_total{path="/prometheus"} 4
http_requests_total{path="/recipes"} 2
# HELP promhttp_metric_handler_requests_in_flight Current number of scrapes being served.
# TYPE promhttp_metric_handler_requests_in_flight gauge
promhttp_metric_handler_requests_in_flight 1
# HELP promhttp_metric_handler_requests_total Total number of scrapes by HTTP status code.
# TYPE promhttp_metric_handler_requests_total counter
promhttp_metric_handler_requests_total{code="200"} 3
promhttp_metric_handler_requests_total{code="500"} 0
promhttp_metric_handler_requests_total{code="503"} 0
```

Figure 10.2 – Instrumenting Gin code

> **Note**
>
> Your output might not display as much data as mine since you have not
> accessed the application that often. The best way to get more data is to issue
> multiple HTTP requests to the Recipes API.

Another useful metric you can expose is the number of HTTP requests that have been
received per HTTP method. Similarly, define a global counter and increment the counter
for the corresponding HTTP method:

```
var totalHTTPMethods = prometheus.NewCounterVec(
    prometheus.CounterOpts{
        Name: "http_methods_total",
        Help: "Number of requests per HTTP method",
    },
    []string{"method"},
)
```

```
func PrometheusMiddleware() gin.HandlerFunc {
    return func(c *gin.Context) {
        totalRequests.WithLabelValues(
            c.Request.URL.Path).Inc()
        totalHTTPMethods.WithLabelValues(
            c.Request.Method).Inc()
        c.Next()
    }
}
```

Register the `totalHTTPMethods` counter within the `init()` method body and restart the application.

Once the application has been restarted, in the response payload, you should see the number of requests partitioned by the HTTP method:

```
# HELP http_methods_total Number of requests per HTTP method
# TYPE http_methods_total counter
http_methods_total{method="GET"} 2
http_methods_total{method="POST"} 2
# HELP http_requests_total Number of incoming requests
# TYPE http_requests_total counter
http_requests_total{path="/prometheus"} 2
http_requests_total{path="/recipes"} 2
# HELP promhttp_metric_handler_requests_in_flight Current number of scrapes being served.
# TYPE promhttp_metric_handler_requests_in_flight gauge
promhttp_metric_handler_requests_in_flight 1
# HELP promhttp_metric_handler_requests_total Total number of scrapes by HTTP status code.
# TYPE promhttp_metric_handler_requests_total counter
promhttp_metric_handler_requests_total{code="200"} 1
promhttp_metric_handler_requests_total{code="500"} 0
promhttp_metric_handler_requests_total{code="503"} 0
```

Figure 10.3 – Number of requests per HTTP method

You can also record the HTTP request latencies in seconds with the following code block. We're using `Histogram` instead of `Counter` to count individual observations from incoming HTTP requests:

```
var httpDuration = promauto.NewHistogramVec(
    prometheus.HistogramOpts{
        Name: "http_response_time_seconds",
        Help: "Duration of HTTP requests",
    },
    []string{"path"},
)
```

```
func PrometheusMiddleware() gin.HandlerFunc {
    return func(c *gin.Context) {
        timer := prometheus.NewTimer(httpDuration.
            WithLabelValues(c.Request.URL.Path))
        totalRequests.WithLabelValues(
            c.Request.URL.Path).Inc()
        totalHTTPMethods.WithLabelValues(
            c.Request.Method).Inc()
        c.Next()
        timer.ObserveDuration()
    }
}
```

As a result, you should have something similar to the following:

```
# HELP http_response_time_seconds Duration of HTTP requests
# TYPE http_response_time_seconds histogram
http_response_time_seconds_bucket{path="/prometheus",le="0.005"} 1
http_response_time_seconds_bucket{path="/prometheus",le="0.01"} 1
http_response_time_seconds_bucket{path="/prometheus",le="0.025"} 1
http_response_time_seconds_bucket{path="/prometheus",le="0.05"} 1
http_response_time_seconds_bucket{path="/prometheus",le="0.1"} 1
http_response_time_seconds_bucket{path="/prometheus",le="0.25"} 1
http_response_time_seconds_bucket{path="/prometheus",le="0.5"} 1
http_response_time_seconds_bucket{path="/prometheus",le="1"} 1
http_response_time_seconds_bucket{path="/prometheus",le="2.5"} 1
http_response_time_seconds_bucket{path="/prometheus",le="5"} 1
http_response_time_seconds_bucket{path="/prometheus",le="10"} 1
http_response_time_seconds_bucket{path="/prometheus",le="+Inf"} 1
http_response_time_seconds_sum{path="/prometheus"} 0.001169575
http_response_time_seconds_count{path="/prometheus"} 1
http_response_time_seconds_bucket{path="/recipes",le="0.005"} 0
http_response_time_seconds_bucket{path="/recipes",le="0.01"} 1
http_response_time_seconds_bucket{path="/recipes",le="0.025"} 1
http_response_time_seconds_bucket{path="/recipes",le="0.05"} 1
http_response_time_seconds_bucket{path="/recipes",le="0.1"} 1
http_response_time_seconds_bucket{path="/recipes",le="0.25"} 1
http_response_time_seconds_bucket{path="/recipes",le="0.5"} 1
http_response_time_seconds_bucket{path="/recipes",le="1"} 1
http_response_time_seconds_bucket{path="/recipes",le="2.5"} 1
http_response_time_seconds_bucket{path="/recipes",le="5"} 1
http_response_time_seconds_bucket{path="/recipes",le="10"} 1
http_response_time_seconds_bucket{path="/recipes",le="+Inf"} 1
http_response_time_seconds_sum{path="/recipes"} 0.006760148
http_response_time_seconds_count{path="/recipes"} 1
# HELP promhttp_metric_handler_requests_in_flight Current number of scrapes being served.
```

Figure 10.4 – Duration of the HTTP requests

Now that the metrics have been exposed, you can store them in a time-series database and build an interactive dashboard on top of that. Getting regular insights into how the app works can help you identify ways to optimize its performance.

> **Note**
> Another alternative is to use the following Go library, written by the open source community: `https://github.com/zsais/go-gin-prometheus`. It comes with a generic set of metrics.

To get started, follow these steps:

1. Deploy Prometheus by using the official Docker image with the following `docker-compose.yml` file:

```yaml
version: "3"

services:
  api:
    build: .
    environment:
      - MONGO_URI=mongodb://admin:password@
                    mongodb:27017/test?authSource=admin
                    &readPreference=primary&ssl=false
      - MONGO_DATABASE=demo
      - REDIS_URI=redis:6379
      - API_VERSION=1.0.0
    ports:
      - 8080:8080
    external_links:
      - mongodb
      - redis
    restart: always

  redis:
    image: redis
    restart: always

  mongodb:
```

```
    image: mongo:4.4.3
    environment:
      - MONGO_INITDB_ROOT_USERNAME=admin
      - MONGO_INITDB_ROOT_PASSWORD=password
    restart: always

  prometheus:
    image: prom/prometheus:v2.27.0
    volumes:
      - ./prometheus.yml:/etc/prometheus/prometheus.yml
    ports:
      - 9090:9090
    restart: always
```

The Prometheus container uses a `prometheus.yml` configuration file, which defines a background job to scrape the Golang Prometheus metrics endpoint:

```
global:
  scrape_interval:     15s
  evaluation_interval: 15s

scrape_configs:
  - job_name: prometheus
    static_configs:
      - targets: ['localhost:9090']
  - job_name: recipes-api
    metrics_path: /prometheus
    static_configs:
      - targets:
        - api:8080
```

2. Redeploy the application stack with the following command:

```
docker-compose up -d
```

The stack logs should look similar to this:

```
,"attr":{"remote":"172.24.0.3:33978","connectionId":2,"connectionCount":2}}
mongodb_1    | {"t":{"$date":"2021-05-12T23:49:05.391+00:00"},"s":"I",  "c":"NETWORK", "id":51800,   "ctx":
:{"remote":"172.24.0.3:33978","client":"conn2","doc":{"driver":{"name":"mongo-go-driver","version":"v1.4.5"},
md64"},"platform":"go1.16.4"}}}
mongodb_1    | {"t":{"$date":"2021-05-12T23:49:05.402+00:00"},"s":"I",  "c":"ACCESS",  "id":20250,   "ctx":
on","attr":{"mechanism":"SCRAM-SHA-256","principalName":"admin","authenticationDatabase":"admin","client":"17
redis_1      |   1:C 12 May 2021 23:49:02.222 # o000o000o000o Redis is starting o000o000o000o
redis_1      |   1:C 12 May 2021 23:49:02.222 # Redis version=6.0.10, bits=64, commit=00000000, modified=0, pi
redis_1      |   1:C 12 May 2021 23:49:02.222 # Warning: no config file specified, using the default config. I
edis-server /path/to/redis.conf
redis_1      |   1:M 12 May 2021 23:49:02.225 * Running mode=standalone, port=6379.
redis_1      |   1:M 12 May 2021 23:49:02.225 # WARNING: The TCP backlog setting of 511 cannot be enforced bec
et to the lower value of 128.
redis_1      |   1:M 12 May 2021 23:49:02.225 # Server initialized
redis_1      |   1:M 12 May 2021 23:49:02.227 * Ready to accept connections
mongodb_1    | {"t":{"$date":"2021-05-12T23:49:12.392+00:00"},"s":"I",  "c":"NETWORK", "id":22943,   "ctx":
,"attr":{"remote":"172.24.0.3:33984","connectionId":3,"connectionCount":3}}
mongodb_1    | {"t":{"$date":"2021-05-12T23:49:12.393+00:00"},"s":"I",  "c":"NETWORK", "id":51800,   "ctx":
:{"remote":"172.24.0.3:33984","client":"conn3","doc":{"driver":{"name":"mongo-go-driver","version":"v1.4.5"},
md64"},"platform":"go1.16.4"}}}
api_1        | [GIN] 2021/05/12 - 23:49:14 |   200 |    6.695766ms |      172.24.0.5 | GET      "/prometheus"
api_1        | [GIN] 2021/05/12 - 23:49:29 |   200 |    2.990317ms |      172.24.0.5 | GET      "/prometheus"
```

Figure 10.5 – Docker stack logs

3. Navigate to the Prometheus dashboard by visiting localhost:9090 in your favorite browser. You can explore the available metrics by using the search bar and writing queries using the **Prometheus Query Language** (**PromQL**). Prometheus collects metrics by polling (scraping) instrumented Gin code:

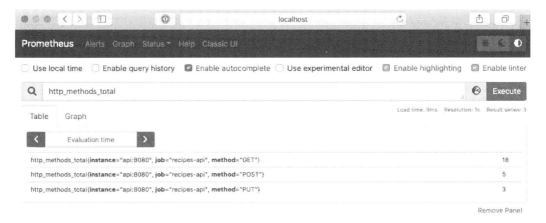

Figure 10.6 – Exploring metrics from the Prometheus dashboard

4. Turn the metrics into a chart by clicking on the **Graph** tab:

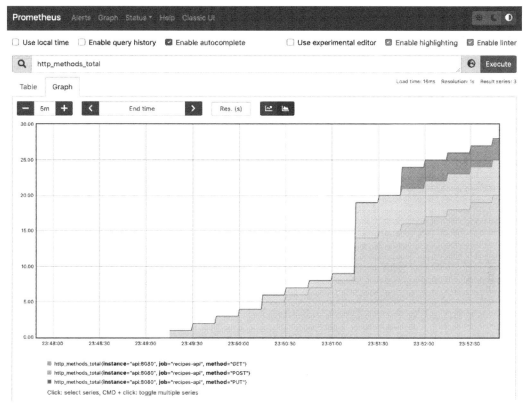

Figure 10.7 – Using the built-in graph feature of Prometheus

You can build advanced charts by using a visualization platform such as Grafana. It summarizes and visualizes data stored in Prometheus and provides a wide range of UI components to build user-friendly dashboards. The monitoring workflow is illustrated in the following schema:

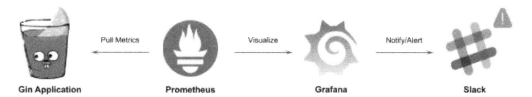

Figure 10.8 – Collecting Gin metrics with Prometheus and Grafana

5. Deploy Grafana inside a Docker container with the following code snippet:

```
grafana:
    image: grafana/grafana:7.5.6
    ports:
      - 3000:3000
    restart: always
```

6. Spin up the container using the following command:

```
docker-compose up -d
```

7. Head to `localhost:3000`; you'll be asked to enter some user credentials. The defaults are admin for both the username and password:

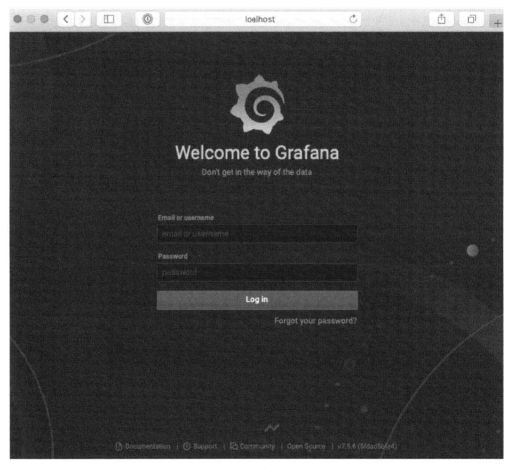

Figure 10.9 – Grafana login page

8. Next, connect to Prometheus by creating a data source. Click on
    Configuration from the sidebar. Within the **Data Sources** tab, click on the
    Add data source button:

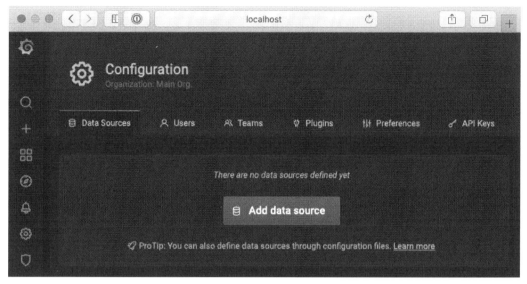

Figure 10.10 – Adding a new data source

9. After that, select **Prometheus** and then fill in the fields, as shown in the following
    screenshot. Then, click on the **Save & Test** button at the bottom of the page:

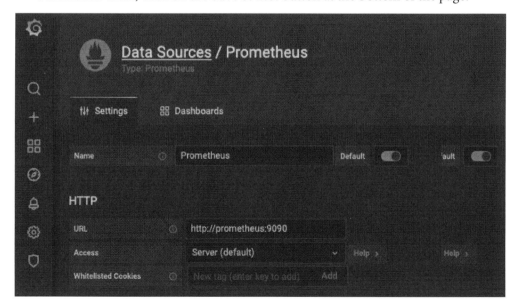

Figure 10.11 – Configuring a Prometheus data source

You're now ready to create your first Grafana dashboard!

You can start by clicking on **New Dashbord/Add panel** to create a chart. Enter the `http_ requests_total` expression into the query field while using the **Metrics** dropdown to look up metrics via autocompletion. Show only the path label of the returned results by typing the `{{path}}` keyword in the `legend` field.

You should now have the following graph configuration, which represents the total number of HTTP requests over time per path:

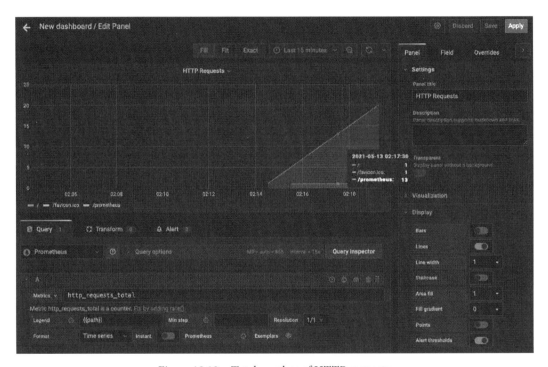

Figure 10.12 – Total number of HTTP requests

Save the panel and create a new one to display the response time of the served HTTP requests over time by using the `http_response_time_seconds_sum` expression:

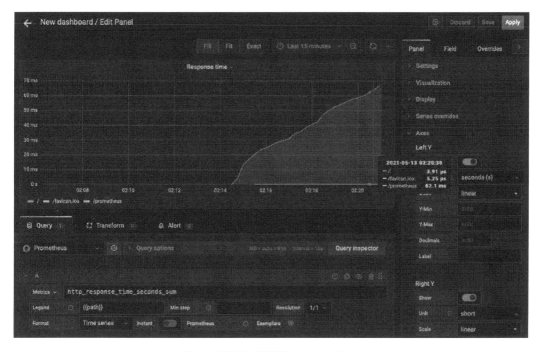

Figure 10.13 – HTTP response time

You can also create a single stat counter to display the total number of requests per HTTP method using the following configuration:

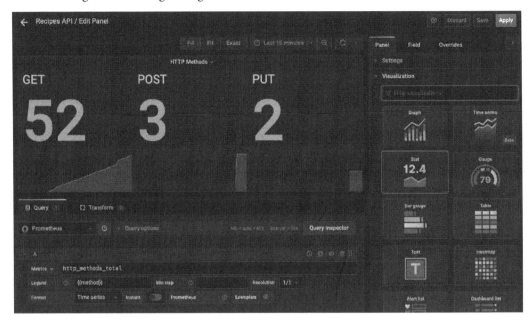

Figure 10.14 – Using Grafana's single stat component

You can experiment with the dashboard by adding other panels with metrics and customize it to your liking:

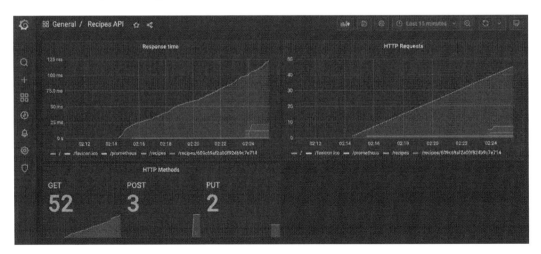

Figure 10.15 – Interactive and dynamic Grafana dashboard

> **Note**
>
> You can download `dashboard.json`, which contains the Grafana configuration for the preceding dashboard, from the GitHub repository under the `chapter10` folder.

Monitoring server-side metrics

So far, you have learned how to monitor application-side metrics by instrumenting the Gin application code. In this section, you will learn how to expose server-side metrics and monitor the overall health of the containers running on the Gin distributed web application.

To collect server-side metrics, you can use an open source solution called **Telegraf** (`https://github.com/influxdata/telegraf`), a **data collection agent** (**DCA**) that can collect metrics from multiple inputs and forward them to different sources:

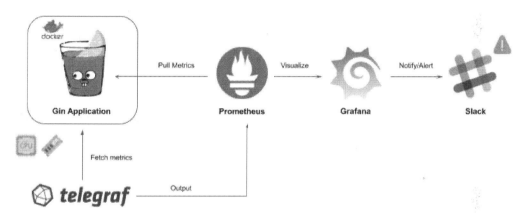

Figure 10.16 – Collecting server-side metrics with the Telegraf agent

Telegraf can be easily deployed using Docker. Add the following code block to `docker-compose.yml`:

```
telegraf:
    image: telegraf:latest
    volumes:
        - ./telegraf.conf:/etc/telegraf/telegraf.conf
        - /var/run/docker.sock:/var/run/docker.sock
```

`telegraf.conf` contains a list of data sources (**inputs**) where Telegraf will fetch data from. It also contains a list of destinations (**outputs**) where the data will be forwarded to. In the following configuration file, Telegraf will collect the metrics about the server resources (memory, CPU, disk, and network traffic) and Docker daemon (usage of resources per container), and then forward these metrics to the Prometheus server:

```
[[inputs.cpu]]
 percpu = false
 totalcpu = true
 fieldpass = [ "usage*" ]

[[inputs.disk]]
 fielddrop = [ "inodes*" ]
 mount_points=["/"]

[[inputs.net]]
 interfaces = [ "eth0" ]
 fielddrop = [ "icmp*", "ip*", "tcp*", "udp*" ]

[[inputs.mem]]

[[inputs.swap]]

[[inputs.system]]

[[inputs.docker]]
 endpoint = "unix:///var/run/docker.sock"
 container_names = []

[[outputs.prometheus_client]]
 listen = "telegraf:9100"
```

> **Note**
>
> You can also forward these metrics to InfluxDB (`https://github.com/influxdata/influxdb`), a scalable time-series database, and connect it to Grafana.

Next, define a new job in `prometheus.yml` to scrape the metrics that have been exposed by the Telegraf container:

```yaml
global:
  scrape_interval:     15s
  evaluation_interval: 15s

scrape_configs:
  - job_name: prometheus
    static_configs:
      - targets: ['localhost:9090']
  - job_name: recipes-api
    metrics_path: /prometheus
    static_configs:
      - targets:
        - api:8080
  - job_name: telegraf
    scrape_interval: 15s
    static_configs:
      - targets: ['telegraf:9100']
```

With that done, restart the stack with the following command:

```
docker-compose up -d
```

Then, head back to the Prometheus dashboard and navigate to **Targets** from the **Status** dropdown list. A Telegraf target should have been added to the list:

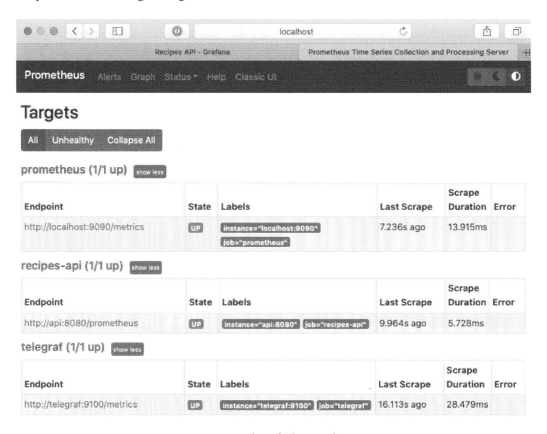

Figure 10.17 – Telegraf job up and running

With the server-side metrics now available in Prometheus, you can create additional panels in Grafana.

For instance, you can select the `docker_container_mem_usage_percent` expression from the **Metrics** dropdown to monitor the memory usage per container over time:

Figure 10.18 – Memory usage per container

Add additional metrics so that you can monitor the CPU, disk usage, or the overall health metrics of the running containers:

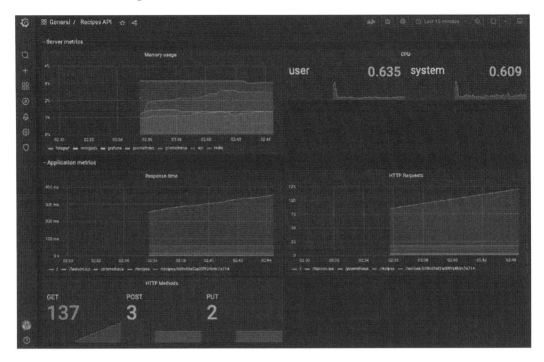

Figure 10.19 – Server-side and application-side metrics

Well done! Now, you have a pretty interactive dashboard for a minimum amount of time.

Creating a Grafana notification channel

In the previous chapter, you learned how to use Slack to raise awareness about the CI/ CD status for teams to take immediate actions. You can use the same approach while monitoring Gin applications by configuring a Slack alert on your **Grafana** dashboard when a certain threshold is reached.

From the Grafana dashboard, click on the **Alerting** icon and click on **Notification channels**. Click on the **Add Channel** button and change the type to **Slack**. Then, input a Webhook URL:

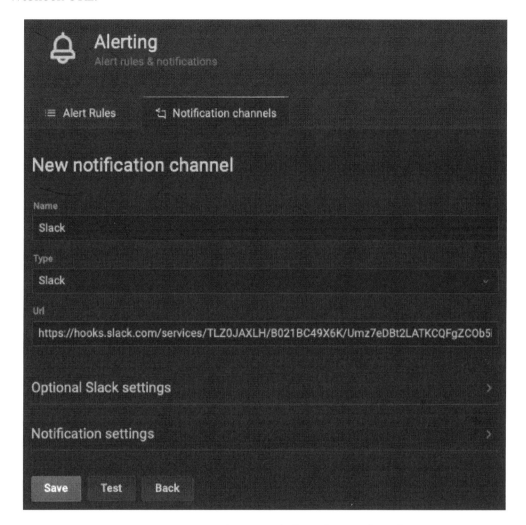

Figure 10.20 – Configuring a Slack notification channel

> **Note**
> For a step-by-step guide on how to create a Slack application and generate a Webhook URL, check out *Chapter 9, Implementing a CI/CD Pipeline.*

To test out the configuration, click on the **Test** button. You should get a message similar to the following in your configured Slack channel:

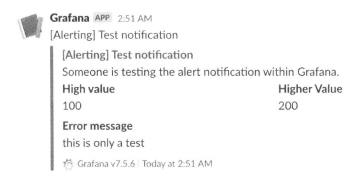

Figure 10.21 – Slack test message from Grafana

Now that you have a notification channel, you can create an alerting rule on the dashboard panel. For instance, create an alert rule on the **HTTP Requests** graph that you created earlier and select the notification channel in the **Notifications** section. The rule will look as follows:

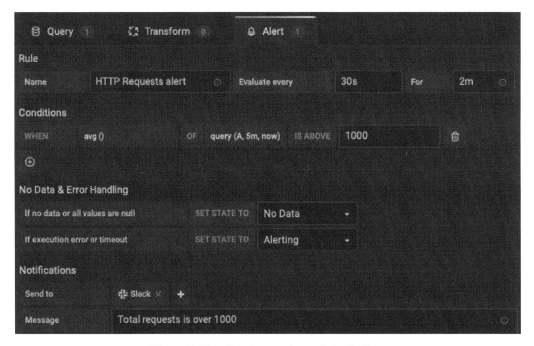

Figure 10.22 – Creating an alert rule in Grafana

Every 30 seconds, Grafana will evaluate if the average number of HTTP requests is over 1,000 requests. If the metrics violate this rule, Grafana will wait for 2 minutes. If, after 2 minutes, the metrics have not been recovered, Grafana will trigger an alert and a Slack notification will be sent.

To test out the alert rule, you need to generate a workload. You can use **Apache Benchmark** to send 1,500 requests in parallel to the Recipes API with the following command:

```
ab -n 1500 http://localhost:8080/recipes
```

Here, the number of requests for the /recipes endpoint will cross the 1,000 threshold, as shown in the following graph:

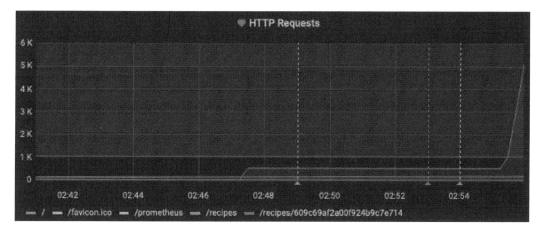

Figure 10.23 – Reaching the 1,000 requests limit

After 2 minutes, the alert will be triggered, and you will see the following message on your Slack channel:

Figure 10.24 – Slack alert from Grafana

> **Note**
>
> Another option for setting up metrics alerts is using Prometheus Alertmanager (`https://prometheus.io/docs/alerting/latest/alertmanager`).

Having Slack notifications can help you take immediate action before things go horribly wrong in your production environment.

Streaming Gin logs to the ELK platform

Another beneficial aspect to keep an eye on while deploying a Gin web application in production is **logs**. Logs can help you find the root cause of bad application performance or crashes.

However, logs can be verbose and spammy – that's why you'll need a centralized platform to be able to apply filters and keep an eye on important events. That's where a solution such as **Elasticsearch**, **Logstash**, and **Kibana** (**ELK**) is needed. The following schema illustrates how such a solution can be implemented:

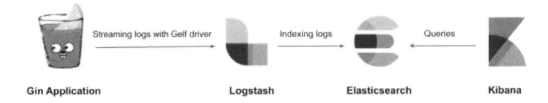

Figure 10.25 – Streaming Gin logs to ELK

Gin application logs will be shipped to Logstash using the Docker GELF driver (`https://docs.docker.com/config/containers/logging/gelf/`). From there, Logstash will process the incoming logs and store them in Elasticsearch. Finally, the logs can be visualized in Kibana through interactive dashboards.

Deploying the ELK stack with Docker

By now, you should be familiar with Docker and be able to use it to deploy a Dockerized ELK stack using Docker Compose. To do so, follow these steps:

1. Start with **Logstash**. Add the following YAML block to `docker-compose.yml`. The container uses the latest Docker image v7.12.1 (at the time of writing this chapter):

```yaml
logstash:
    image: docker.elastic.co/logstash/logstash:7.12.1
    command: logstash -f /etc/logstash/logstash.conf
    volumes:
        - ./logstash.conf:/etc/logstash/logstash.conf
    ports:
        - "5000:5000"
        - "12201:12201"
        - "12201:12201/udp"
```

2. The container uses a `logstash.conf` with the following content:

```
input {
    gelf {
        type => docker
        port => 12201
    }
}
output {
    elasticsearch {
        hosts => "elasticsearch:9200"
        index => "containers-%{+YYYY.MM.dd}"
    }
}
```

3. Next, deploy the second component responsible for storing and indexing incoming logs. Elasticsearch can be deployed in a single-node mode with the following configuration:

```
elasticsearch:
    image: docker.elastic.co/elasticsearch
        /elasticsearch:7.12.1
    ports:
        - 9200:9200
    environment:
        - discovery.type=single-node
```

> **Note**
>
> For production usage, it's highly recommended deploying Elasticsearch in a cluster mode with multiple data nodes to achieve high availability and resiliency.

4. Then, deploy the third component to visualize the incoming Gin logs in an interactive way. The following YAML block is responsible for deploying Kibana:

```
kibana:
    image: docker.elastic.co/kibana/kibana:7.12.1
    ports:
        - 5601:5601
    environment:
        - ELASTICSEARCH_HOSTS=http://elasticsearch:9200
```

Your ELK stack is now configured!

With the ELK stack configured, you need to stream the Gin application logs to Logstash. Luckily, Docker has a built-in `GELF` driver that supports Logstash. To stream the Gin application logs to Logstash, apply the following steps:

1. Add the following `logging` section to the Recipes API YAML block:

```
api:
    build: .
    environment:
        - MONGO_URI=mongodb://admin:password
            @mongodb:27017/test?authSource=admin
```

```
            &readPreference=primary&ssl=false
      -  MONGO_DATABASE=demo
      -  REDIS_URI=redis:6379
      -  API_VERSION=1.0.0
    ports:
      -  8080:8080
    restart: always
    logging:
      driver: gelf
      options:
        gelf-address: "udp://127.0.0.1:12201"
        tag: "recipes-api"
```

2. Redeploy the entire stack with `docker-compose up -d`. You can check whether all the services are up and running by running the `docker-compose ps` command:

```
Name                       Command                        State    Ports
chapter10_api_1            ./app                          Up       0.0.0.0:8080->8080/tcp
chapter10_elasticsearch_1  /bin/tini -- /usr/local/bi ... Up       0.0.0.0:9200->9200/tcp, 9300/tcp
chapter10_grafana_1        /run.sh                        Up       0.0.0.0:3000->3000/tcp
chapter10_kibana_1         /bin/tini -- /usr/local/bi ... Up       0.0.0.0:5601->5601/tcp
chapter10_logstash_1       /usr/local/bin/docker-entr ... Up       0.0.0.0:12201->12201/udp, 5044/tcp, 9600/tcp
chapter10_mongodb_1        docker-entrypoint.sh mongod    Up       27017/tcp
chapter10_prometheus_1     /bin/prometheus --config.f ... Up       0.0.0.0:9090->9090/tcp
chapter10_redis_1          docker-entrypoint.sh redis ... Up       6379/tcp
chapter10_telegraf_1       /entrypoint.sh telegraf        Up       8092/udp, 8094/tcp, 8125/udp
```

Figure 10.26 – List of running Docker services

> **Note**
>
> Make sure Docker Engine is allotted at least 4 GiB of memory. In Docker Desktop, you can configure resource usage of the **Advanced** tab in **Preferences**.

3. Then, point your browser to `localhost:5601`. You should be welcomed with the Kibana dashboard:

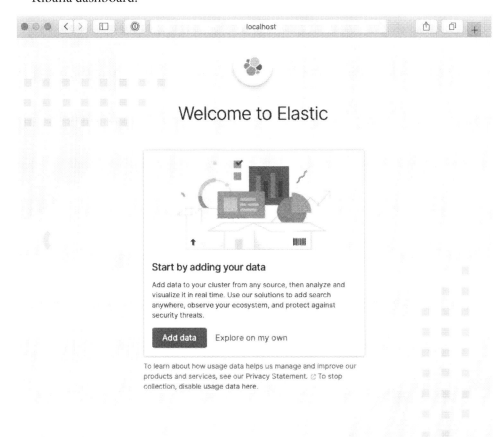

Figure 10.27 – Kibana welcome page

4.   Next, click on **Add data** and select **Elasticsearch logs** as a data source:

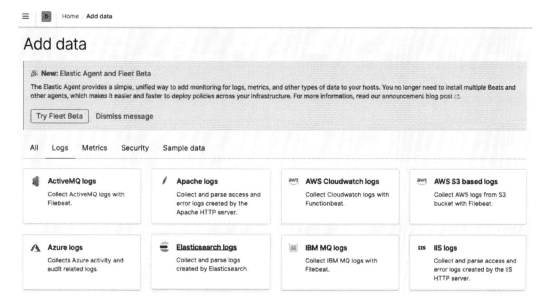

Figure 10.28 – Adding data from Elasticsearch

5. Click on **Create index pattern** and type `containers-*` in the **Index pattern name** field. The *asterix* is used to include all the logs coming from Logstash. Then, click on the **Next step** button:

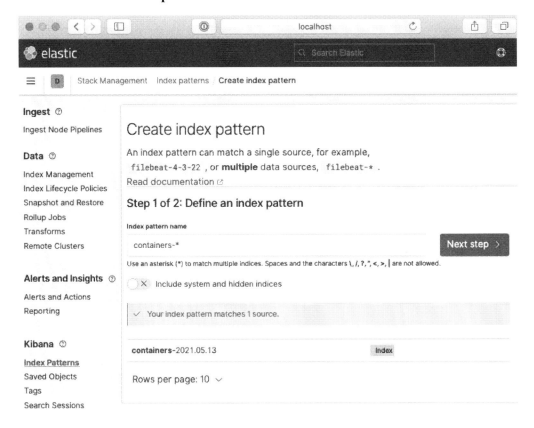

Figure 10.29 – Creating an index pattern

6. Select @timestamp as the primary time field to use with the global time filter. Then, click on **Create index pattern**:

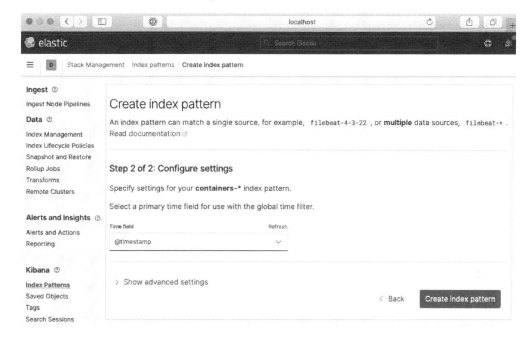

Figure 10.30 – Configuring a timestamp field for logs

On the subsequent page, you should see a list that contains every field in the `containers` index:

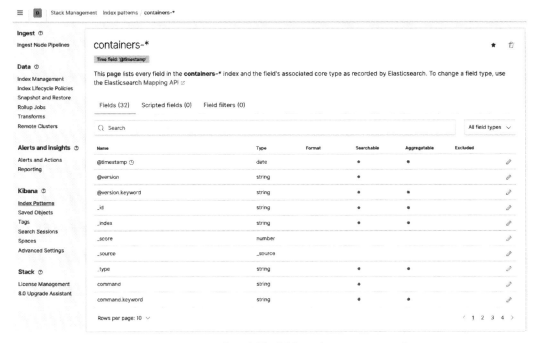

Figure 10.31 – List of available fields in the containers index

7. With Elasticsearch being connected with Kibana, click on **Discover** from the sidebar in the **Analytics** section. You should see a stream of logs coming from the Gin RESTful API:

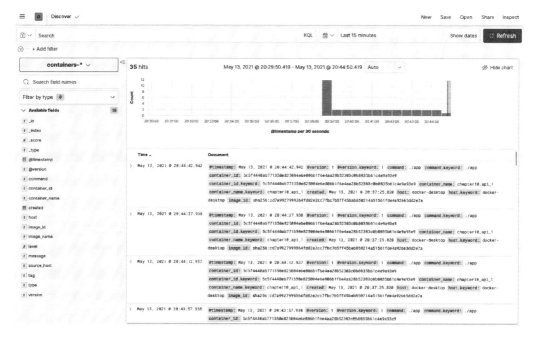

Figure 10.32 – Gin logs in Kibana

> **Note**
>
> For production usage, you can use the curator tool (`https://www. elastic.co/guide/en/elasticsearch/client/curator/ index.html`) to remove indices that are older than X days from Elasticsearch.

8.   Expand a row from the list of logs.

You should see that the Gin application log is stored in a field called `message`:

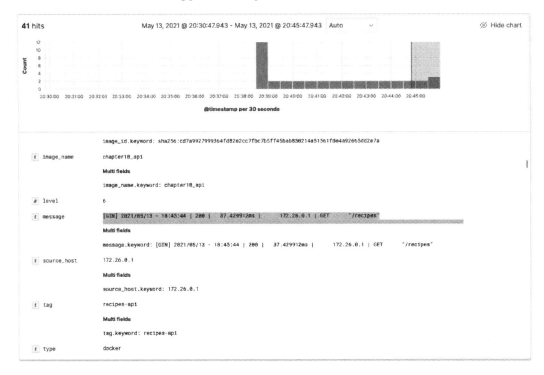

Figure 10.33 – Message field content

Now, you have a working pipeline that reads Gin logs. However, you'll notice that the format of the log messages is not ideal. You can parse this field and split the important information into multiple fields using Grok expressions.

Writing Grok expressions

Grok expressions work by parsing text patterns by using regular expressions and assigning them to an identifier. The syntax is `%{PATTERN:IDENTIFIER}`. We can write a sequence of Grok patterns and assign various pieces of the following log message to various identifiers:

```
[GIN] 2021/05/13 - 18:45:44 | 200 |     37.429912ms |
172.26.0.1 | GET    "/recipes"
```

The Grok pattern is as follows:

```
%{DATE:date} - %{TIME:time} \| %{NUMBER:status} \|
%{SPACE} %{NUMBER:requestDuration}%{GREEDYDATA:unit} \|
%{SPACE} %{IP:clientIp} \| %{WORD:httpMethod} %{SPACE}
%{QUOTEDSTRING:url}
```

> **Note**
>
> Grok comes with its own dictionary of patterns that you can use out of the box.
> However, you can always define your own custom pattern.

You can test the pattern using the **Grok Debugger** feature on the **Dev Tools** page. In the **Sample Data** field, enter the previous message and in **Grok Pattern**, enter the Grok pattern.

Then, click on **Simulate**; you'll see the simulated event that results from applying the Grok pattern:

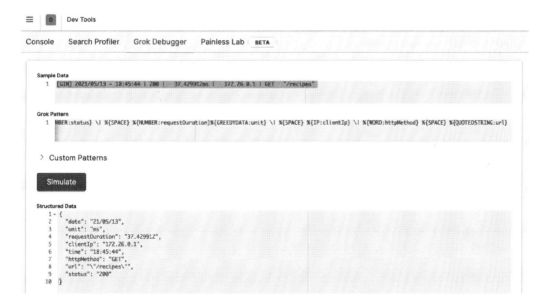

Figure 10.34 – Applying a Grok pattern to sample data

> **Note**
>
> If an error occurs, you can continue iterating over the custom pattern until the output matches the event that you expect.

Now that you have a working Grok pattern, you can apply parsing at the Logstash level. To do this, update the `logstash.conf` file so that it includes a filter section, as follows:

```
input {
    gelf {
        type => docker
        port => 12201
    }
}

filter {
    grok {
        match => {"message" => "%{DATE:date} - %{TIME:time}
                  \| %{NUMBER:status} \| %{SPACE}
              %{NUMBER:requestDuration}%{GREEDYDATA:unit}
                  \| %{SPACE} %{IP:clientIp}
                  \| %{WORD:httpMethod} %{SPACE}
              %{QUOTEDSTRING:url}"}
    }
}

output {
    elasticsearch {
        hosts => "elasticsearch:9200"
        index => "containers-%{+YYYY.MM.dd}"
    }
}
```

Now, if you restart the Logstash container, the incoming logs should be parsed and split into multiple fields:

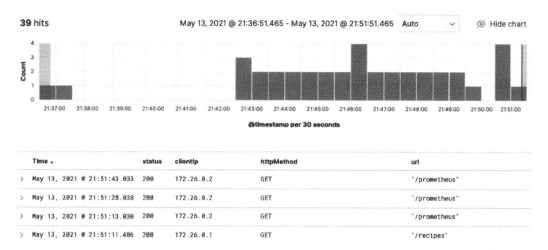

Figure 10.35 – Message field split into multiple fields

Create a new dashboard and click on **Create panel** to create a new chart:

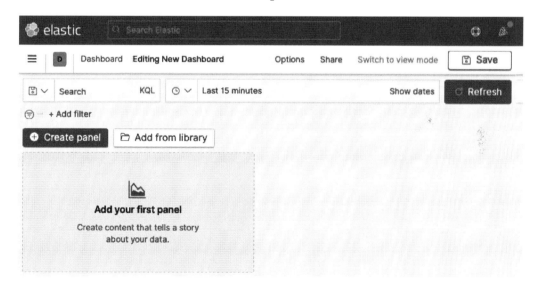

Figure 10.36 – Creating a new Kibana dashboard

Drag the `status.keyword` field and drop it into the panel. Then, select a **Stacked bar** chart. You should get the following chart, which represents the number of requests per HTTP status code:

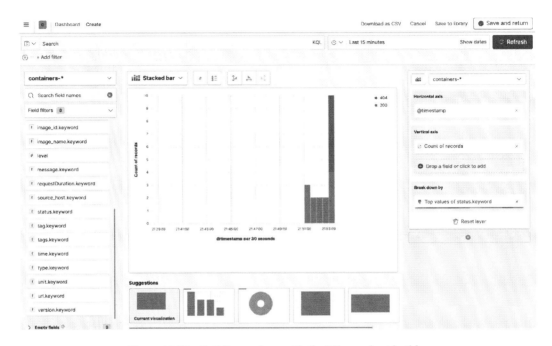

Figure 10.37 – Building a chart with the Kibana chart builder

You can save the stacked bar chart as a widget and import it into a dashboard. With a dashboard, you can combine multiple visualizations onto a single page, then filter them by providing a search query or by selecting filters by clicking elements in the visualization. Dashboards are useful when you want to get an overview of your Gin application logs and make correlations among various visualizations and logs.

Updating the Gin logging format

By default, Gin records every request field to **standard output** (**stdout**), which is awesome for troubleshooting and debugging HTTP request errors. However, this can be too verbose for other developers and they can get lost easily and miss the important events. Luckily, you can override this default behavior by creating a custom log formatter.

To create a custom log format with Gin, start with the following code block:

```
router.Use(gin.LoggerWithFormatter(func(
                    param gin.LogFormatterParams) string {
        return fmt.Sprintf("[%s] %s %s %d %s\n",
            param.TimeStamp.Format("2006-01-02T15:04:05"),
            param.Method,
            param.Path,
            param.StatusCode,
            param.Latency,
    )
}))
```

The code will log the request timestamp, HTTP method, path, status code, and duration:

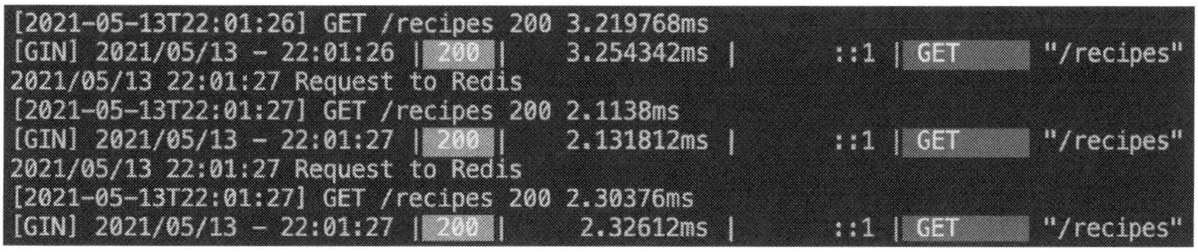

Figure 10.38 – Gin custom log format

By default, Gin will output all logs to `stdout`, but you can disable them by setting GIN_ MODE to release mode with the following command:

```
GIN_MODE=release go run main.go
```

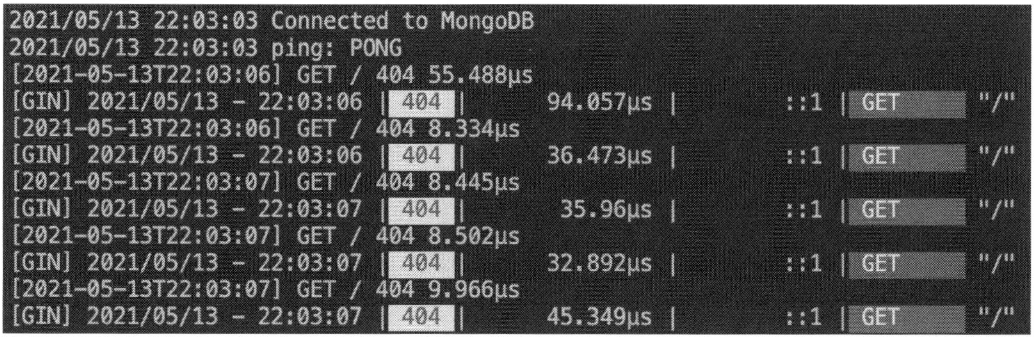

Figure 10.39 – Running Gin in release mode

You can also override the log destination so that it's a file instead of stdout with the following code block:

```
gin.DisableConsoleColor()
f, _ := os.Create("debug.log")
gin.DefaultWriter = io.MultiWriter(f)
```

As a result, a new file called debug.log should be created alongside the application logs:

```
Building-Distributed-Applications-in-Gin > chapter10 >  ☰ debug.log
1    [GIN] 2021/05/13 - 22:04:35 | 200 |     2.659571ms |          ::1 | GET      "/recipes"
2    [GIN] 2021/05/13 - 22:04:36 | 200 |     2.525996ms |          ::1 | GET      "/recipes"
3    [GIN] 2021/05/13 - 22:04:36 | 200 |     1.721515ms |          ::1 | GET      "/recipes"
4    [GIN] 2021/05/13 - 22:04:36 | 200 |     1.926928ms |          ::1 | GET      "/recipes"
5    [GIN] 2021/05/13 - 22:04:36 | 200 |     1.941609ms |          ::1 | GET      "/recipes"
6    [GIN] 2021/05/13 - 22:04:36 | 200 |     2.071787ms |          ::1 | GET      "/recipes"
7
```

Figure 10.40 – Streaming logs to a file

You can stream the file's content to Elasticsearch with Filebeat. **Filebeat** can be used as a replacement for Logstash:

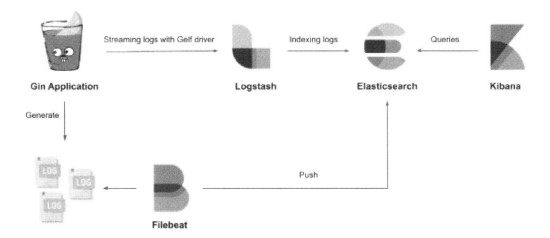

Figure 10.41 – Shipping log files with Filebeat to ELK

Add the following YAML block to `docker-compose.yml` to deploy a container based on the Filebeat v7.12.1 image:

```
filebeat:
    image: docker.elastic.co/beats/filebeat:7.12.1
    volumes:
        - ./filebeat.yml:/usr/share/filebeat/filebeat.yml
        - ./debug.log:/var/log/api/debug.log
```

The container will look in `/usr/share/filebeat` for the configuration file. The configuration file is provided through bind mounts (see the *volumes* section). The file's content is as follows. It will listen for logs coming from `/var/log/api/debug.log` and echo any that are received by Elasticsearch:

```
filebeat.inputs:
- type: log
  paths:
    - /var/log/api/debug.log


output.elasticsearch:
    hosts: 'http://elasticsearch:9200'
```

Restart the stack with the `docker-compose up -d` command. The list of running Docker services is as follows:

```
mlabouardy@Mohameds-MBP-001 chapter10 % docker-compose ps
         Name                    Command            State                      Ports
chapter10_elasticsearch_1  /bin/tini -- /usr/local/bi ...   Up    0.0.0.0:9200->9200/tcp, 9300/tcp
chapter10_filebeat_1       /usr/bin/tini -- /usr/loca ...   Up
chapter10_grafana_1        /run.sh                          Up    0.0.0.0:3000->3000/tcp
chapter10_kibana_1         /bin/tini -- /usr/local/bi ...   Up    0.0.0.0:5601->5601/tcp
chapter10_logstash_1       /usr/local/bin/docker-entr ...   Up    0.0.0.0:12201->12201/tcp, 0.0.0.0:12201->12201/udp,
                                                                  0.0.0.0:5000->5000/tcp, 5044/tcp, 9600/tcp
chapter10_mongodb_1        docker-entrypoint.sh mongod      Up    0.0.0.0:27017->27017/tcp
chapter10_prometheus_1     /bin/prometheus --config.f ...   Up    0.0.0.0:9090->9090/tcp
chapter10_redis_1          docker-entrypoint.sh redis ...   Up    0.0.0.0:6379->6379/tcp
chapter10_telegraf_1       /entrypoint.sh telegraf          Up    8092/udp, 8094/tcp, 8125/udp
```

Figure 10.42 – Filebeat running as a Docker container

Issue a few requests to the Recipes API. At this point, Gin will forward the logs to debug. log and Filebeat will stream them into Elasticsearch. From there, you can visualize them in real time in Kibana:

Figure 10.43 – Visualizing logs coming from Filebeat

Great! You can now use the Kibana dashboard to analyze Gin logs in real time. Analyzing those logs can provide a lot of information that helps with troubleshooting the root cause of Gin application failure.

Summary

In this chapter, you learned how to instrument Gin application code to expose application-side metrics using Prometheus. You saw how to build a dynamic dashboard with Grafana to monitor the overall health of a Gin application in near-real time, as well as how to trigger a Slack alert when certain thresholds are crossed.

Then, you learned how to stream Gin logs to a centralized logging platform built using open source tools such as Logstash, Elasticsearch, and Kibana. Along the way, you learned how to parse Gin logs with Grok patterns and how to build charts on top of these parsed fields.

Congratulations! Now, you can design, build, and deploy a distributed Gin application from scratch. You also have a solid foundation regarding how to automate the deployment workflow and monitor a running Gin application in production.

Further reading

- *Learn Grafana 7.0* by Eric Salituro, Packt publishing
- *Hands-On Infrastructure Monitoring with Prometheus* by Joel Bastos and Pedro Arajo, Packt publishing

Conclusion

We're at the end of our journey through this book! You've made it to the very end. I hope that you're proud of the journey you've taken. You've learned the ins and outs of the Gin framework and put together a fully functional distributed Gin application.

By now, you should know all you need to know to build a scalable Dockerized Gin application, from handling multiple Git branches with GitFlow to automating the build on AWS with a CI/CD pipeline, troubleshooting and monitoring in near-real-time, and generating API documentation with OpenAPI.

There's a lot to absorb and learn in this book, especially if this is your first exposure to the Gin framework. I find that the best way to learn is by doing, so take the RESTful API you've built and add new features to it. And if you do build something, reach out to me and tell me what you've done.

Assessments

This section contains answers to the questions from all chapters.

Chapter 1 – Getting started with Gin

1. **Golang** is currently one of the fastest growing programming languages in the software development industry. It is a lightweight, open-source language suited for today's microservices architectures.

2. Multiple web frameworks exist, the most popular are **Gin**, **Martini**, and **Gorilla**.

3. A Go module is a way to group together a set of packages and give it a version number to mark its existence at a specific point in time.

4. The default port of an HTTP server backed by Gin framework is 8080.

5. You can use the c.JSON() or c.XML() methods to return literal JSON or XML structs.

Chapter 2 – Setting up API Endpoints

1. **GitFlow** is a branching strategy that developers can follow when using version control. To apply the GitFlow model, you need a central Git repository with two main branches:

   Master: It stores the official release history.

   Develop: It serves as an integration branch for features.

2. A model is a normal structs with basic Go types. To declare a struct in Go, use the following format:

```
Type ModelName struct{
    Field1 TYPE
    Fiel2 TYPE
}
```

3. To bind a request body into a type, we use Gin model binding. Gin supports binding of JSON, XML and YAML. Gin provides two sets of methods for binding:

Should Bind: `ShouldBindJSON()`, `ShouldBindXML()`, `ShouldBindYAML()`

Must Bind: Binds the struct pointer using the specified binding engine. It will abort the request with HTTP 400 if any error occurs.

4. First, define a route with an ID as a path parameter:

```
router.GET("/recipes/:id", GetRecipeHandler)
```

The `GetRecipeHandler` function parses the ID parameter and `go` loop through the recipes list. If the ID matches a recipe of the list, it will be returned, otherwise a `404 error` will be thrown as follows:

```
func GetRecipeHandler(c *gin.Context) {
    id := c.Query("id")
    for i := 0; i < len(recipes); i++ {
        if recipes[i].ID == id {
            c.JSON(http.StatusOK, recipes[i])
        }
    }
    c.JSON(http.StatusNotFound, gin.H{"error": "Recipe
                                      not found"})
}
```

5. To define a parameter, we use the swagger:parameters annotation:

```
// swagger:parameters recipes newRecipe
type Recipe struct {
    //swagger:ignore
    ID string `json:"id"`
    Name string `json:"name"`
    Tags []string `json:"tags"`
    Ingredients []string `json:"ingredients"`
    Instructions []string `json:"instructions"`
    PublishedAt time.Time `json:"publishedAt"`
}
```

Generate the specification with `swagger` generate command and load the results on **Swagger UI**.

You can now issue a POST request by filling the recipe fields directly from the Swagger UI.

Chapter 3 – Managing Data Persistence with MongoDB

1. You can delete recipes using `collection.DeleteOne()` or `collection.DeleteMany()`. Here you pass `bson.D({})` as the filter argument, which will match all documents in the collection.

   Update the `DeleteRecipeHandler` as follows:

```
func (handler *RecipesHandler) DeleteRecipeHandler(c
*gin.Context) {
    id := c.Param("id")
    objectId, _ := primitive.ObjectIDFromHex(id)
    _, err := handler.collection.DeleteOne(handler.ctx,
bson.M{
        "_id": objectId,
    })
    if err != nil {
        c.JSON(http.StatusInternalServerError,
            gin.H{"error": err.Error()})
        return
    }
    c.JSON(http.StatusOK, gin.H{"message": "Recipe has
                        been deleted"})
}
```

   Make sure to register the handler on DELETE `/recipes/{id}` resource as follows:

```
router.DELETE("/recipes/:id", recipesHandler.
DeleteRecipeHandler)
```

2. To find a recipe, you will need a filter document, as well as a pointer to value into which the result can be decoded. To find a single recipe, use `collection.FindOne()`. This method returns a single result which can be decoded into a Recipe struct. You'll use the same filter variable you used in the update query to match a recipe where ID is `600dcc85a65917cbd1f201b0`.

Register a handler on the `main.go` file:

```
router.GET("/recipes/:id", recipesHandler.
GetOneRecipeHandler)
```

Then, declare the `GetOneRecipeHandler` in `handler.go` with the following content:

```
func (handler *RecipesHandler) GetOneRecipeHandler(c
*gin.Context) {
    id := c.Param("id")
    objectId, _ := primitive.ObjectIDFromHex(id)
    cur := handler.collection.FindOne(handler.ctx, bson.M{
        "_id": objectId,
    })
    var recipe models.Recipe
    err := cur.Decode(&recipe)
    if err != nil {
        c.JSON(http.StatusInternalServerError,
            gin.H{"error": err.Error()})
        return
    }

    c.JSON(http.StatusOK, recipe)
}
```

3. JSON documents in MongoDB are stored in a binary representation called **BSON** (**Binary-encoded JSON**). This format includes additional types such as:

    a. Double

    b. String

    c. Object

    d. Array

    e. Binary data

    f. Undefined

    g. Object ID

    h. Boolean

i. Date

j. Null

This makes it much easier for applications to reliably process, sort, and compare data.

4. **Least Recently Used** (**LRU**) algorithm uses the recent past to approximate the near future. It simply deletes the keys that has not been used for the longest period of time.

Chapter 4 – Building API Authentication

1. In order to create a user or sign them up, we need to define a HTTP handler with `SignUpHandler` as follows:

```go
func (handler *AuthHandler) SignUpHandler(c *gin.Context) {
    var user models.User
    if err := c.ShouldBindJSON(&user); err != nil {
        c.JSON(http.StatusBadRequest, gin.H{"error":
                                            err.Error()})
        return
    }
    cur := handler.collection.FindOne(handler.ctx, bson.M{
        "username": user.Username,
    })
    if curTalent.Err() == mongo.ErrNoDocuments {
        err := handler.collection.InsertOne(handler.ctx,
                                            user)
        if err != nil {
            c.JSON(http.StatusInternalServerError,
                gin.H{"error": err.Error()})
            return
        }
        c.JSON(http.StatusAccepted, gin.H{"message":
            "Account has been created"})
    }
    c.JSON(http.StatusInternalServerError, gin.H{"error":
        "Username already taken"})
}
```

```
Then, register the handler on POST /signup route:
router.POST("/signup", authHandler.SignUpHandler)
```

To ensure the username field is unique in all your users' entries, you can create a unique index for the username field.

2. Define a `ProfileHandler` with the following body:

```
func (handler *AuthHandler) ProfileHandler(c *gin.
Context) {
    var user models.User
    username, _ := c.Get("username")
    cur := handler.collection.FindOne(handler.ctx, bson.M{
        "username": user.Username,
    })
    cur.Decode(&user)
    c.JSON(http.StatusAccepted, user)
}
Register the HTTP handler on the router group as below:
authorized := router.Group("/")
authorized.Use(authHandler.AuthMiddleware()){
        authorized.POST("/recipes",
                        recipesHandler.NewRecipeHandler)
        authorized.PUT("/recipes/:id",
                        recipesHandler.UpdateRecipeHandler)
        authorized.DELETE("/recipes/:id",
                        recipesHandler.DeleteRecipeHandler)
        authorized.GET("/recipes/:id",
                        recipesHandler.GetOneRecipeHandler)
        authorized.GET("/profile",
                        authHandler.ProfileHandler)
}
```

3. Add the following Swagger annotation in top of `SignOutHandler` signature:

```
// swagger:operation POST /signout auth signOut
// Signing out
// ---
// responses:
//      '200':
```

```
//          description: Successful operation
func (handler *AuthHandler) SignOutHandler(c *gin.
Context) {}
```

Chapter 5 – Serving Static HTML in Gin

1. Create a `header.tmpl` file with the following content:

```
<head>
    <title>Recipes</title>
    <link rel="stylesheet" href="/assets/css/app.css">
    <link href="https://cdn.jsdelivr.net/npm/
bootstrap@5.0.0-beta2/dist/css/bootstrap.min.css"
rel="stylesheet">
</head>
```

Then, reference the file in the `recipe.tmpl` with the following code block:

```
{{template "/templates/header.tmpl.tmpl"}}
```

Follow the same approach to create a reusable template for the footer part.

2. The full-source code of the `NewRecipe.js` component is available on the GitHub repository under the folder for *Chapter 5, Serving static HTML in Gin*.

3. Cross-compiling works by setting required environment variables that specify the target operating system and architecture. We use the variable GOOS for the target operating system, and GOARCH for the target architecture. To build an executable, the command would take this form:

```
GOOS=target-OS GOARCH=target-architecture go build -o
main *.go
```

For instance, to build the binary for Windows, you can use the following command:

```
GOOS=windows GOARCH=amd64 go build -o main main.go
```

Chapter 7 – Testing Gin HTTP Routes

1. Define a `TestUpdateRecipeHandler` in `main_test.go` as follows:

```
func TestUpdateRecipeHandler(t *testing.T) {
    ts := httptest.NewServer(SetupServer())
    defer ts.Close()
```

```go
    recipe := Recipe{
        ID:    "c0283p3d0cvuglq85log",
        Name: "Oregano Marinated Chicken",
    }

    raw, _ := json.Marshal(recipe)
    resp, err := http.PUT(fmt.Sprintf("%s/recipes/%s",
ts.URL, recipe.ID), bytes.NewBuffer(raw))
    defer resp.Body.Close()
    assert.Nil(t, err)
    assert.Equal(t, http.StatusOK, resp.StatusCode)
    data, _ := ioutil.ReadAll(resp.Body)

    var payload map[string]string
    json.Unmarshal(data, &payload)

    assert.Equal(t, payload["message"], "Recipe has been
updated")
}
```

Define TestDeleteRecipeHandler in main_test.go as
follows:

```go
func TestDeleteRecipeHandler(t *testing.T) {
    ts := httptest.NewServer(SetupServer())
    defer ts.Close()

    resp, err := http.DELETE(fmt.Sprintf("%s/recipes/
c0283p3d0cvuglq85log", ts.URL))
    defer resp.Body.Close()
    assert.Nil(t, err)
    assert.Equal(t, http.StatusOK, resp.StatusCode)
    data, _ := ioutil.ReadAll(resp.Body)

    var payload map[string]string
    json.Unmarshal(data, &payload)
```

```
        assert.Equal(t, payload["message"],
                "Recipe has been deleted")
}
```

2. Define `TestFindRecipeHandler` in `main_test.go` as follows:

```
func TestDeleteRecipeHandler(t *testing.T) {
    ts := httptest.NewServer(SetupServer())
    defer ts.Close()

    resp, err := http.DELETE(fmt.Sprintf("%s/recipes
            /c0283p3d0cvuglq85log", ts.URL))
    defer resp.Body.Close()
    assert.Nil(t, err)
    assert.Equal(t, http.StatusOK, resp.StatusCode)
    data, _ := ioutil.ReadAll(resp.Body)

    var payload map[string]string
    json.Unmarshal(data, &payload)

    assert.Equal(t, payload["message"],
            "Recipe has been deleted")
}
```

3. Define `TestFindRecipeHandler` in `main_test.go` as follows:

```
func TestFindRecipeHandler(t *testing.T) {
    ts := httptest.NewServer(SetupServer())
    defer ts.Close()

    expectedRecipe := Recipe{
        ID:   "c0283p3d0cvuglq85log",
        Name: "Oregano Marinated Chicken",
        Tags: []string{"main", "chicken"},
    }

    resp, err := http.GET(fmt.Sprintf("%s/recipes/
```

```
c0283p3d0cvuglq85log", ts.URL))
    defer resp.Body.Close()
    assert.Nil(t, err)
    assert.Equal(t, http.StatusOK, resp.StatusCode)
    data, _ := ioutil.ReadAll(resp.Body)


    var actualRecipe Recipe
    json.Unmarshal(data, &actualRecipe)


    assert.Equal(t, expectedRecipe.Name,
                actualRecipe.Name)
    assert.Equal(t, len(expectedRecipe.Tags),
len(actualRecipe.Tags))
}
```

Chapter 8 – Deploying the Application on AWS

1. Create a Docker volume with the following command:

```
docker volume create mongodata
```

Then mount the volume while running the Docker container:

```
docker run -d -p 27017:27017 -v mongodata:/data/db --name
mongodb mongodb:4.4.3
```

2. To deploy RabbitMQ, you can use the docker-compose.yml to deploy an additional service based on the RabbitMQ official image as follows:

```
rabbitmq:
    image: rabbitmq:3-management
    ports:
      - 8080:15672
    environment:
      - RABBITMQ_DEFAULT_USER=admin
      - RABBITMQ_DEFAULT_PASS=password
```

3. Create the user's credentials in the form of a Kubernetes secret:

```
kubectl create secret generic mongodb-password --from-
literal="password=YOUR_PASSWORD"
```

Once we have created the secret, we need to update `mongodb-deployment.yaml` to use the Kubernetes secret:

```
apiVersion: apps/v1
kind: Deployment
metadata:
  annotations:
    kompose.cmd: kompose convert
    kompose.version: 1.22.0 (955b78124)
  creationTimestamp: null
  labels:
    io.kompose.service: mongodb
  name: mongodb
spec:
  replicas: 1
  selector:
    matchLabels:
      io.kompose.service: mongodb
  strategy: {}
  template:
    metadata:
      annotations:
        kompose.cmd: kompose convert
        kompose.version: 1.22.0 (955b78124)
      creationTimestamp: null
      labels:
        io.kompose.service: mongodb
    spec:
      containers:
        - env:
            - name: MONGO_INITDB_ROOT_PASSWORD
              valueFrom:
                secretKeyRef:
                  name: mongodb-password
                  key: password
            - name: MONGO_INITDB_ROOT_USERNAME
              value: admin
```

```
        image: mongo:4.4.3
        name: mongodb
        ports:
            - containerPort: 27017
        resources: {}
    restartPolicy: Always
status: {}
```

4. To scale the API pods with `kubectl`, issue the following command:

```
kubectl scale deploy
```

Chapter 9 – Implementing a CI/CD Pipeline

1. The pipeline will have the following stages:

   a. Checkout the source code from the GitHub repository.

   b. Install the NPM packages with `npm install` command.

   c. Generate the assets with `npm run build` command.

   d. Install the AWS CLI and push the new assets to an S3 bucket.

   e. The `config.yml` is given here:

```
version: 2.1

executors:
  environment:
    docker:
       - image: node:lts
    working_directory: /dashboard

jobs:
  build:
    executor: environment
    steps:
       - checkout
       - restore_cache:
           key: node-modules-{{checksum "package.json"}}
       - run:
```

```
        name: Install dependencies
        command: npm install
    - save_cache:
        key: node-modules-{{checksum "package.json"}}
        paths:
          - node_modules
    - run:
        name: Build artifact
        command: CI=false npm run build
    - persist_to_workspace:
        root: .
        paths:
          - build

deploy:
  executor: environment
  steps:
    - attach_workspace:
        at: dist
    - run:
        name: Install AWS CLI
        command: |
          apt-get update
          apt-get install -y python3-pip
          pip3 install awscli
    - run:
        name: Push to S3 bucket
        command: |
          cd dist/build/dashboard/
          aws configure set preview.cloudfront true
          aws s3 cp --recursive . s3://YOUR_S3_BUCKET/
--region YOUR_AWS_REGION
workflows:
  ci_cd:
    jobs:
      - build
```

```
  - deploy:
      requires:
        - build
      filters:
        branches:
          only:
            - master
```

Before running the pipeline, you will need to give access `S3:PutObject` permission to the **CircleCI IAM** user.

2. You can configure the Slack ORB to send a notification on a successful pipeline as follows:

```
- slack/notify:
    event: pass
    custom: |
      {
        "blocks": [
          {
            "type": "section",
            "text": {
              "type": "mrkdwn",
              "text": "Current Job: $CIRCLE_JOB"
            }
          },
          {
            "type": "section",
            "text": {
              "type": "mrkdwn",
              "text": "New release has been successfully
                       deployed!"
            }
          }
        ]
      }
```

Packt.com

Subscribe to our online digital library for full access to over 7,000 books and videos, as well as industry leading tools to help you plan your personal development and advance your career. For more information, please visit our website.

Why subscribe?

- Spend less time learning and more time coding with practical eBooks and Videos from over 4,000 industry professionals

- Improve your learning with Skill Plans built especially for you

- Get a free eBook or video every month

- Fully searchable for easy access to vital information

- Copy and paste, print, and bookmark content

Did you know that Packt offers eBook versions of every book published, with PDF and ePub files available? You can upgrade to the eBook version at packt.com and as a print book customer, you are entitled to a discount on the eBook copy. Get in touch with us at customercare@packtpub.com for more details.

At www.packt.com, you can also read a collection of free technical articles, sign up for a range of free newsletters, and receive exclusive discounts and offers on Packt books and eBooks.

Other Books You May Enjoy

If you enjoyed this book, you may be interested in these other books by Packt:

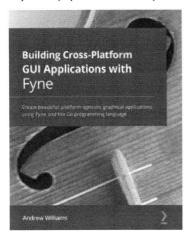

Building Cross-Platform GUI Applications with Fyne

Andrew Williams

ISBN: 9781800563162

- Become well-versed with the history of GUI development and how Fyne and the Golang programming language make it easier
- Explore how the Fyne toolkit is architected and the various modules are provided
- Discover how Fyne apps can be tested and constructed using best practices
- Construct five complete applications and deploy them to your devices
- Customize the design of your apps by extending widgets and themes
- Understand the separation and presentation of data and how to test and build applications that present dynamic data

Hands-On High Performance with Go

Bob Strecansky

ISBN: 9781789805789

- Organize and manipulate data effectively with clusters and job queues

- Explore commonly applied Go data structures and algorithms

- Write anonymous functions in Go to build reusable apps

- Profile and trace Go apps to reduce bottlenecks and improve efficiency

- Deploy, monitor, and iterate Go programs with a focus on performance

- Dive into memory management and CPU and GPU parallelism in Go

Packt is searching for authors like you

If you're interested in becoming an author for Packt, please visit authors. packtpub.com and apply today. We have worked with thousands of developers and tech professionals, just like you, to help them share their insight with the global tech community. You can make a general application, apply for a specific hot topic that we are recruiting an author for, or submit your own idea.

Share Your Thoughts

Now you've finished *Building Distributed Applications in Gin*, we'd love to hear your thoughts! Scan the QR code below to go straight to the Amazon review page for this book and share your feedback or leave a review on the site that you purchased it from.

https://packt.link/r/1801074852

Your review is important to us and the tech community and will help us make sure we're delivering excellent quality content.

Index

Printed in Great Britain
by Amazon

76461167R00273